GEOFFREY CHAUCER

THE CANTERBURY TALES

RANDOM HOUSE NEW YORK

THE CANTERBURY TALES

A PROSE VERSION
IN MODERN ENGLISH BY
DAVID WRIGHT

TO FRANK RUDMAN

Though I come after hym with hawebake
I speke in prose, and lat hym rymes make.

CONTENTS

viii   Contents

INTRODUCTION

The Canterbury Tales is one of the most astonishing productions of the Middle Ages. Not only is it completely original in concept and method, but its range and variety have never been surpassed within the confines of a single work. The idea of the pilgrimage to Canterbury, in which men and women drawn from all classes of life lighten their journey by telling tales in keeping with their various characters and callings, is much more than a mechanic peg on which to hang a miscellany of stories: it is a dramatic concept, a dynamic device by which the different tales are made to set one another off and throw light on the characters of the tellers, till the whole furnishes an unparallelled panorama not only of life in the fourteenth century but of life itself. Chaucer is more than 'The Father of English Poetry', that somewhat depressive title which is often bestowed upon him. He is one of the greatest and most original of European poets, and his work has a quality of universality which is only matched and exceeded by Shakespeare, who of all poets he most nearly resembles in his range and understanding, and in the quality of his irony, his detachment and his humour.

Geoffrey Chaucer was born in the reign of Edward III, shortly after the beginning of the Hundred Years' War between England and France. It was an exciting period, the last flowering of the age of chivalry; the days of the Black Prince, when the English came within an ace of conquering the whole of France with the victories of Crécy and Poitiers. It was also a time when the common people, after the visitation of the Black Death (the plague that wiped out a third of the population and undermined the economic structure of the feudal system), first began to assert themselves against their overlords—the time of the Jacquerie (the French peasants' insurrection in 1358) and of the Peasants' Revolt in 1381 when John of Gaunt's palace at the Savoy was sacked and burnt and Wat Tyler very nearly made himself master of England. For the Church, too, it was a critical period; the Great Schism, with two rival and warring Popes, began in 1378, while at the same time Wyclif was beginning his attacks on the clergy and on

Church dogma which were the first harbingers of the Reformation.

Chaucer, though a poet, was by no means a recluse; for he had a varied and distinguished career as a courtier, diplomat, and administrator. He was probably born about 1343 (the exact date is not known) and came of a prosperous upper-middle-class family that had been in the wine trade for several generations: his father was a well-off London vintner who had held public office. The family had court connections, and Chaucer began his career as a page in the household of the Countess of Ulster, wife of Prince Lionel, a son of Edward III.

Chaucer took part in at least two military campaigns, and was once taken prisoner by the French near Rheims (Edward III ransomed him for £16—a sum worth probably a hundred times as much in present-day money). John of Gaunt (Shakespeare's 'time-honour'd Lancaster') seems to have been his chief patron. It is known that Chaucer's wife, Philippa, was the sister of Katherine Swynford who was the governess of John of Gaunt's children, then became his mistress and eventually his third wife. In the 1370's Chaucer went abroad several times on a series of diplomatic missions, to Flanders and France, and twice to Italy, where he visited Florence and may conceivably have met Petrarch. These Italian visits were crucial, for quite apart from his becoming acquainted with the work of Dante, Petrarch, and Boccaccio, it was the impact on Chaucer of the Italy of the Quattrocento, of cities like Milan, Florence, and Pisa which were then building, that probably helped to turn him into the great artist he afterwards became. It must be remembered that for his age Chaucer was a very learned man—he read and spoke French and Italian fluently as well as Latin, was expert in astrology and astronomy, and had more than a smattering of history, theology, medicine, law, and even alchemy; he owned (if we are to believe his claim in *The Legend of Good Women*) a library of sixty books, which was more than many university colleges possessed in those days. By 1374 he was a man of considerable standing and substance, for in that year he was appointed to the important post of Controller of Customs and Subsidies on Wools, Skins, and Hides in the Port of London (wool customs were a main source of the king's revenue). This post he held until 1386, when he became a Justice of the

Peace and Knight of the Shire (i.e. Member of Parliament) for Kent. It was about this time he began to write *The Canterbury Tales*. But his public career was by no means over; in 1389 he was appointed Clerk of the King's Works, in charge of the upkeep and repair of eight of the royal residences, including Westminster Palace, the Tower, and St. George's Chapel at Windsor. Two years later this appointment was exchanged for the less onerous one of Deputy Forester of the royal forest of North Peterton in Somerset. According to the date on the tomb that was erected to him in Westminster Abbey in the fifteenth century, he died on 25th October 1400.

This is a full life by any standards, and the wonder is that Chaucer found time for his achievement as a poet, which included two masterpieces—*Troilus and Cressida,* and *The Canterbury Tales*—besides lesser works that would have been enough to ensure the immortality of half a dozen other poets. But it is the great variety of contacts that his involvement in affairs afforded the poet, no less than his travels and campaigns, that lies behind the immense experience of men and women and life that is apparent in his work and nowhere more than in *The Canterbury Tales*. These include every variety of medieval story—romances of courtly love like the Knight's Tale, pious legends like the Prioress's Tale and the Second Nun's Tale, fairy stories such as the Tales of the Wife of Bath and the Squire, and last but not least racy *fabliaux* (or what used to be called smoking-room stories) like the Miller's, Reeve's, and Summoner's Tales and others. These, whose downright acceptance of life as it is incurred some Victorian headshaking at Chaucer's coarseness, are in fact the most original and technically the most masterly of his poems, and among the best descriptions of common or everyday life ever written.

I have thought it worth while to make the experiment of translating *The Canterbury Tales* into straightforward contemporary prose, in an attempt to give the general reader, who might otherwise be deterred by the Middle English that Chaucer wrote (which is not really so very difficult to follow, though translating it is another matter), some glimpse of their freshness, and of the skill, humour, irony, pathos, and immediacy of Chaucer's narrative. The trouble with most verse translations (with the exception of Dryden's paraphrases of *The Knight's Tale* and *The Nun's*

Priest's Tale) has been the pedestrian versification of the translators. One result has been to obscure not only the view of Chaucer's poetry, but too many of his other qualities, by the cataract of the makeshift and often downright bathetic rhyme-carpentry into which their efforts to reproduce the Tales in verse has led.

This translation has been based on the text of F. N. Robinson's edition of *The Canterbury Tales*. Chaucer never completed them, and does not seem to have made up his mind about their final order; what has come down to us is fragmentary in parts. I have followed the order of Skeat's Oxford Edition, which is generally accepted as the best. Here I should like to record my grateful thanks to Mr S. S. Hussey of London University for his invaluable advice and assistance in the interpretation of crucial passages and in the revision of the final draft of my translation; and to Mr Brian Higgins for his advice on Yorkshire dialect phrases in *The Reeve's Tale*.

DAVID WRIGHT

THE CANTERBURY TALES

THE GENERAL PROLOGUE

When the sweet showers of April have pierced the dryness of March to its root and soaked every vein in moisture whose quickening force engenders the flower; when Zephyr with his sweet breath has given life to tender shoots in each wood and field; when the young sun has run his half-course in the sign of the Ram; when, nature prompting their instincts, small birds who sleep through the night with one eye open make their music—then people long to go on pilgrimages, and pious wanderers to visit strange lands and far-off shrines in different countries. In England especially they come from every shire's end to Canterbury to seek out the holy blessed martyr St Thomas à Becket, who helped them when they were sick.

It happened one day at this time of year, while I was lodging at the Tabard in Southwark, ready and eager to go on my pilgrimage to Canterbury, a company of twenty-nine people arrived in the hostelry at nightfall. They were of various sorts, accidentally brought together in companionship, all pilgrims wishing to ride to Canterbury. The rooms and stables were commodious and we were very well looked after. In short, by the time the sun had gone down I had talked with every one of them and soon become one of their company. We agreed to rise early to set out on the journey I am going to tell you about. But nevertheless before I take the story further it seems right to me to describe, while I have the time and opportunity, the sort and condition of each of them as they appeared to me: who they were, of what rank, and how dressed. I shall begin with the Knight.

The KNIGHT was a very distinguished man. From the beginning of his career he had loved chivalry, loyalty, honourable dealing, generosity, and good breeding. He had fought bravely in the king's service, besides which he had travelled further than most men in heathen as well as in Christian lands. Wherever he went he was honoured for his valour. He was at Alexandria when it fell. When he served in Prussia he was generally given the seat of honour above the knights of all other nations; no Christian soldier

of his rank had fought oftener in the raids on Russia and Lith-
uania. And he had been in Granada at the siege of Algeciras,
fought in Benmarin and at the conquests of Ayas and Attalia,
besides taking part in many armed expeditions in the eastern
Mediterranean. He had been in fifteen pitched battles and fought
three times for the faith in the lists at Tramassene, and each time
killed his foe. This same distinguished Knight had also fought at
one time for the king of Palathia against another heathen enemy
in Turkey. He was always outstandingly successful; yet though
distinguished he was prudent, and his bearing as modest as a
maid's. In his whole life he never spoke discourteously to any kind
of man. He was a true and perfect noble knight. But, speaking of
his equipment, his horses were good, yet he was not gaily dressed.
He wore a tunic of thick cotton cloth, rust-marked from his coat of
mail; for he had just come back from his travels and was making
his pilgrimage to render thanks.

With him came his son, a young SQUIRE; a spirited apprentice-
knight, a lover with hair as curly as if it had just been pressed in
the tongs—I suppose his age was about twenty. He was of average
height, wonderfully active and strong. In Flanders, Artois, and
Picardy he had taken part in cavalry forays and in that short space
of time had borne himself well, for he hoped to win favour in his
lady's eyes. He was decked out like a meadow full of fresh flowers,
white and red; he whistled or sang the whole day long, as lively
as the month of May. His gown was short, with long wide sleeves.
He was a good rider and sat his horse well; he was able to com-
pose songs and set them to music, joust and also dance; and he
could draw and write. Being passionately in love, at night he
slept no more than a nightingale. Courteous, modest, and willing
to serve, he carved for his father at table.

The Knight had a YEOMAN, and no other servants, for that was
how he preferred to travel on this occasion. The Yeoman was clad
in a green coat and hood and carried a sheaf of sharp bright
peacock-feathered arrows slung handily from his belt (he knew
how to look after his gear in soldierly fashion; his arrows did not
fall short because of poor feathering) while in his hand he car-
ried a mighty bow. He had a brown face, short-cropped hair, and
was adept in everything to do with woodcraft. On his arm he
wore a gay arm-guard, and a sword and buckler on one side;

upon the other a bright well-mounted dagger as sharp as a spear-point; and on his breast a shining silver image of St Christopher. He carried a horn slung from a green belt; I'd say he was a forester.

There was also a NUN, a Prioress, who smiled in an unaffected and quiet way; her greatest oath was only, 'By St Loy!' Her name was Madame Eglantine. She sang the divine service prettily, becomingly intoned through the nose. She spoke French elegantly and well but with a Stratford-at-Bow accent, for she did not know the French of Paris. At table she showed her good breeding at every point: she never let a crumb fall from her mouth or wetted her fingers by dipping them too deeply into the sauce; and when she lifted the food to her lips she took care not to spill a single drop upon her breast. Etiquette was her passion. So scrupulously did she wipe her upper lip that no spot of grease was to be seen in her cup after she had drunk from it; and when she ate she reached daintily for her food. Indeed she was most gay, pleasant and friendly. She took pains to imitate courtly behaviour and cultivate a dignified bearing so as to be thought a person deserving of respect. Speaking of her sensibility, she was so tender-hearted and compassionate that she would weep whenever she saw a mouse caught in a trap, especially if it were bleeding or dead. She kept a number of little dogs whom she fed on roast meat, milk, and the best bread. But if one of them died or someone took a stick to it she would cry bitterly, for with her all was sensitivity and tender-heartedness. Her wimple was becomingly pleated; her nose well-shaped, her eyes grey as glass, her mouth small, but soft and red. Certainly she had a fine forehead, I daresay almost a span in breadth; for indeed there was nothing diminutive about her. I noticed that she wore a most elegant cloak. On her arm she carried a rosary of small coral beads interspersed with large green ones, from which hung a shining golden brooch that had inscribed upon it a crowned A, and underneath, *'Amor vincit omnia'*.* With her she had another NUN, her chaplain, and three PRIESTS.

There was a remarkably fine-looking MONK, who acted as estate-steward to his monastery and loved hunting: a manly man, well fitted to be an abbot. He kept plenty of fine horses in his stable,

---

* 'Love conquers all.'

and when he went out riding people could hear the bells on his bridle jingling in the whistling wind as clear and loud as the chapel bell of the small convent of which he was the head. Because the Rule of St Maur or of St Benedict was old-fashioned and somewhat strict, this Monk neglected the old precepts and followed the modern custom. He did not give two pins for the text which says hunters cannot be holy men, or that a monk who is heedless of his Rule—that is to say a monk out of his cloister—is like a fish out of water. In his view this saying was not worth a bean; and I told him his opinion was sound. Why should he study and addle his wits with everlasting poring over a book in cloisters, or work with his hands, or toil as St Augustine commanded? How is the world to be served? Let St Augustine keep his hard labour for himself! Therefore the Monk, whose whole pleasure lay in riding and the hunting of the hare (over which he spared no expense) remained a hard rider and kept greyhounds swift as birds.

I saw that his sleeves were edged with costly grey fur, the finest in the land. He had an elaborate golden brooch with a love-knot at the larger end to fasten his hood beneath his chin. His bald head shone like glass; and so did his face, as if it had been anointed. He was a plump and personable dignitary, with prominent, restless eyes which sparkled like fire beneath a pot. His boots were supple and his horse in perfect condition. To be sure he was a fine-looking prelate, no pale and wasting ghost! His favourite dish was a fat roast swan. The horse he rode was as brown as a berry.

A begging FRIAR was there, a gay, pleasant Limiter* with an imposing presence; nobody in all the four Orders was so adept with flattery and tittle-tattle. He had had to pay for the marriages of a good many young women†; still, he was a noble pillar of his Order. He was well-liked and on easy terms with rich landowners everywhere in the district in which he begged, and also with the wealthy townswomen, for he was a licentiate of his Order and qualified, so he said, to hear confession of graver sins than parish priests were allowed to absolve. He heard confession sweetly, and

---

* A Limiter was a begging friar who was assigned a certain district or *limit* in which he was allowed to solicit alms. (Skeat.)
† i.e. because he had seduced them himself.

his absolution was pleasant; when he was sure of a good thank-offering he was an easy man in giving penance. For if a man gives generously to a poor Order it is a sign he has been well shriven. Once a man opened his purse-strings the Friar could vouch for it that he was penitent, for many people—though truly remorseful —are so hardened that they cannot weep. Therefore, instead of prayers and tears, people might as well give money to the poor friars.

The pockets of his hood were always stuffed with knives and pins to give to young women. And he certainly had a pleasant voice; he could sing and play the fiddle well, and was a champion ballad-singer. His neck was white as a lily, but for all that he was as strong as a prize-fighter. In every town he knew all the taverns and innkeepers and barmaids better than the lepers and beggars, for it hardly befitted a man of his ability and distinction to mix with diseased lepers. It is not seemly, and gets a man nowhere, to have dealings with rabble of that type, but only with merchants and the rich. Above all, wherever profit might be had he offered his services with polite submission. Nowhere would you find so capable a man; he was the best beggar in his friary. He paid a fixed fee for the district in which he begged; none of his brethren poached on his preserves. Even if a widow had no shoes, he had only to begin saying the first words of the Gospel of St John in his pleasant voice and he'd get at least a sixpence out of her before he left. But he made his biggest profits on the side.

He would romp about like a puppy on settling days, when he was of great help as an arbitrator; for on these occasions he did not appear like some poor cloistered student in threadbare vestment, but like a Master of Divinity, or the Pope. His outer cloak was of double-worsted, as rounded as a bell just out of its mould. He lisped a little—this was a mannerism to make his English sound attractive. And when he played the harp and had finished his song his eyes twinkled in his head like stars on a frosty night. This excellent Friar was called Hubert.

Next there was a MERCHANT with a forked beard who rode seated on a high saddle, wearing a many-coloured dress, boots fastened with neat handsome clasps, and upon his head a Flanders beaver hat. He gave out his opinions with great pomposity and never stopped talking about the increase of his profits. In his view the high seas between Harwich and Holland should be cleared of pirates at all costs. He was an expert at the exchange of currency. This worthy citizen used his head to the best advantage, conducting his money-lending and other financial transactions in a dignified manner; none guessed he was in debt. He was really a most estimable man; but to tell the truth his name escapes me.

Also there was a SCHOLAR from Oxford who had long been studying Logic. His horse was as lean as a rake, and I give you my word that he himself was no fatter, but looked both melancholy and hollow-cheeked. As he had not yet found himself a benefice and was too unworldly to take secular employment, his overcoat was pretty threadbare. For he preferred his library of Aristotle's philosophical works bound in black calf and red sheepskin at the head of his bed, to fine clothes, the fiddle and psalter; yet for all his philosophy and science he had but little gold in his coffer. He spent everything he could get from his friends on books and learning, and in return prayed assiduously for the souls of those who gave him the money to pursue his studies. Learning was his whole solicitude and care. He never spoke a word more than necessary, and then it was with due formality and respect, brief and to the point, and lofty in theme. His conversation was eloquent with goodness and virtue; he was as glad to learn as to teach.

A sage and cautious SERGEANT-AT-LAW, a well-known figure at the portico of St Paul's, where the lawyers meet, was also present. He was a man of excellent parts, discreet, and of great distinction —or so he seemed, he spoke with such wisdom. He had often acted as Judge of the Assize by the King's Letters Patent and had authority to hear all types of cases. His skill and great reputation earned him many fees, and robes given in lieu of money. Nowhere was there a better conveyancer; he could untie any entail and get unrestricted possession of the property, while his conveyances were never invalidated. There was no busier man anywhere; and yet he seemed busier than he was. He could quote precisely all the cases and judgements since the Conquest, besides which he could compose and draw up a deed so that none could fault it; and he knew all the statutes word for word. He was dressed simply in a particoloured coat girt by a silk belt with narrow stripes. I'll say no more of his appearance.

His companion was a FRANKLIN with a ruddy complexion and daisy-white beard, who was more than partial to a drink of sops-in-wine early in the morning. It was always his custom to live well, for he was a true son of Epicurus who held the opinion that the only real happiness lies in sensual pleasures. The Franklin kept up a magnificent establishment where he was as famous for hospitality as St Julian, its patron saint. The quality of his bread and wine never varied; his cellar was unsurpassed; his house never lacked food (whether fish or meat) in such plenty that in his house it seemed to snow food and drink and every kind of delicacy one can think of. Different dishes were served according to the season of the year. An abundance of fat partridges filled his coops, while his fishponds were plentifully stocked with bream and pike. His cook found himself in trouble if the sauce was not sharp and piquant or if he were caught unprepared. The hall table was kept laid and ready the livelong day. This Franklin presided at the sessions of justices of the peace and was often Member of Parliament for the shire. A dagger and a silk purse hung from his belt, which was white as milk. He had been Sheriff and Auditor of his county; nowhere would you find a better specimen of the landed gentry.

Among the rest were a HABERDASHER, a CARPENTER, a WEAVER, a DYER, and a TAPESTRY-MAKER, all dressed in uniform livery belonging to a rich and honourable Guild. Their apparel was new and freshly trimmed; their knives were not tipped with brass but finely mounted with wrought silver to match their belts and purses. Each seemed a proper burgess worthy of a place on the dais of a guildhall; and every one of them had the ability and judgement, besides sufficient property and income, to become an alderman. In this they would have the hearty assent of their wives—else the ladies would certainly be much to blame. For it's very pleasant to be called 'Madam' and take precedence at church festivals, and have one's mantle carried in state.

They had taken a COOK with them for the occasion, to boil chickens with marrowbones, tart flavouring-powder and spice. Well did he know the taste of London ale! He knew how to roast, fry, seethe, broil, make soup and bake pies. But it was the greatest pity, so I thought, that he'd got an ulcer on his shin. For he made chicken-pudding with the best of them.

A SEA-CAPTAIN, whose home was in the West Country, was also there; as far as I can tell he came from Dartmouth. He rode, after a fashion, upon a farm-horse; and wore a gown of coarse serge reaching to the knee. Under his arm he carried a dagger slung from a lanyard round his neck. The hot summer had tanned him brown; and he was certainly a bit of a lad, for he had lifted any amount of wine from Bordeaux while the merchants were napping. He had no time for the finer feelings; if he fought and got the upper hand, he threw his prisoners overboard and sent them home by water to wherever they came from. From Hull to Cartagena there was none to match his seamanship in calculating tides, currents, and the hazards around him; or his knowledge of harbours, navigation, and the changes of the moon. He was a shrewd and hardy adventurer; his beard had been shaken in many a storm. He knew every harbour there was from Gottland to Cape Finisterre, and every inlet of Brittany and Spain. The name of his ship was the *Magdalen*.

A DOCTOR OF MEDICINE accompanied us. There was none to touch him in matters of medicine and surgery, for he was well grounded in astronomy. His astrological knowledge enabled him to select the most favourable hour to administer remedies to his patients; and he was skilled in calculating the propitious moment to make talismans for his clients. He could diagnose every kind of disease and say in what organ and from which of the four humours—the hot, the cold, the wet, or the dry—the distemper arose. He was a model practitioner. Once he had detected the root of the trouble he gave the sick man his medicine there and then, for he had his apothecaries ready at hand to send him drugs and sirops. In this way each made a profit for the other—their partnership was not new. The Doctor was well versed in the ancient medical authors: Aesculapius, Dioscorides, Rufus, Hali, Galen, Serapion, Rhazes, Avicenna, Averroes, Constantine, Bernard, Gaddesden, and Gilbert. In his own diet he was moderate: it contained nothing superfluous but only what was nourishing and digestible. He seldom read the Bible. The clothes he was dressed in were blood-red and grey-blue, lined with silk and taffeta; yet he was no free spender, but laid by whatever he earned from the plague. In medicine gold is the great restorative; and therefore he was particularly fond of it.

There was among us a worthy WIFE from near Bath, but she was a bit deaf, which was a pity. At cloth-making she beat even the weavers of Ypres and Ghent. There was not a woman in her parish who dared go in front of her when she went to the offertory; if anybody did, you may be sure it put her into such a rage she was out of all patience. Her kerchiefs were of the finest texture; I daresay those she wore upon her head on Sundays weighed ten pounds. Her stockings were of the finest scarlet, tightly drawn up above glossy new shoes; her face was bold, handsome, and florid. She had been a respectable woman all her life, having married five husbands in church (apart from other loves in youth of which there is no need to speak at present). She had visited Jerusalem thrice and crossed many foreign rivers, had been to Rome, Boulogne, the shrine of St James of Compostella in Galicia, and Cologne; so she knew a lot about travelling around—the truth is, she was gap-toothed.* She rode comfortably upon an ambling horse, her head well covered with a wimple and a hat the size of a shield or buckler. An outer skirt covered her great hips, while on her feet she wore a pair of sharp spurs. In company she laughed and rattled away. No doubt she knew all the cures for love, for at that game she was past mistress.

With us there was a good religious man, a poor PARSON, but rich in holy thoughts and acts. He was also a learned man, a scholar, who truly preached Christ's Gospel and taught his parishioners devoutly. Benign, hardworking, and patient in adversity —as had often been put to the test—he was loath to excommunicate those who failed to pay their tithes. To tell the truth he would rather give to the poor of his parish what had been offered him by the rich, or from his own pocket; for he managed to live on very little. Wide as was his parish, with houses few and far between, neither rain nor thunder nor sickness nor misfortune stopped him from going on foot, staff in hand, to visit his most distant parishioners, high or low. To his flock he set this noble example: first he practised, then he preached. This was a precept he had taken from the Gospel; and to it he added this proverb: 'If gold can rust, what will iron do?' For if the priest in whom we trust be rotten, no wonder an ordinary man

---

* This was supposed to be a certain sign of luck and travel; and the physiognomists regarded it as a sign of a lascivious disposition.

corrupts. Let priests take note: shame it is to see the shepherd covered in dung while his sheep are clean! It's for the priest to set his flock the example of a spotless life! He did not farm his benefice and leave his sheep to flounder in the mud while he ran off to St Paul's in London to seek some easy living such as a chantry where he would be paid to sing masses for the souls of the dead, or a chaplaincy in one of the guilds; but dwelt at home and kept watch over his flock so that it was not harmed by the wolf. He was a shepherd, not a priest for hire.

And although he was saintly and virtuous he did not despise sinners. His manner of speaking was neither distant nor severe; on the contrary he was considerate and benign in his guidance. His endeavour was to lead folk to heaven by the example of a good life. Yet if anyone—whatever his rank—proved obstinate, he never hesitated to deliver a stinging rebuke. I'd say that there was nowhere a better priest. He never looked for ceremony and deference, nor was his conscience of the over-scrupulous and specious sort. He taught the Gospel of Christ and His twelve apostles: but first he followed it himself.

With him came his brother, a PLOUGHMAN. Many a load of dung had been carted by this good and faithful labourer, who lived in peace and charity with all. First he loved God with his whole heart, in good times and in bad; next he loved his neighbour as himself. He threshed and dug and ditched, and for Christ's love would do as much for any poor fellow without payment, if he could manage it. He paid his tithes on both his crops and the increase of his livestock fairly and in full. He rode humbly upon a mare and wore a loose labourer's smock.

Finally there was a REEVE, a MILLER, a SUMMONER, a PARDONER, a MANCIPLE, and last of all myself.

The MILLER was a great brawny fellow, big-boned, with powerful muscles which he turned to good account at wrestling matches up and down the land; for he carried off the prize every time. He was thickset, broad, and muscular; there was no door that he couldn't heave off its hinges, or break down by running at it with his head. His beard was as red as a fox or a sow, and wide as a spade at that. Upon the tip of his nose, on the right side, was a wart on which stood a tuft of hairs red as bristles in a pig's ear. His nostrils were squat and black. At his side he carried a sword and buckler. He had a great mouth, wide as a furnace-door; and his talk was mostly bawdy and vicious. He was a ribald joker and a chatterer. Well did he know all the tricks of his trade, how to filch corn and charge three times his proper due; yet he was honest enough, as millers go. He wore a white coat and a blue hood and led us out of town lustily blowing and tooting upon the bagpipes.

There was a worthy MANCIPLE of one of the Inns of Court, who might have served as a model to caterers for shrewdness in the purchase of provisions; for whether he paid cash or bought on credit, he watched prices all the time, so that he always got in first and did good business. Now is it not a remarkable example of God's grace that the wit of an uneducated man like this should outmatch the wisdom of a pack of learned men? His superiors numbered more than thirty and were all erudite and expert in the law; there were a dozen men in his college capable of so managing the rents and land of any peer in England as to enable him (unless he were mad) to live honourably and free of debt upon his income, or else as plainly as he pleased; capable too of advising a whole county in any lawsuit that might conceivably arise; yet this Manciple could hoodwink the lot of them!

The REEVE was a slender, choleric man. He shaved his beard as close he could, and cropped his hair short round the ears; the top of his head was shorn in front like a priest's. He had long thin legs like sticks; the calves were invisible. He kept his bins and granaries ably; no auditor could get the better of him. By noting the drought and rainfall he could make a good estimate of the yield of his seed and grain. All his master's livestock, sheep, cattle, dairy, pigs, horses, and poultry was entirely managed by this Reeve, who had undertaken to render accounts ever since his master was twenty years old. None could prove he was in arrears. He knew every dodge and swindle of every one of the bailiffs, herdsmen, and farm-labourers; they feared him like death itself. He lived in a beautiful house standing in a meadow shaded by green trees. At bargaining he was better than his master and had feathered his nest very comfortably. For he was adroit at putting his master under an obligation by a gift or loan of his own property, thus earning his thanks besides the present of a gown or a hood. As a young man he had learned a good

trade; he was a skilled workman, a carpenter. This Reeve rode a
sturdy dapple-grey cob called Scot. He wore a long blue over-
coat with a rusty sword by his side. The Reeve of whom I
speak came from near the town of Bawdeswell in Norfolk. He
had his coat hitched up by a girdle like a friar, and always rode
the hindmost of our party.

Among us at the inn was a SUMMONER* with slit eyes and a
flaming red visage like a cherub's, all covered with pimples. He
was as randy and lecherous as a sparrow. Children were afraid
of his face with its scabbed black eyebrows and scraggy beard.
No mercury, white lead, sulphur, borax, ceruse, cream of tartar,
or other oinments that cleanse and burn could rid him of his
white pustules or the pimply knobs on his cheeks. He had a great
love of garlic, onions, and leeks, and of drinking strong wine
red as blood, which made him roar and gabble like a madman.
When really drunk on wine he'd speak nothing but Latin. He
knew two or three tags that he'd learned from some decree or
other—and no wonder, for he heard Latin all day long; but as
you know a jaybird can call out 'Wat' as well as the Pope him-
self. Yet if you tried him further you found he was out of his
depth; all he could do was parrot *'questio quid juris'†* over and
over. He was a tolerant easy-going dog, as good a fellow as you
might hope to find. For a quart of wine he'd allow any rascal
of a priest to keep his concubine for a twelvemonth and excuse
him altogether; on the other hand he was well able to fleece a
greenhorn on the sly. And if he found a fellow with a girl he'd
tell him not to worry about the Archdeacon's excommunication
in such a case, unless he thought his purse was where his soul was
kept, for it was in his purse he'd be punished. 'Your purse is
the Archdeacon's Hell,' he would say. But I am sure he lied in
his teeth; the guilty must fear excommunication because it
destroys the soul just as absolution saves it—and they should also
beware of the writ that sends them to prison. All the young
people of his diocese were wholly under his thumb, for he was

---

* A summoner was an officer or constable whose task was to summon
delinquents to appear before the ecclesiastical courts, enforce payment of
tithes and church dues, etc. He also had power to punish adultery, fornica-
tion, and other sins not punishable by common law. *The Friar's Tale* is a
satire on the abuses practised by Summoners.

† 'What is the law on this point?'

their confidant and sole adviser. Upon his head the Summoner had set a garland as big as one of those they hang outside ale-houses. He had a great round cake which he carried like a shield.

With him rode a worthy PARDONER* of Rouncival at Charing Cross, his friend and bosom companion, who had come straight from the Vatican at Rome. He loudly carolled 'Come hither, love, to me', while the Summoner sang the bass louder than the loudest trumpet. This Pardoner's hair was waxy yellow and hung down as sleek as a hank of flax; such locks of hair as he possessed fell in meagre clusters spread over his shoulders, where it lay in thinly scattered strands. For comfort he wore no hood; it was packed in his bag. With his hair loose and uncovered except for a cap, he thought he was riding in the latest style. He had great staring eyes like a hare's. Upon his cap he'd sewn a small replica of St Veronica's handkerchief. His wallet lay on his lap in front of him, chockful of pardons hot from Rome. He'd a thin goatlike voice and no vestige or prospect of a beard; and his skin was smooth as if just shaven. I took him for a gelding or a mare. But as for his profession, from Berwick down to Ware there was not another pardoner to touch him. For in his wallet he kept a pillow-slip which, he said, was Our Lady's veil. He claimed to have a bit of the sail belonging to St Peter when he tried to walk on the waves and Jesus Christ caught hold of him. He had a brass cross set with pebbles and a glass reliquary full of pig's bones. Yet when he came across some poor country parson he could make more money with these relics in a day than the parson got in two months; and thus by means of barefaced flattery and hocus-pocus he made the parson and the people his dupes. To do him justice, in church at any rate he was a fine ecclesiastic. Well could he read a lesson or a parable; but best of all he sang the offertory hymn, because after it was sung he knew he must preach, as he well knew how, to wheedle money from the congregation with his smooth tongue. Therefore he sang all the louder and merrier.

Now I have told you in a few words the class of person, dress, and number of our party and the reason why it assembled in

---

* Pardoners were sellers of papal indulgencies, i.e. commutations of penances imposed for sins. The profits were supposed to go to religious organizations, or to be used for some pious purpose.

this excellent inn at Southwark, the Tabard hard by the Bell. And now it's time to tell you how we comported ourselves the night of our arrival at the inn; and afterwards I'll speak of our journey and the rest of our pilgrimage. But first I must beg you to be good enough not to put it down to my lack of refinement if in this matter I use plain language to give an account of their conversation and behaviour and when reporting their actual words. For you know as well as I do that whoever repeats a story told by another must reproduce as nearly as he can every word entrusted to him, no matter how uncouth or free the language; or else falsify the tale, or invent, or find new words for it. Be the man his brother, he may not shrink, but whatever words are used he also must use. In the Bible the language of Christ Himself is outspoken; but as you well know, it's no breach of taste. Besides, Plato says (as anyone who can read him may see), 'The words must relate to the action.' Also I beg you to forgive me if in this account I have not paid due attention to people's rank and the order in which they should appear. My wits aren't too bright, as you may suppose.

Our HOST welcomed each of us with open arms and soon led us to our places at the supper-table. He served us with the finest viands; the wine was strong and we were in a mood to drink. Our Host was a striking-looking fellow, a fit master of ceremonies for any hall. He was a big man with prominent eyes (there's no better-looking City burgess in Cheapside), racy in his talk, shrewd yet civil; a proper man in every respect. What's more, he was a bit of a wag, for after supper, when we'd settled our bills, among other things he began to talk of amusing us, saying: 'Ladies and gentlemen, you're all most heartily welcome, for on my honour I'm telling you no lie when I say I've not seen such a jolly company as this under my roof at any one time this year. I'd like to provide you with some entertainment if I knew how to see about it. And I've just thought of a game that will amuse you and not cost a penny.

'You're off to Canterbury—Godspeed, and the blessed martyr reward you! And you mean to entertain yourselves by telling stories on the way, I'll be bound; for there's certainly no sense or fun in riding along as dumb as stones; and so, as I said before, I'll devise a game that'll give you some amusement. If it pleases

you all to accept my decision unanimously and to do as I'll tell
you when you ride off tomorrow, then I swear by my father's
soul you can have my head if you don't enjoy yourselves! Not
another word—hands up, everyone!'

It did not take us long to make up our minds. We saw no point
in deliberating, but agreed to his proposal without further argu-
ment and asked him to give what commands he liked.

'Ladies and gentlemen,' began the Host, 'do yourselves a good
turn and listen to what I say, and please don't turn up your noses
at it. This is the point in a nutshell: each of you, to make the
road seem shorter, shall tell two stories on the journey—I mean
two on the way to Canterbury and two others on the way home
—tales of once upon a time. Whoever tells his story best—that's
to say whoever spins the most edifying and amusing tale—is to
be given a dinner at the expense of the rest of us, here in this
inn and under this very roof, when we return from Canterbury.
And just to make it the more fun for you I'll gladly ride with
you myself at my own cost and be your guide. Anybody who
gainsays my judgement shall pay all our expenses on the road!
Now if you agree, let me know here and now without more ado,
and I'll make my arrangements early.'

The matter was agreed; we gave our promises gladly, begging
him to do as he proposed and be our leader, judge and arbiter
of our tales, and arrange a dinner at a set price. We agreed to
be ruled by his decision in every respect; and thus we unani-
mously submitted ourselves to his judgement. Thereupon more
wine was fetched, and when we had drunk it we all went to
bed without further delay.

Next morning our Host rose up at break of day, roused us all
and gathered us together in a flock. We rode off at little more
than a walking-pace until we came to the watering-place of St
Thomas, where our Host reined his horse and said, 'Attention,
please, ladies and gentlemen! You know what you promised;
remember? If you're of the same mind this morning as you were
last night, then let's see who's to tell the first tale. Whoever
rebels against my ruling must pay for everything we spend upon
the road, or may I never drink another drop! Now let's draw lots
before going further. Sir Knight,' said he, 'will your honour
draw lots, for that is my decree. Come nearer, my lady Prioress,

and you too, Master Scholar; lay aside that diffidence and come out of your brown study—all hands draw lots.'

Upon this everybody began drawing lots, and in fine, whether by luck, or fate, or chance, the truth is that to everyone's delight the lot fell to the Knight. Now he must tell his tale, as was right and proper according to the bargain I've described. What more can I say? And when that good man saw how things were, he very sensibly obeyed the promise he had freely given and said, 'Since I must begin the game, why, then, welcome be the luck of the draw, in God's name! Now let us ride on; and listen to what I say.' With that we began to ride forward on our way, and at once he cheerfully began his tale, which went like this.

THE KNIGHT'S TALE

he old legends tell us there was once a Duke called Theseus who was lord and ruler of Athens. In his time there was no mightier conqueror under the sun. He had overrun many rich kingdoms, and by his generalship and knightly valour had conquered the land of the Amazons, then called Scythia, and wedded Hippolyta their queen, whom he brought home with him to his own land in the greatest pomp and splendour, together with her younger sister Emily. And so I leave this noble Duke and his armed host riding victoriously and with music towards Athens. If it weren't too long to listen to I would certainly describe in detail how the land of women was vanquished by Theseus and his knights; and especially the pitched battle between the Athenians and the Amazons; how Hippolyta, the fierce and beautiful queen of Scythia, was besieged; the feast that took place at their wedding, and the great storm that blew up on their voyage home. But for the time being I must pass over all these things—God knows I have a big field to plough and weak oxen in my team. The rest of my tale is long enough; and I don't want to stand in the way of the others in our party. Let everyone tell his tale in turn and we'll see who wins the dinner. So I'll begin again where I left off.

The Duke I spoke of had just approached the outskirts of the town when, in the midst of all his joy and triumph, he noticed out of the corner of his eye a band of ladies dressed in black kneeling two by two in a row on the highway. They were weeping and wailing, making a lamentation the like of which no living creature ever heard; nor would they stop their clamour until they had laid hold of his bridle-rein.

'Who may you be who disturb my homecoming and the general joy with these outcries?' asked Thesus. 'Is it because you grudge me these honours that you complain and cry out like this? Or has somebody insulted or injured you? Tell me if it can be redressed, and why you are thus clothed in black.'

Almost fainting, with a deathlike countenance pitiful to see, the eldest of these ladies began to speak: 'My lord, to whom Fortune has granted victory and all the honours of a conqueror, we do not grudge you your laurels or your triumph, but beg for aid and mercy. Have mercy on our distress and grief! Out of the nobility of your heart let some drop of pity fall upon us wretched women— for indeed, my lord, there is not one of us who was not once a duchess or a queen. But now, as anyone can see, we are the most miserable of women, thanks to Fortune's treacherous wheel which sees to it that no state of affairs continues happy. Indeed, my lord, we have been waiting your arrival here in the temple of the Goddess of Pity for a whole fortnight. Now help us, Sir, since it lies in your power!

'I who weep here in misery was once the wife of King Capaneus who perished at Thebes. Cursed be that day! And all of us who are lamenting in this dress lost their husbands while the town was being besieged. Alas! alas! at this very moment old Creon, who is now lord of the city of Thebes, is filled with wrath and iniquity and dishonours their corpses: in his tyrannic spite he has dragged the bodies of our slain husbands upon a heap and will not hear of their being burned or given burial, but contemptuously gives them to the dogs to eat.'

Saying this they immediately fell upon their faces, pitifully crying out, 'Have mercy upon us wretched women, and let our grief sink into your heart.'

When the Duke heard them speak he leapt from his horse with his heart full of pity; seeing how forlorn and dejected they were who had once been of such high estate, he felt as if his heart must break. He raised each of them in his arms and tried to give comfort, swearing upon his knighthood that he would exert his utmost might to avenge them upon the tyrant till all Greece should resound with the manner in which Theseus awarded Creon the death he so richly deserved. Then without waiting further he displayed his banner to summon his men and rode against Thebes with his whole army. Nor would he approach any nearer Athens, even to rest half a day, but lodged that night on the road to Thebes. He sent his queen Hippolyta and her young and lovely sister Emily into the city of Athens there to remain while he rode forth. What more can I say?

The red image of Mars with spear and shield gleamed from his

great white banner till its reflection glittered up and down all the
fields through which they rode. Beside the banner was borne his
pennon of rich gold embroidered with the figure of the Minotaur
he had slain in Crete. So the conquering Duke rode with his
army, the flower of chivalry, until he came to Thebes where he
drew up in splendid array before the field of battle. But to cut the
story short, he fought with Creon king of Thebes and slew him
in fair combat like a valiant knight; then having routed his men
he took the city by storm, tearing down walls, beams, and rafters.
Next Theseus restored to the women the bones of their slain hus-
bands so that they might be accorded the customary funeral rites.
It would take much too long to describe the din of lamentation the
ladies made at the burning of the corpses, or the great courtesy
the noble conqueror Theseus paid them when they took leave
of him, for I mean to tell my story as briefly as I can.

Having slain Creon, taken Thebes and disposed of the whole
kingdom as he thought fit, the noble Duke Theseus camped
quietly in the field that night. But after the battle and the flight of
the Thebans, pillagers busily ransacked the pile of dead bodies,
stripping them of arms and clothing. It so happened that among
the heaped corpses they found two young knights lying bleeding
side by side, clad in the same richly-wrought armour and pierced
through with many grievous wounds. Arcite was the name of
one; the other knight was called Palamon. Half-dead and half-
alive though they were, the heralds identified them, particularly
from their coats-of-arms and equipment, as cousins and members
of the royal house of Thebes. The looters dragged them from the
pile of corpses and carried them gently to the tent of Theseus,
who, refusing to hear of any ransom, immediately sent them to
perpetual imprisonment in Athens. This done, the noble Duke
and his army rode straight home, crowned with conquering
laurels. And there, needless to say, he lives in honour and in joy
for the remainder of his days, while Palamon and his friend Arcite
are shut up for ever in a tower, in misery and grief; no amount of
gold can secure their release.

Thus passed the days and years, till one May morning it
chanced that Emily—she was lovelier to look upon than a lily on
its stalk of green, and fresher than May with all its budding
flowers; for her hue competed with the rose, and I don't know

which was the prettier—had risen and dressed herself before day-light as she often did.

The nights of May are not for sleep, for the time of year stirs each noble heart, rousing it from slumber with the bidding, 'Arise and pay homage to the season.' This made Emily remember to do honour to the month of May, and she got up. Picture her clothed in bright colours, her yellow hair falling down her back and braided in a tress perhaps a yard long, wandering at will in the garden at the rising of the sun to gather white and scarlet flowers to weave a delicate garland for her head; and singing with a heavenly voice like an angel's.

A mighty tower, thick and strong, the principal keep of the castle in which the two knights who are the subject of my tale were shut up, adjoined the garden wall where Emily was amusing herself. The sun was bright and clear that morning; and poor captive Palamon had risen as usual. By leave of his jailer he was roaming about in an upper room from which he could see the noble prospect of the city and also the green-branched garden where Emily, so radiant and fresh, was walking up and down. As the captive Palamon sadly paced to and fro in the chamber, com-miserating with himself and often crying out: 'Alas that I was born!' it happened that, whether by chance or fate, his glance fell on Emily through a window thickly fenced with iron bars as square and massive as stakes of timber: at which he started back with a cry, sung to the heart. And at the noise Arcite leapt to his feet and said, 'What is the matter, cousin? Why do you look so deadly pale? Why did you cry out? Who has upset you? For the love of God be patient in our imprisonment—there is no alterna-tive. This hardship is the gift of Fortune; some malign aspect or disposition of Saturn and the constellations has allotted it to us in spite of all we can do. It was in our stars when we were born; the long and short of it is, we must endure our fate.'

Palamon replied, 'Indeeed, cousin, you've got hold of the wrong idea. It was not this prison which made me cry out, for just now my eye was pierced right through to my heart with a wound that I fear will prove mortal. The beauty of that lady I see wandering in the garden there is the sole cause of my crying out and of my grief. Whether she is a goddess or a woman I cannot tell, but by my guess it is Venus herself.' And with that he fell down on his knees and said, 'Venus, if it be your will to manifest yourself in this garden to so sorrowful and wretched a creature as I, help us to escape from this prison; yet if my destiny is irrevocably fixed by an eternal fiat to die in captivity, have some pity upon our noble blood brought low by tyranny.'

But while he was speaking Arcite caught a glimpse of the lady as she walked to and fro. At the sight of her beauty he was so shaken that if Palamon was sorely wounded, Arcite was as badly hit or more. Sadly he said, 'The fresh beauty of that girl wandering there has dealt me a blow as sudden as it is mortal; unless I obtain her pity and favour so that I can at least see her, I am no better than a dead man—that's all I can say.'

When he heard these words Palamon replied sharply, 'Do you say that in game or in earnest?'

'In earnest and good faith,' returned Arcite, 'So help me God, I am in no mood to joke.'

Palamon knitted his brows and answered, 'It would do you no great honour were you to prove faithless or a traitor to me, seeing that I am not only your cousin but your sworn brother. We are each bound to the other by the most solemn oaths: that never till death do us part—not even death by torture—shall either stand in the other's way in matters of love or of anything else. On the contrary you, dear brother, must always come faithfully to my aid just as I must come to yours. That was your sworn oath, and mine also, and I know perfectly well that you dare not gainsay it. For this reason I trustfully confided in you; but now you are treacherously seeking to love the lady whom I must always love and serve till my heart stops beating. No, you won't, false Arcite, that's certain! I was first to love her; I told you about it only because, as I said before, you are the confidant of my secrets, my sworn brother pledged to come to my help, and therefore bound as a knight to give me what aid you can—otherwise I dare call you forsworn.'

Arcite disdainfully retorted: 'You are more likely to prove forsworn than I—and you are utterly forsworn, I tell you plainly! For I loved her passionately before you did. What can you say? Just now you did not know whether she is a woman or a goddess. Yours is a spiritual affection, while mine is love of a human being

—that's why I told you what had happened to me, as to my cousin and sworn brother.

'Suppose for the sake of argument that you loved her first. Have you never heard the old philosopher's adage: "Who can lay down the law to a lover?" Upon my soul, love is a greater law than any decreed by mortal men; and therefore all man-made laws and like injunctions are broken every day for love by all kinds of people. A man must love, against all reason. Even if it should cost him his life there's no escaping it, whether she be maid, widow or wife. And anyway it is hardly likely you will ever win her favour any more than I shall, for as you well know we are both condemned to a perpetual imprisonment from which no ransom will buy us out. We are quarrelling like the two dogs who fought all day over a bone but got no share of it: while they bickered a kite came along and carried off the bone from between them both. And so, brother, as in high politics, it's every man for himself—that's all there is to it. Love her if you wish, for I love her and always will. Dear brother, each of us must endure this prison and take his chance, that's all.'

Had I the time I would describe their long and bitter quarrel. But to cut a long story short, in the end a noble Duke called Perotheus, who had been a friend of Duke Theseus since they were small children, came to Athens one day, as he often did, to take a holiday and visit his old companion; for there was nobody he loved more in the world, and Theseus loved him just as tenderly in return. So great indeed was their love, ancient writers say that when one of them died his friend went and looked for him down in hell. But that's another story.

Duke Perotheus loved Arcite greatly, having known him for many years in Thebes. And finally, at Perotheus' request and entreaty Duke Theseus let him out of prison without ransom, free to go wherever he pleased upon the following condition.

In plain terms the covenant between Theseus and Arcite was this: it was agreed that if Arcite were ever caught alive at any time by day or night in any of Theseus' dominions, his head was to be struck off with a sword. There was no help for it; Arcite had no alternative but to take his leave and hasten home. He'd better watch out: his neck is forfeit!

Then what anguish Arcite suffered! He felt death strike into his heart; he wept and wailed and made a pitiful clamour, and watched secretly for a chance to kill himself. 'Alas the day I was born!' he cried, 'for now my prison is worse than it was before: I am eternally doomed to live, not in purgatory but in hell! Alas that I ever met Perotheus! Otherwise I might have remained with Theseus, fettered in his prison for ever. Then I would have been living in happiness instead of misery. The mere sight of her whom I serve would have been more than enough for me even if I may never deserve her favour. Dear cousin Palamon,' he went on, 'in this case you have come out best. How happily may you remain in prison—not prison, but paradise! Fortune has certainly loaded the dice in your favour: you have Emily's presence, I her absence. And it is possible (for you are near her, and a doughty and resourceful knight) that by some chance—Fortune is changeable—you will sooner or later attain your desire. But as for me, exiled and barren of all hope, in such despair that neither earth, fire, water, nor air nor any creature made of the elements can afford me comfort or remedy—well may I perish in desperation and distress. Farewell, life, joy and felicity! Alas, why is it that people in general complain against the providence of God or Fortune, which so often and in so many ways dispose events far better than they could devise for themselves? One would have riches—which may cause his murder or loss of health; another would be freed from prison, only to be slain by his servants on reaching home. Endless disasters come from this: we do not know what it is that we pray for here below. We behave like a man who's drunk as an owl—he knows well enough that he has a home to go to but doesn't know where it is; and a drunk man walks a slippery road. And that's just how we go about the world, searching desperately for happiness but generally in the wrong quarter. This is true of all of us and particularly myself—I who conceived a great notion that if I could only escape from prison my happiness and well-being would be assured, and now find myself exiled from all peace of mind. If I cannot see you, Emily, I am no better than a corpse; there's no remedy.'

On the other hand when Palamon realized that Arcite had gone, he made such an outcry that the great tower resounded with his bellowing and clamour. The huge fetters on his shins were wet with his salt, bitter tears. 'Alas,' he cried, 'my cousin Arcite,

God knows you have had the better of our quarrel, for you now walk at large in Thebes and care nothing for my misery. Being a shrewd and resolute man you are in a position to muster our kinsfolk and make such fierce war on Athens that by some bold stroke, or by some treaty, you may yet have Emily for your lady and your wife—she for whom I here must perish. When one weighs the possibilities, your position is so much better than mine, here dying in a cage. For you are a Prince, no longer in prison but at liberty. But I must weep and lament out my life with all the misery prison brings; and with the added pangs of love, which doubles my whole torment and grief.'

Then the flame of jealousy sprang up within his breast and took hold of his heart with such fury that he turned the colour of box-wood, or of ashes when they are cold and dead; and he cried: 'O you cruel Gods who rule this world, binding it with your eternal fiat, and writing on tables of adamant your eternal decisions and decrees, how can mankind be of greater concern to you than the sheep that cower in the fold? For man dies like any other beast, and often suffers arrest and imprisonment besides, or endures plagues and adversity, for no guilt whatever. What method is in your foreknowledge if it torments the innocent and guiltless? And what increases the whole penance, man is bound to walk according to the laws of God and must curb his desires, while a beast may do what it pleases; when it dies it feels no pain, yet after death man must weep and suffer, though enduring trouble and grief in this world. No doubt of it, that's how things stand. I leave it to the divines to provide the answer, but I am sure of one thing: there is great misery here on earth. Alas! I see some viper, a thief who has done mischief to many good men, go free to wander where he likes; but I must languish in prison because Saturn and Juno in their jealous rage destroyed well-nigh all the best blood of Thebes, whose broad walls lie waste and broken. And on the other hand Venus murders me with jealousy and fear of Arcite.'

Now I'll give Palamon a rest, and leave him to stay in his prison while I tell you more about Arcite.

The summer passes and its long nights double the violent torments of the lover, Arcite, and the prisoner, Palamon. I don't know which of them has the most to bear. In short, Palamon is condemned to perpetual imprisonment in chains and fetters till he dies, while Arcite, exiled on pain of death from Theseus' dominions for ever, is never to see his lady again.

Now, you lovers, let me pose the question: who has the worst of it, Arcite or Palamon? The one can see his lady every day, but is lodged in prison for ever; the other, while free to go where he pleases, may never again see his lady. Those who can may choose between them as they please; as for me, I will continue as I began.

ii

When Arcite arrived in Thebes, many times a day he fainted and cried out; for he was never again to see his lady. To sum up, his anguish was so great that no living creature ever suffered or is likely to suffer as much as he while the world endures. Bereft of sleep, food and drink, Arcite became as thin and dry as a stick, while his eyes grew hollow and cadaverous, his face ash-white and sallow. He was always solitary and alone, bewailing his woes the whole night long and bursting into uncontrollable tears at the sound of music or singing. His spirits became so weak and enfeebled and himself so altered that no one could recognize his voice or speech even if they heard it. As for his appearance, he went about for all the world as though he were not merely suffering from lovesickness but actual mania engendered by some melancholic humour in the forehead, where the imagination has its seat. In short, the behaviour as well as the character of Prince Arcite, that woebegone lover, had been turned entirely upside down.

But I needn't take all day to describe his sufferings. When he had endured this cruel anguish and torment for a year or two in Thebes (his native land as I have said), one night as he lay down to sleep he imagined the winged god Mercury stood before him, telling him to cheer up. He had his sleep-giving wand upright in his hand and wore a helmet upon his gleaming hair. Here let me note that the god was dressed as he was when he lulled Argus to slumber. To Arcite he said: 'You are to go to Athens. There your troubles are destined to end.' At these words Arcite awoke and started up. 'Indeed I will go to Athens at once, no matter how heavy the cost,' he said. 'No fear of death is going to stop me from seeing the lady whom I love and serve. In her presence I care nothing if I die.'

Saying this he picked up a large mirror; and noticed that his colour was wholly changed and his face completely altered. It immediately occurred to him that since his face had been so dis-figured by the illness he had suffered, he might easily live unrecognized in Athens and see his lady almost every day so long as he behaved inconspicuously. At once he changed his apparel, dressed himself in workman's clothes and took the quickest route to Athens, accompanied only by a squire as shabbily disguised as himself, to whom he had confided his whole story.

One day he went to the palace and offered his services at the gate for any kind of rough work, whatever might be required. To cut the story short, he got a job under a chamberlain who belonged to Emily's establishment: a shrewd fellow who kept a sharp eye on every one of her servants to see they did their work. As he was young, tall, powerfully built and exceptionally strong, Arcite did well as a hewer of wood and drawer of water, for he could perform anything that was asked of him. Saying that his name was Philostrate, he spent a year or two in service as chamber-page to Emily the fair: and no one of his station at the court was half so well-liked. His character was so noble that it became famous throughout the palace. It was said that it would be a gracious act were Theseus to promote him and give him a worthier position in which to exercise his talents. And so in time his reputation for courtesy and helpfulness spread until Theseus took him into his personal service, making him his chamber squire and giving him money to maintain his new position. Not only that, but each year money was secretly brought to him from his own land, which he spent with such prudence and discretion that no one wondered how he came by it. In this manner he lived three years, acquitting himself so well in peace and war that there was none whom Theseus valued more. Now I will leave Arcite in this happy condition and speak of Palamon for a little.

Palamon, wasted away with anguish and distress, has lodged these seven years in the horrible darkness of his impregnable prison. Who feels twofold grief and pain if not Palamon, whom love so afflicts that he is about to go out of his wits from sheer misery? On top of all this he is a prisoner, not for a year or so but for life. Who can put into English a just idea of his martyrdom? Certainly not I; so I pass over it as quickly as I can.

According to the ancient writers who tell this story so much more fully, on the third night of May in the seventh year of his imprisonment it came about (either by chance or fate; for once a thing is decreed it must take place) that Palamon, helped by a friend, broke out of his prison shortly after midnight and fled from Athens as fast as he could go. For he had given his jailer a drink of a kind of spiced honeyed cup made from a certain wine mixed with narcotics and fine Theban opium. As a result the jailer slept the whole of that night; no amount of shaking could have roused him. And so Palamon fled as fast as his heels could carry him.

The night being short and day near at hand, Palamon had to hide himself at all costs; so he tiptoed cautiously towards a grove near by. In short, his idea was to hide all day in the grove and then make his way to Thebes by night and beg his friends to help him make war on Theseus. In a word, his intention was either to perish or win Emily for his bride.

Now I'll turn again to Arcite, who little guessed how close he was to trouble till Fortune sprang the trap.

The busy lark, messenger of day, saluted in her song the grey dawn, while burning Phoebus rose in splendour till the whole East laughed in his radiance and his beams dried the silver drops hanging upon the leaves of the brakes. Arcite, chief squire at the royal court of Theseus, arose and looked out upon the cheerful day. In order to pay homage to the month of May—and thinking all the while upon the object of his desire—to amuse himself he rode a fiery courser into the fields a mile or two away from the court. By chance he began to steer his course towards the grove I mentioned, to make himself a garland from leaves of hawthorn or woodbine. And he sang lustily in the sunlight:

> May with all your flowers and greenery,
> Welcome to you, fair, fresh May,
> I hope to get for you some greenery.

He leapt lightheartedly from his horse and quickly made his way into the grove, where he wandered along a path near the thicket in which Palamon, in fear of his life, happened to be hidden from view. Palamon had not the least idea it was Arcite—heaven knows he would hardly have believed it—but as the old proverb truly says, 'Fields have eyes, and woods have ears.' It's a good idea to keep a level head, for people are always meeting when they least expect it. Little did Arcite imagine that his friend, crouching motionless in a bush, was near enough to hear his every word.

Tired of wandering, Arcite gaily finished his song. Then suddenly he fell into a brown study—as is the odd habit of lovers, whose moods go up and down like a bucket in a well, now high in the treetops and now sunk among the undergrowth. In fact capricious Venus overcasts the hearts of her followers exactly like a Friday, fine one moment and pouring the next; and just as Friday (which is her day) is fickle, so she changes mood—a Friday is seldom like the rest of the week.

When his song was finished Arcrite began to sigh, and sat down without further ado. 'Alas the day that I was born!' he said. 'O pitiless Juno, how much longer will you make war against the city of Thebes? Alas! The royal blood of Cadmus and Amphion is brought to destruction—Cadmus, who founded Thebes before the town first began, and was the first crowned king of the city. I am of his blood, descended in the true line from the royal stock; and now so miserable a slave am I that I serve my deadliest enemy as a menial squire. Yet Juno heaps still more shame upon me, for I dare not acknowledge my own name—whereas I used to be called Arcite I am now called Philostrate—fiddlestick! O relentless Mars! O Juno! Thus has your wrath wiped out the whole of our family save only myself and wretched Palamon, whom Theseus martyrs in prison. And on top of all this, as if to annihilate me utterly, Love has thrust his flaming dart so scorchingly through my troubled faithful breast that it seems as if my death had been prepared for me before I was born. O Emily, one look from your eyes has destroyed me! I die because of you. I wouldn't give a straw for the rest of my troubles if only I could do anything that would please you.' And with this he fell into a long trance—and then jumped up.

As for Palamon, who felt as if a cold sword had suddenly slid through his heart, he shook with anger, he could stand it no longer. After hearing Arcite to the end, he leapt out of the thick undergrowth, his face dead white like a madman's, crying, 'Black traitor Arcite! I've got you now—you who love the lady for whom I suffer misery and anguish—you, my blood-brother, my sworn confidant as I've reminded you often enough! You who slyly changed your name and hoodwinked Duke Theseus here! One of us must die! You're not going to love the lady Emily—no one but I alone—for I'm your deadly enemy Palamon! Although I've no weapon here with me, since I've only just had the luck to break out of prison, never fear, you must either die or give up your love for Emily—take your choice; for you shan't escape.'

As soon as Arcite recognized him and heard his story, his heart filled with contemptuous rage. Fierce as a lion, he pulled out his sword and exclaimed, 'By God in heaven, if it weren't that you're sick and crazed with love, and weaponless besides, before you left this grove you'd die by my hand. For I disown those covenants which you say I made with you. You fool, get this into your head: Love is free!—and I shall love her in spite of anything you can do. But as you're an honourable knight, ready to support your claim to her in battle, here is my word of honour that I will not fail to turn up in this spot tomorrow without anyone knowing, clad as a knight and bringing sufficient armour for you as well—you can choose the best and leave me the worst. Tonight I'll fetch you enough to eat and drink, and clothes for your bedding. And should you win my lady and kill me in this thicket, then she's yours as far as I am concerned.'

Palamon answered, 'Agreed.' And when each had pledged his word they parted till next day.

Inexorable Cupid, whose dominion admits no rival partner! It has truly been said, 'Neither Love nor Power will tolerate friendship', as Arcite and Palamon are learning only too well. Arcite rode straight back to the city. Next morning, before daylight, he secretly prepared two complete sets of armour with which the pitched battle between the pair of them might suitably be decided. Alone he carried this armour before him on his horse. And at the fixed time and place Arcite and Palamon faced one another in the grove.

Their faces began to change colour, as when Thracian huntsmen, guarding a gap in the thickets with their spears while hunting bear or lion, hear the beast come rushing through the brake, crashing through leaves and branches, and think: 'Here comes my mortal enemy—whatever happens one of us must be killed—I must either slay it when it breaks cover or it must kill me if I make a mistake.' Just so the two knights changed colour, each knowing the other's prowess.

They exchanged neither greeting nor salutation, but straight-away without a word or preliminary each helped to arm the other as amicably as if they were brothers. Then they lunged and thrust at one another with their strong sharp spears for hours on end. To see them fight you'd have thought Palamon was a raging lion and Arcite a relentless tiger. In their mad fury they went at each other like wild boars frothing white foam, until they fought in blood up to the ankles.

Let me leave them fighting like this while I return to Theseus.

So strong is Destiny, the paramount minister, which everywhere carries out the providence foreseen by God, that events which everyone swears impossible are sooner or later brought to pass, if only once in a thousand years. Certainly our passions are wholly governed by a providence above, whether they be of war, or peace, or hate, or love. All this applies to great Theseus, who was so eager for the chase, and especially to hunt the stag in May, that dawn never found him in his bed but dressed and ready to ride out with huntsmen, horn, and hounds. Such was his delight in hunting that the killing of the stag had become his ruling passion: next to the god of war he followed the huntress Diana.

The day was fine, as I said before, when Theseus gaily set out hunting with his beautiful queen Hippolyta and Emily, all dressed in green and riding in royal array. Duke Theseus held his course directly towards a nearby grove, in which he had been told there was a stag. He rode straight towards the clearing where the stag was likely to break cover, leaping the brook and so off on his way. The Duke hoped to try a course or two at him with the hounds he had picked.

When the Duke came to the clearing he looked round, shielding his eyes from the sun, and at once saw Arcite and Palamon fiercely fighting like two boars. The flashing swords swung back and forth so fearsomely that it seemed the least of their strokes was enough to fell an oak. Who they were he had no notion. The Duke clapped spurs to his courser and at a bound was between the pair of them. He pulled out his sword, crying, 'Stop! No more, on pain of death! By mighty Mars, whoever I see strike another blow dies on the spot! But tell me what manner of men you are, who make so bold as to fight here without a judge or other referee as if it were a royal tournament?'

Palamon made haste to answer: 'Sir, there is nothing to be said. Both of us deserve death. We are two miserable wretches, captives whose lives are burdens to themselves. As you are a lawful prince and judge, grant us neither mercy nor escape. For charity's sake, kill me first; but slay my companion together with me, or first kill him, for you little know he is your mortal enemy: Arcite whom you banished from your country on pain of death—for that alone he deserves the penalty! For he's the man who came to your palace door calling himself Philostrate. All these years he's fooled you till you made him your chief squire—and that's the man who loves Emily! Now that my last day has come I'll make a clean breast of it: I am the wretched Palamon who criminally broke out of your prison. I am your mortal foe! And I am so passionately in love with the fair Emily that I am ready to die before her eyes this instant. Therefore I ask for the penalty of death. But kill my companion along with me, for we both deserve to be slain.'

To this the noble Duke at once returned, 'That would seem to sum it up. By this confession your own mouth has condemned you, and I confirm the sentence. There is no need for a rope to make you talk! By red almighty Mars, you die!'

Then the Queen began to weep out of sheer womanly sympathy, and so did Emily and all the ladies of the party. They thought it a great pity such a fate should befall them, since they were noblemen of high rank and love alone the cause of their quarrel. And when they saw their bloodstained wounds, deep and gaping, they one and all cried out: 'Take pity, Sir, upon us women!' and fell down upon their bare knees ready to kiss the feet of Theseus where he stood, till at last his angry mood abated; for pity quickly flows in noble hearts. Though he shook with rage at first, he soon reconsidered their transgression and its cause; and while his anger accused their guilt, his reason found excuses for them both. To himself he argued that anyone in love will help himself and escape from prison if he can. And in his heart he took pity on the women who were weeping together; and in his magnanimity he reflected, saying under his breath, 'Shame upon a ruler without mercy, who acts and speaks like a lion towards those who are penitent and fearful, as well as to the proud and disdainful who persist in their ways! A prince has little discernment if he cannot make distinctions in such cases but gives pride the same weight as humility.' So in a minute or two, when his anger had subsided, he looked up cheerfully and said aloud:

'How great and mighty a potentate (Lord bless us) is the God of Love! No obstacles can prevail against his strength. His miracles entitle him to be called a god, for in his own way he can twist hearts to whatever shape he pleases. Look at Arcite and Palamon here: free of my prison, they might have lived in Thebes like princes. They know I am their mortal enemy and that their lives are in my hands. Yet love has brought them with their eyes open to die in this spot. When you come to think of it, isn't it the height of folly? Is there any bigger fool than a lover? God in heaven, look at them! See how they bleed! Look at the state they're in! This is how their ruler, the God of Love, pays them wages and rewards for their services. Yet the devotees of Love consider themselves perfectly rational no matter what happens. And the biggest joke of all is that the occasion of this frolic has no more reason to thank them than I have. For heaven's sake, she knows as much about these fiery goings-on as a March hare or a cuckoo. However, one tries anything once, no matter what; a man's either a young fool or an old fool. I found that out for myself a long time ago, for in my time I was one of Love's servants. And because—as one who has often been caught in his snare—I understand the pangs of love and how sorely they can afflict a man, at the request of both the Queen kneeling here and of my dear sister Emily I entirely forgive your offence. But both of you must swear never to harm my country again or ever make war upon me, but show me friendship in every way you can. I freely pardon you this transgression.'

They swore what he had asked, doing him homage in proper form, and begging him for protection and mercy, which Theseus granted. Then he said, 'Though she were a queen or a princess, so far as royal blood and wealth is concerned each of you is perfectly eligible to marry her in due course. But nevertheless—I speak on behalf of my sister Emily, the cause of your jealousy and contention—as you yourselves know, you might fight for ever but she cannot marry two men at once; and therefore one of you, whether he likes it or not, must go whistle for her. In other words, she can't have both, no matter how jealous or angry you may be. Therefore the best I can do is so to order matters that each of you shall have whatever destiny is decreed him. If you listen I'll explain how. This is your part in the arrangement I propose.

'Here is my decision: to end the matter once for all without further argument—and you may as well make up your minds to accept—each of you is free to go, without ransom and in safety, wherever he pleases; but within twelve months from this day, neither more nor less, must each bring a hundred knights fully equipped and armed for tournament, ready to do battle to vindicate his claim to Emily. And I faithfully promise you upon my honour as a knight that whichever of you gains the upper hand—that's to say, if either slays his opponent or drives him from the lists with the aid of the hundred knights I spoke of—I shall give Emily to the one whom Fortune grants so fair a favour. I shall build the lists in this very spot: and as God may have mercy on my soul, I shall prove a true and fair judge. One of you must be slain or taken prisoner: no other conclusion will satisfy me. If this seems good to you, say so and count yourselves fortunate. That is the end of the matter for you.' C602918

How happy Palamon looks! How Arcite leaps for joy! How can I describe the delight of everyone there at the generous gesture of Theseus? They all went down on their knees and thanked him again and again from the bottom of their hearts—especially the two Thebans. Then with light hearts, filled with hope, they took leave of him and rode homeward to the broad and ancient walls of Thebes.

iii

I suppose I would be accounted remiss were I to omit to describe Theseus' lavish expenditure when he busily set to work erecting the royal lists. I dare say there was no more magnificent an arena in the world. Walled with stone and ditched without, the circuit was a mile in radius. It was round in shape like a compass, with tiers to the height of sixty feet, so that a man sitting in any one row did not obstruct his neighbour's view. A gate of white marble stood at the eastern end; a similar one stood opposite at the western side. In short, there was no building like it, considering the small space it occupied. For in the land there was no craftsman skilled in geometry or arithmetic, no painter or sculptor to whom Theseus did not pay board and wages for the building and decoration of the arena. Above the eastern gate he set up an altar and temple for the worship of Venus, goddess of Love, in which to perform due rites and sacrifices. Over the western gate he erected one just like it dedicated to Mars, costing the best part of a cartload of gold. He also ordered a gorgeous chapel, dedicated to chaste Diana and marvellous to look at, to be built of white alabaster and red coral in a turret on the northern wall.

But I had almost forgotten to describe the splendid carvings, pictures, forms, faces and figures in these three temples.

First of all you saw, executed upon the walls in the temple of Venus, moving representations of the broken sleep, shuddering sighs, sacred tears, lamentations and fiery longings that Love's servants endure in this life; the oaths that bind their vows; Pleasure, Hope, Desire, Foolhardiness, Beauty, Youth, Gaiety, Riches, Love-Potions and Force, Lies, Flattery, Extravagance, Intrigue; Jealousy wearing a garland of yellow marigolds with a cuckoo perched upon her hand; Feasts, Music, Songs, Dances, Joy and Display. All the phenomena of Love I have enumerated or am about to enumerate were painted in order upon the walls, besides more than I can mention. Indeed the whole mountain of Citherea where Venus has her principal seat was figured in the frescoes with all its gardens and gaiety. Idleness, the porter, was not forgotten, nor beautiful Narcissus of bygone days; the folly of King Solomon; the huge might of Hercules; the witcheries of Medea and Circe; the fierce stern courage of Turnus; and wealthy Croesus in misery and chains. The moral was that neither wisdom, wealth, beauty, cunning, strength, nor courage may compare with Venus, who can rule the world as she pleases: for all these people were caught in her snare till in their agony they cried out again. One or two examples will serve, though I could give a thousand more.

There was a splendid statue of Venus, naked, floating upon a boundless sea. From the navel down she was hidden by green waves that shone like glass. She held a cithern in her right hand, while doves fluttered above a beautiful garland of fresh-smelling roses upon her head. Cupid her son stood before her, winged and blind (as he is often represented), bearing a bow and bright sharp arrows.

I may as well go on to describe the frescoes on the walls of the temple of red Mars. The whole length and breadth of them were painted, as in the case of the interior of that dismal building known as the Great Temple of Mars in Thrace—a frigid, icy region where Mars has his principal palace.

The first fresco was a forest inhabited by neither man nor beast: a forest of knotted, barren, gnarled and ancient trees; of jagged ugly stumps through which ran the rumbling noise of wind, as if a gale were breaking every bough. And halfway down a hill, under a slope, stood the temple of Mars Armipotent built entirely of burnished steel. It had a long, narrow, and forbidding entrance, out of which there came a furious blast of wind shaking the whole gate. A wintry glimmer shone in at the doors, since there were no windows in the walls to give light. The door was made of everlasting adamant clenched with tough iron bolts crosswise and lengthwise. To give the temple greater strength every one of the supporting pillars was as thick as a barrel and made of gleaming iron.

There you could perceive the dark imaginings of Treachery and all its intrigues; cruel Anger, red as burning coal; the pickpocket and pale Fear; the smiler with the knife under his cloak; black smoke rolling over burning farmsteads; the treacherous murdering in a bed; rank War, bloodied with wounds; Discord, with dripping knife and threatening looks. A grating noise filled this dreadful place.

And there you saw the self-slaughtered, his heart's blood drenching his hair; the sleeping head split by a driven nail; stark on his back, Death with gaping mouth. Sad-faced and comfortless in the midst of the temple sat Mischance. You saw Madness laugh in frenzy; armed rebellion, the hue and cry, and fierce outrage; the carrion corpse flung in a bush, with slit throat; a thousand slain—victims of Mars, not one killed by the plague; the tyrant wrestling with his despoiled prey; towns gutted and laid waste. You saw the reeling ships burn on the sea, the huntsman crushed by wild bears, the sow devouring the child in its very cot, the cook, for all his long ladle, scalded to the bone; the carter ground beneath his cart, pinned under the wheel; none of the bad luck brought by Mars was forgotten. And those under Mars' influence were also represented: the barber, the butcher, and the smith who forges keen blades upon his anvil. High above, depicted on a tower, I saw Conquest sitting in state, over his head a sharp sword hanging from a slender thread of twine.

The murders of Julius Caesar, Nero, and Antonius were there portrayed, though none of them had yet been born; nevertheless their deaths were foreshadowed in the temple with the menacing omens of Mars, shown in those paintings just as the stars in heaven portray who is to be murdered and who is to die for love. One example from legend should serve—even if I wished I could not give them all.

The armed effigy of Mars, with dire and frenzied face, stood in a chariot. Over his head sparkled two starry figures named in ancient works of astrology and geomancy—one was Puella and the other Rubeus. The god of war was represented with a wolf glowering red-eyed at his feet, about to devour a man. All this was delineated with subtle brush in reverence of the glory of Mars.

Now I will make haste as quickly as I can to the temple of chaste Diana and give you a full description. The walls were covered with hunting scenes and images of modest chastity. You saw how sad Callisto was changed from a woman into a bear when Diana became angry with her: later she became the Pole Star. Or so it was pictured: I cannot tell you more. But her son is also a star, as you can see.

And there was Dana—I don't mean the goddess Diana, but Penneus' daughter Dana who became a tree.

You saw Actaeon turned into a stag as a punishment because he saw Diana naked; and how he was caught and eaten by his own hounds which no longer knew him.

A little further on was a painting of Atalanta hunting the wild boar with Meleager and many others; Diana plagued him for this. There were many other wonderful scenes which I shall not trouble to recall.

High on a stag the goddess was seated; small dogs played about her feet, beneath which was set a moon that waxed and waned. The statue was clad in green, with a bow in hand and a quiver-

ful of arrows, the eyes cast down in the direction of Pluto's
dark kingdom. In front of her a woman in labour plaintively
called on her name for her unborn child to be delivered at long
last: 'Only you can help me!' Whoever made it did not grudge
money on the colours and could paint in the most lifelike fashion.

When the lists were ready, Theseus, who had furnished the
temples and all the arena at great expense, was much pleased
with the finished result. But let me leave Theseus for a moment
to speak of Palamon and Arcite.

The day approached when they were to return, each bringing
a hundred knights to decide the battle, as I explained. Each of
them, in honour of their promise, brought to Athens a hundred
well-armed knights in fighting trim. Indeed many thought that
never on sea or land had so few made up a company more im-
pressive in knightly prowess; for every man who delighted in
chivalry and was eager to make a name for himself had begged
to be allowed to take part in the contest. Those chosen were
lucky: were such a tournament to take place tomorrow in Eng-
land or elsewhere, you can imagine how every able-bodied knight
and lover would want to be there to do battle for a lady. I can
tell you it would be a sight worth seeing!

And that's how it was with the many knights with Palamon.
Some were armed in coats of mail, some in breastplates and
tunics, some wore plated body-armour, some carried Prussian
shields or else light bucklers; some cased their legs carefully in
armour and carried a battleaxe or a steel mace—all these new
weapons come from older models. So everyone was armed as he
thought best, just as I have described.

Riding with Palamon you would have seen the powerful black-
bearded countenance of the great king of Thrace, Lycurgus him-
self. The pupils of his eyes glowed with a light between red and
yellow under his beetling shaggy brows. He looked about him
with the air of an eagle-headed gryphon. Huge-limbed, broad-
shouldered, with hard, powerful thews and long muscular arms,
he stood high in a golden chariot drawn by four white bulls in
traces, as was the custom of his country. Instead of a surcoat he
wore over his armour a bearskin coal-black with age, its painted
claws glittering with gold. His long hair, combed behind his
back, shone blacker than a raven's feather under an immensely

heavy golden wreath, thick as your arm, set with gleaming jewels, fine rubies and diamonds. More than twenty white wolfhounds followed his chariot, each as large as a steer and trained for the hunting of deer and lion. They were tightly muzzled and wore golden collars studded with eyeholes. His entourage consisted of a hundred stout-hearted and well-armed noblemen.

The legends say that Emetreus the great king of India came with Arcite, riding like the god of war upon a bay horse sheathed in steel, covered with an elaborately embroidered cloth of gold. He wore a surcoat of Tartar silk inlaid with large round white pearls. His saddle was of burnished new-beaten gold. From his shoulder fell a mantle swarming with red rubies sparkling like fire. Yellow and glittering like the sun, his crisp hair was arranged in ringlets. With his high nose and eyes the colour of citron, full lips, sanguine complexion, and a few black and yellow freckles sprinkled over his face, as he glanced about him he had the aspect of a lion. I put his age at twenty-five. His beard had sprouted and was nearly full; and his voice was like the blast of a trumpet. Upon his head he wore a gay garland of fresh green laurel. For sport he carried a lily-white falcon on his wrist. With him there rode a hundred noblemen, bareheaded but otherwise fully armed and sumptuously equipped in every respect. Believe me, dukes, earls, and kings had willingly gathered in this noble assembly for the exaltation of chivalry. Many tame lions and leopards gambolled around the king.

In this manner these lords arrived together in the city about nine in the morning on the Sunday, and there alighted.

Then when the noble Duke Theseus had escorted them into his city and housed each according to his rank, he took such pains to feast and entertain them and do them honour that people still say nobody could have shown better judgement or improved his hospitality.

I shall say nothing of the minstrelsy, the service at the banquet, the gifts bestowed on high and low, the rich decorations of Theseus' palace, the order of precedence on the dais, which lady was the best dancer or the most beautiful, or which could best dance and sing, or speak of love most feelingly; or what hawks perched above, what dogs lay on the floor—I'll say nothing of all this, but give the gist of it; I think that's the best thing to do. Now here comes the point—listen if you will.

On the Sunday night, before daybreak, Palamon heard the lark sing, although dawn was not due for another two hours. Yet the lark sang; and so did Palamon. He rose in high spirits to make his pilgrimage with devout heart to the blessed and gracious Cythera—I mean Venus the worshipful and august. It was in the hour ruled by her that he slowly walked to the lists where her temple stood, and humbly knelt down with full heart, saying something like this:

'Fairest of the fair, daughter of Jove and bride of Vulcan, Lady Venus who brings joy to the mount of Cythera: by that love you bore for Adonis have pity upon my burning, bitter tears and take my humble prayer to your heart. Alas! I have no words to give an idea of the hell that torments me. My heart cannot reveal its hurt. I am so confused that I can only say, "Mercy, radiant Lady, for you understand my thoughts and see the wounds that I feel!" Consider all this and take pity on my pain, inasmuch as ever after as far as in me lies I shall be your true servant and wage eternal war on chastity. That is my vow if you will help me: I have no wish to brag of feats of arms, nor do I ask for victory tomorrow, nor to win fame or any kind of vain renown in this affair, nor to have my prowess in battle trumpeted up and down—but only to possess Emily and die in your service: by what means, and in what manner, I leave it to you to decide. Whether I win victory over them or they over me means nothing if I can hold my lady in my arms. Though Mars is god of war, your power in heaven above is so great that I may easily possess my love if you so wish. Ever after I shall worship at your shrine; I shall kindle fires and perform sacrifice at your altars wherever I go. But if this should not be your will, sweet Lady, then I pray that tomorrow Arcite may drive a spear through my heart. Being dead I shall not care if Arcite wins her for his bride. This is the sum and total of my prayer: O dear and blissful Lady, grant me my love!'

As soon as Palamon had finished his prayer he sacrificed humbly with due ceremonial, though I shall not here describe his devotions. But in the end the statue of Venus shook and made a sign by which he understood his prayer that day had been accepted. Although the sign hinted at a delay, it was clear to him that his request had been granted: so he went home quickly with a glad heart.

Three hours after Palamon had set out for the temple of Venus the sun rose: and up rose Emily to hasten to the temple of Diana. The maidens whom she took with her brought the fire with them ready prepared, as well as incense, vestments, and all the rest that pertains to sacrifice—horns brimming with mead as was the custom, and whatever else was needed.

Smoking incense filled the temple, which was hung with splendid draperies. With light heart Emily washed her body in well-water—but I dare not describe how she performed her rites except in a general way, although it would be great fun to hear it all. If one is a man of goodwill it's no harm; still, it's best to leave it to the imagination.

Her shining hair was combed and loose, and a crown of evergreen oakleaves set neatly and becomingly upon her head. She began to kindle two fires upon the altar and performed those ceremonies you can read of in Statius' *Thebiad* and other ancient books.

When the fire had been lit she began to implore Diana in these words:

'O chaste goddess of the greenwood, to whom heaven, earth, and sea are visible; Queen of Pluto's dark kingdom below, Goddess of virgins: for so many years you have understood my heart and know what I desire. Keep me from your anger and the terrible punishment suffered by Actaeon. Chaste Goddess, you know my wish is to live as a virgin, never, never a wife or mistress. As you know I am still one of your train: a virgin huntress who would far rather roam the wild woods than marry and be with child. I do not wish for the company of men. Now help me, Lady, since you have the ability and the knowledge in all three aspects of your divinity. As for Palamon who has such longing for me, and Arcite, who loves me so desperately, this is the only favour I ask of you: set peace and amity between the two, turn their hearts from me, quench or direct elsewhere their burning passion and desire, all their fiery ceaseless torment. But if you will not grant me this boon, if one of the two must be my destiny, let it be him who desires me most. Goddess of pure chastity, look upon the bitter tears that fall from my cheeks. Virgin guardian of us all, keep and guard my maidenhood, that I may live a virgin in your service.'

While Emily prayed the fires burned clear upon the altar. But suddenly she saw a curious sight: all at once one of the fires went out, then blazed up again; immediately afterwards the other fire was completely quenched, and as it went out made a whistling noise like that made by wet branches burning; what seemed to be drops of blood collected at the end of each faggot. At this Emily was terrified almost out of her senses and cried aloud, not understanding what it meant; from sheer fright she began to weep piteously. Thereupon Diana appeared, bow in hand, in the shape of a huntress, and said, 'Daughter, dry your tears: it has been decided among the gods on high, set down and confirmed in their eternal decree, that you must be wedded to one of these two who are undergoing so much trouble and suffering on your account—but to which of them I may not say. Farewell, for I can stay no longer; but the fires burning upon my altar will make plain to you before you leave what your destiny is to be in this affair.'

When she had spoken the arrows in the quiver of the goddess clattered and rang. She stepped forward and vanished. Emily said in amazement, 'What does this mean? I place myself under your protection and disposal, O Diana!' Then she went home by the shortest way; that was all—there is no more to tell.

At the next hour belonging to Mars, Arcite strode to the temple of the fierce God of War to make his sacrifice with all the rites of his pagan faith. With suppliant and devoted heart he made his prayer to Mars:

'O you strong God, honoured in the cold region of Thrace where you are accounted lord; who in all lands and kingdoms holds the reins of war and sways its fortunes as you please— accept this my humble sacrifice. If my youth merits your favour, if my strength fits me to serve your godhead as one of your devotees, then I pray you take pity on my sufferings, by those pangs and scorching flames with which you once burned with desire when the beauty of Venus, fair, young, fresh and free was yours to enjoy, and you had her in your arms at will—

although unfortunately things went badly for you on the occasion when Vulcan caught you in his trap and found you lying with his wife. By the pain and passion that you felt then, take pity also upon my sufferings. As you know, I am young and ignorant; and as I suppose more racked by love than any living creature —for she who makes me suffer this torment does not care if I sink or swim. And I am well aware that before she grants me her love I must win her by force in the lists. And I know that my strength will avail nothing without your help and favour. Then help me, Lord, in battle tomorrow, not only for the sake of the flames that burned you once but the fire that burns me now; and grant me victory tomorrow. Let the labour be mine and yours the glory. I shall always honour your sovereign temple above all other places, and ever labour at what most delights you, and in your stern arts; in your temple I will hang up my banner and the arms of my companions; I will keep fires eternally burning at your altar until the day I die. Moreover I bind myself with a vow: to you I will dedicate my beard and these long hanging locks untouched by razor or shears, and remain your true servant for the rest of my life. Have pity, Lord, upon my heavy sorrows and give me the victory—I ask no more.'

When mighty Arcite had finished his prayer the rings that hung upon the temple door, and the doors themselves, clattered violently; Arcite flinched. The altar fires blazed up till the whole temple was illuminated, while a sweet smell came up from the ground. Then Arcite raised his hand and threw more incense into the fire, and performed other ceremonies, till at length the coat of mail upon the statue of Mars jingled: and with that sound he heard a low soft murmur saying 'Victory!'; whereupon he rendered praise and homage to the god. Filled with joy and the hope that all would turn out well, Arcite returned to his lodging as gay as a bird in the sunshine.

But in Heaven above a furious row immediately broke out between Venus, the Goddess of Love, and Mars, stern God of War, over the granting of his boon. Jupiter was hard put to it trying to make peace, but at length bleak Saturn, well-versed in past stratagems, from his long experience managed to devise a solution with which he soon satisfied both parties. As has been truly said, age has the advantage. It has wisdom and experience; it can be outdone but not outwitted. Although it is not his nature to discourage strife and fear, Saturn soon found a remedy for the dispute.

'My dear daughter Venus,' said Saturn, 'mine is the widest orbit round the sun, and my power is greater than men suspect: to me belongs death by drowning in the wan sea, imprisonment in dark vaults, strangling and hanging by the neck, the muttering and rebellion of the mob, complaints, clandestine poisonings; when I am in Leo, vengeance and retribution are mine; and mine the ruin of high palaces, the fall of towers and walls upon miner and carpenter; I slew Samson shaking the pillar; and mine are all deadly diseases, black treacheries and conspiracies. Pestilence is fathered by my glance. Now stop weeping: I shall do my best to see that your knight, Palamon, shall have his lady as you promised, though Mars shall help his own knight. Nevertheless, sooner or later there must be peace between you in spite of your diverse temperament, the cause of these daily squabbles. I am your grandfather, ready to listen to your commands: now dry your tears and I will do your pleasure.'

And that's enough about Mars and Venus and the gods above; I shall now come to the climax of my story.

iv

That day there was a great festival in Athens. And besides, the gay season of May put everyone in good spirits, so that all that Monday they danced and jousted or spent their time in the high service of Venus. But as they had to rise early in order to see the great tournament, at night they retired to rest. By daybreak next morning there was a noise and clatter of horses and armour in all the hostelries round about; bands of noblemen rode to the palace on stallions and palfreys. There you might see strange, richly designed armour, splendid examples of goldsmith's work, embroidery, and steelwork; glittering shields, headpieces, and trappings; gold-forged helmets, coats-of-mail, and surcoats; splendidly-accoutred princes upon their coursers; the knights in attendance, and squires fastening spearheads to their shafts, buckling on helmets and strapping shields with lacings of leather thongs. With so much to do, no one was idle. You might have seen foam-flecked horses champing golden bridles, armourers

scurrying busily back and forth with files and hammers; yeo-
men on foot, and dense crowds of common people armed with
short staves; pipes, trumpets, kettledrums, and clarions howling
for blood; the palace everywhere filled with people, here a knot
of three and there a group of ten, debating the odds and spec-
ulating about the two Theban knights. Some said one thing,
some another; some backed Black-beard, others Bald-head, or else
Thatch-hair. 'This one looks tough!'—'That's a fighter!' 'This
fellow's battleaxe weighs twenty pounds!' Long after the sun
was up the hall was filled with conjecture.

Great Theseus, roused from sleep by the music and hubbub,
kept his room until the Theban knights (who were treated with
equal honour) had been brought into the palace. Throned like
a god, Duke Theseus was seated by a window. Quickly the crowd
pressed in to see and pay homage, and hear his commands.

From a scaffold a herald called for silence till the noise of the
people subsided. And when it had quietened he announced the
will and pleasure of the great Duke:

'In his high discretion the Prince considers that the destruction
of noble blood in this affair would be too great were the battle
fought to the death. Therefore he wishes to modify his original
conditions in order to save life.

'On pain of death, therefore, no man may convey or bring into
the lists any kind of missile, poleaxe, or dagger; no man may
draw or wear short, sharp-pointed stabbing swords; no man is
to ride more than one course with spear unblunted against an
opponent; thrusting is permitted when on foot, but only in
self-defence. Anyone at disadvantage is to be taken, not slain, and
brought to a stake which shall be fixed on either side; he must
be taken there by main force and must then remain at the stake.
Should the leader of either side be taken or slay his opponent,
the tournament must end there and then. Now Godspeed! For-
ward, and lay on hard! Fight your fill with long swords and
maces. Go ahead: it is the Duke's will.'

The sky rang with the people's joyful shout: 'God save the
good Duke, who will not allow wholesale bloodshed!'

Up went the trumpets in a fanfare; and the company rode
to the lists in due order through the great city, hung with no
plainer stuff than cloth-of-gold.

The noble Duke rode in princely state with the two Thebans on either side of him, followed by the queen and Emily, and after them in another company came all the rest according to rank. In this way they passed through the city till they duly arrived at the lists.

It was still before nine in the morning when Theseus took his seat in the place of honour with Queen Hippolyta, Emily, and the other ladies in order of rank about them. The crowd pressed to the seats. At the western end Arcite with a red banner and the hundred knights of his party entered by the Mars Gate, while at the same instant Palamon, looking determined, entered with a white banner by the gates of Venus at the eastern end. You would have to search far and wide throughout the world before you found two companies so equally matched; no one could say that either seemed to have the advantage in valour, rank, or age, so evenly had they been picked. They dressed themselves in two imposing formations. When the roll was called (so that there could be no cheating over their numbers) the gates were shut and the cry went up, 'Young knights, do your duty and show your mettle!'

The heralds withdrew and the trumpets and clarions rang out. Without further preliminary, spears were firmly couched in dead earnest for the attack, and both sides clapped spurs to their horses. Who can best joust and ride will soon be seen. Shafts shiver against thick shields, and someone feels the thrust of a lance through his breast-bone. Spears leap twenty feet in the air; out come swords, flashing like silver; helms are hewn and hacked asunder; the blood spurts in harsh red streams, and bones smash under the heavy maces. One man begins to thrust through the thickest of the press, where even the strongest horses stumble; all are overset; a second rolls underfoot like a ball, regains his feet, thrusts with a spear-shaft, and hurtles another knight from his horse; yet another is pierced through the body, is taken, and brought, fighting desperately, to the stake where according to the rules he must remain; and another is similarly captured upon the other side. From time to time Theseus makes them rest and refresh themselves and take a drink if they wish.

The two Thebans met and wounded one another many times in the course of the day. Twice each unhorsed the other. A tiger in the valley of Gargaphia bereaved of its cub is not more savage against the huntsman than Arcite, in his passion of jealousy, is to Palamon; and no lion hunted in Benmarin is more fell, more frenzied with hunger and thirsty for the blood of his prey, than Palamon seeking to slay his enemy Arcite. Their jealous blows gash their helmets and red blood gushes on both sides.

Sooner or later everything comes to an end. Before the sun had gone down, the powerful king Emetrius caught Palamon as he fought with Arcite. His sword bit deeply into his flesh; and it took twenty men to drag Palamon—who would not yield—to the stake. Coming to the rescue of Palamon, the mighty king Lycurgus was overthrown. Before being taken Palamon struck King Emetrius such a blow that in spite of his great strength he was knocked a yard from the saddle. But it was all for nothing. Palamon was dragged to the stake, where his courage could no longer avail him; having been taken, there he had to stay, held by force of arms and the rule of the tournament.

Now Palamon is in miserable case, for he cannot fight again. And when Theseus saw what had happened he called out to all the combatants: 'Stop! No more! It's all over! I will be an honest judge and no partisan: Arcite of Thebes shall have Emily, for it has been his good fortune to win her fairly.'

At this the crowd raised so thunderous a shout of joy it seemed as if the lists would fall.

Now what can lovely Venus do? There is nothing the Queen of Love can do or say except burst out weeping with disappointment until her tears rain down upon the lists. She exclaimed, 'I am disgraced beyond question.' But Saturn replied, 'Hush, daughter! Mars has had his way, for his knight has been granted his boon; but I swear you will soon be satisfied.'

Trumpets and music blared, and the heralds bawled and yelled their delight at the triumph of Prince Arcite. But bear with me, and do not anticipate, and you will hear what kind of miracle happened next.

Fierce Arcite undid his helmet and rode the whole length of the arena to show his face. He looked up at Emily who cast a friendly eye upon him in return (for women, generally speaking, incline to follow the favourites of Fortune). She was the whole delight of his heart. But out of the ground there started an infernal Fury, sent by Pluto at Saturn's request; upon which his horse shied in terror and stumbled as it plunged, and before Arcite was aware he had been pitched upon the crown of his head and lay for dead in the arena, his chest smashed in by his saddle-bow. There he lay, his face turning coal black as the blood rushed to it. Then he was borne sadly from the lists to Theseus' palace, where they cut him out of his armour and put him quickly to bed, still alive and conscious, and calling the whole time for Emily.

Duke Theseus and his company returned to his city of Athens in joyful pomp. In spite of this accident he did not wish to cast a gloom over everyone. It was said Arcite would not die but recover from his injury. Another thing they were just as pleased about: no one had been killed, although some were badly wounded, especially the man whose breast-bone had been run through with a spear. As a remedy for their other wounds and broken arms, some had salves, others had charms and herb-medicines, in particular a concoction of sage which they drank to recover the use of their limbs. So the Duke, who was skilled in these things, made everyone comfortable and did them all honour. As was right and proper he held high revel with the visiting princes all night long. No one felt defeated any more than at a joust or tournament. There was in fact no disgrace, because a fall can happen to anyone. Nor is it shameful for a man on his own to be captured by twenty knights and dragged unyielding to the stake by main force, helped on with kicks and buffets, while his horse is driven by yeomen and boys with sticks. No one can call that cowardice.

And here Duke Theseus, to put a stop to any jealousy or rancour, had it proclaimed that both sides did equally well, and that they matched one another like a pair of brothers. He gave them gifts according to rank and station, and held a great feast lasting three days; after which he provided the knights with an honourable escort out of the city to see them well on their road. Then everyone went home the shortest way—'Goodbye!' 'Good luck!' and it was all over. I shall say no more about the battle but turn to Palamon and Arcite.

Arcite's breast became swollen, while the wound near his heart grew worse and worse. In spite of all the doctors might do, the clotted blood corrupted and festered in his body. Neither cupping, bleeding from the vein, nor herbal draughts were of the slightest help. The expelling, or animal force, called 'natural' because of this function, could neither dislodge nor expel the venom from the life-giving blood. The lung-vessels began to swell. Poison and gangrene ravaged the muscles of his chest. He could get no benefit from laxatives or vomiting, though his life depended on it. All that part of him was shattered; Nature no longer had the mastery, and where Nature will not work one can only say goodbye to physic and carry the man off to church. The long and short of it was that Arcite had to die. So he sent for Emily and his dear cousin Palamon, and spoke as you shall hear:

'To you, Lady whom I most love, the anguished spirit in my breast cannot express the least part of the sharpness of my sorrow. But since my life may no longer endure, to you, more than any other living creature, I bequeath the service of my ghost. O, the violent sorrow and pain I have suffered for you for so long! O Death! O Emily! O separation! O queen of my heart, my wife, lady of my heart, ender of my life! What is this world? What does man ask to have? One moment with his love: the next alone in the cold grave without a friend! Farewell, Emily, my sweet enemy! Take me gently in your two arms, for the love of heaven; and let me speak.

'For love of you and because of my jealousy there has been rancour and contention between my cousin Palamon and me for many a long day. But let wise Jupiter direct my soul to speak truly and fittingly of the lover and his attributes—that is to say truth, honour, chivalry, wisdom, humility, rank, noble blood, and openheartedness, and all things that belong to love—for, as I trust that Jupiter will protect my soul, at this moment I know of no one in this world more worthy of love than Palamon, who serves you and will serve you all his life. And if you should ever marry, do not forget that good man, Palamon.'

With these words his speech began to falter. The chill of death rose from feet to breast and overcame him, while from his arms the vital power dispersed and was wholly lost. Very soon the intellect, which alone remained in his sick and injured breast, began to fail as death touched his heart. His eyes dimmed and his breath began to flag, but still he looked upon his lady; and his last word was, 'Mercy, Emily!' His spirit left its house and went—where, I cannot say, for I have never been there; being no theologian, I will keep my mouth shut. Souls do not come within the scope of this story and I have no wish to discuss theories about them, though books have been written on the subject. Arcite is dead; may Mars look after his soul. Now I will speak of Emily.

Emily shrieked; Palamon groaned; then Theseus took his fainting sister and led her away from the body. There is no point in dragging out my tale with a description of how she wept night and day: in cases like this women who have lost husbands feel the deepest grief and most of them either mourn in this way or fall into a decline from which in the end they never recover.

Throughout the town the tears and lamentations of young and old for the death of the Theban were unending. Man and boy wept for him. Indeed there was not half such a lamentation when Hector was brought, newly slain, to Troy. What a lamentation it was, with scratching of cheeks and tearing of hair! The women cried, 'Why did you have to die? You had gold enough—and Emily!'

No one could comfort Theseus except his old father Aegeus, who understood the transmutations of this world, having seen its ups and downs—joy following grief, and grief following happiness. He provided examples and illustrations. 'Just as no man ever died,' said he, 'without having lived some length of time on earth, so no man,' he went on, 'ever lived anywhere in the world without dying sooner or later. The world is no more than a thoroughfare of grief, and we are pilgrims travelling to and fro upon it. Death is the end of all earthly troubles.' And over and above this he repeated much more to the same effect, sagely exhorting people to take comfort.

Duke Theseus diligently turned his attention to the problem of where best to build the tomb of good Arcite, and how best to make it honourable, in keeping with his rank. He finally came to the conclusion that the place where Arcite and Palamon first fought one another for their love—in that very grove, so sweet and green, where Arcite felt the hot flame of love and amorous desire, and sang his complaint—he would build a pyre where the funeral service could be fitly performed. Then he gave orders to cut down the ancient oaks and lay them in rows of logs, properly disposed for burning. His officers sped hotfoot to fulfil his commands. Next Theseus sent for a bier, over which he spread the richest cloth of gold in his possession, and swathed Arcite in the same material, placing white gloves upon his hands, a crown of green laurel on his head, and in his grasp a sharp bright sword. He laid him upon the bier with the face uncovered, and then broke down and wept. When it was day, so that all the people should see him he brought Arcite to the palace, which re-echoed with the noise of mourning.

Then came the heartbroken Theban, Palamon, with disordered beard and unkempt hair matted with ashes, in black clothes spotted with tears; and then Emily, weeping more than anyone, the saddest of the whole company. To dignify and enrich the funeral service, Duke Theseus ordered three horses to be brought in trappings of glittering steel, covered with the arms of Prince Arcite. On each of these great white horses sat a rider, one carrying Arcite's shield, another his spear, and the third his Turkish bow, with its quiver and accessories of burnished gold. Then they rode slowly with sad hearts to the grove, as you shall hear. The noblest of the Greeks present shouldered the bier; then with eyes red and wet from weeping they bore it at a slow pace through the city by its principal street. This was entirely draped in black, all its tall houses hung with the same material. Old Aegeus walked on the right hand, with Duke Theseus at the other side, bearing in their hands vessels of the finest gold filled with honey and milk and blood and wine. Next came Palamon with a very great company followed by poor Emily carrying the customary fire for the funeral rites.

Solemn activity and splendid preparation marked the funeral ceremony and the erection of the pyre, whose green summit touched the sky while its base spread twenty fathoms—that is to say, the branches were that wide. First of all load after load of straw was put down: but I have no intention of relating how the towering pyre was built, how the trees were felled, or their names either—oak, fir, birch, aspen, elder, ilex, poplar, willow, elm, plane, ash, box, chestnut, lime, laurel, maple, thorn, beech, hazel, yew, dogwood; how the gods—nymphs, fawns, and hamadryads—ran hither and thither after they had been dispossessed of the homes where they had lived in peace and quiet; how all the beasts and birds fled in panic when the trees were felled; how the ground, unaccustomed to the bright sun, blenched at the light; how the pyre was given a foundation of straw, followed by a layer of dry stumps split in three, then green wood, spices, precious gems, cloth of gold, flowery garlands, heavily scented myrrh and incense; how Arcite lay in the midst of all this, and what treasures lay all round his body; how Emily ritually lit the funeral pyre, and fainted when the fire was built up; what she said or thought; what gems were cast upon the pyre when the flames had taken hold and were burning furiously; how some threw their shields, others their spears, even the clothes they wore, and goblets of wine, milk, and blood, into the raging flames; how a great band of Greeks faced to the left and rode three times round the pyre, shouting together, and thrice again with rattling spears; how thrice the ladies wept, and Emily was led home; how Arcite was burned to cold ashes; how his wake was held the whole night long; how the Greeks played in the funeral games—I am not concerned to tell who wrestled the best, naked and anointed with oil, or who made the best showing; I will not even relate how they went home to Athens after the games, but come quickly to the point and conclude this long tale.

In the course of time, after the passage of some years, the tears and mourning of the Greeks came to an end. It appears that by common consent they held parliament at Athens to discuss certain points at issue, amongst which were debated the question of alliance with certain countries, and the obtainment of full allegiance from the Thebans. On this account Theseus sent for Palamon, without disclosing to him the reason why. At this command he came in haste, sad at heart and clothed in black. Then Theseus sent for Emily. When all were seated and a hush had fallen over the place, Theseus paused for a moment and let his eyes roam over the assembly before speaking from the wisdom of his heart. He sighed quietly, and then spoke his mind with a grave countenance:

'When the First Mover and First Cause originally created the great Chain of Love in heaven, great was His purpose and profound the consequence. He understood all whys and wherefores when He bound with that great Chain of Love fire, air, water, and earth, in certain limits which they may not go beyond. That same Prince and Mover,' he continued, 'established in this wretched world below certain seasons and periods of duration for everything engendered upon the earth, beyond which day they may not last, although they can easily cut short that period—I need quote no authorities, since it can be demonstrated from experience; never-theless I wish to state my opinion. From this Law it is evident that this Mover is immutable and everlasting. And it is clear to anyone but a blockhead that every part derives from a great Whole; for Nature did not originate from some portion or fragment, but from an immutable perfection, descending thence to what is corruptible. And therefore His wise foresight has so ordered matters that all species and processes of seed and growth continue by succession and do not survive for ever. This is the truth: it can be seen at a glance.

'Look at the oak which has so slow a growth after it first germi-nates; as you know it lives to a very great age, but in the end the tree decays.

'Consider the stone we tread under our feet in passing: it wears away as it lies by the roadside.

'The broad river sometimes dries up; great cities are seen to decline and fall. It is evident all things come to an end.

'It is also plain that in the case of men and women it is inevi-table they must die in one of the two periods of life—that is to say in youth or age—some in their beds, some upon the deep, and some on the field of battle, as we know; the king equally with the page. There is no help for it; everyone goes the same road. There-fore I say all things must die.

'Who, truly, contrives all this but majestic Jupiter, Ruler and Cause of all, who converts everything back to its own source, from which it derives? Against this it avails no living creature of any kind to contend.

'Thus it seems wisdom to me to make a virtue of necessity and accept the unavoidable with a good grace, especially those things that are ordained for us all. It is not only futile to repine, but rebellious to Him who governs all things. And certainly the man who dies in his prime and flower while sure of his good name, wins the most honour, for then he brings no shame either to his friends or himself. His friends should be glad of his death if his breath has been yielded up in honour, more so than when his name has grown dim in old age and all his prowess forgotten. To leave a good name behind, it is best to die at the height of one's fame. To deny this would be wilful. Why should we repine or feel heavy-hearted because Arcite, the flower of chivalry, has escaped from the foul dungeon of this life with reverence and honour? Why should his cousin and his wife here grudge him his happiness? He loved them well. Would he thank them? No, God knows, not by any manner of means. They offend both his spirit and themselves without making themselves any happier.

'What conclusion may I draw from this long train of argument but advise that joy should follow our grief, while thanking Jupiter for all his goodness? And before we leave this place I suggest we make of two griefs one perfect joy that shall last for ever. Now watch: there where we find the deepest grief, there shall we begin the cure.

'Sister,' he continued, 'this is my considered opinion, confirmed by my parliament here, that you should be moved to take pity upon noble Palamon—your own knight who has served you with his whole soul, heart, and power, ever since you first knew him— and take him for your lord and husband. Let me have your hand, for this is our decision. Now let us see your womanly compassion. After all, he is a king's nephew—but believe me, were he no more than a poor knight-bachelor, he deserves consideration because he has served you and suffered such great hardship for your sake for so many years. A noble compassion should outdo mere justice.'

Then he spoke to Palamon: 'I think I have little need for argument to obtain your consent to this. Come near, and take your lady by the hand.'

Then between them the bond of matrimony, or marriage as it is called, was made by the assembled council and the barons. Thus Palamon wedded Emily with music and joy. May God who created the wide world send him His love: he earned it dearly. Now all is well with Palamon, living in wealth, health, and happiness. Emily loved him so tenderly and he served her with such devotion that there was never a word of jealousy or vexation between them. So ends the tale of Palamon and Emily: and God bless you all!

When the Knight had finished his tale everyone in the company, young and old—and particularly the gentlefolk—agreed it was a noble story, well worth remembering. Laughing, the Host swore: 'Believe me, we're on the right track! The bag's unbuckled: now let's see who'll tell another story, for indeed the game's begun well. Sir Monk, if you can, tell us something to match the Knight's story.'

The Miller, pallid with drink, could hardly sit upon his horse. He hadn't got the manners to doff his hat or hood, or to wait for anybody, but began shouting and swearing in a booming voice like a stage-villain's: 'Christ's arms and blood and bones, I know a splendid yarn to cap the Knight's tale!' Seeing he was drunk, the Host cried: 'Hold hard, Robin, old man! We need a better man to tell the next one. Pipe down and let's be sensible.' 'By God I won't,' said he. 'I mean to have my say or quit.' 'Say on and be damned,' replied the Host. 'You're a fool and your wits are fuddled.'

'Now listen, all of you,' the Miller began, 'but first let me admit I'm drunk—I can tell by the sound of my voice—so if I trip over a word or two please blame it on the Southwark ale. I want to tell you a story of a carpenter and his wife, and how he was made a fool of by a scholar.'

The Reeve interrupted: 'Hold your noise! Leave off your bumpkin drunken bawdiness. It's sinful, and also it's remarkably foolish, to slander a man and bring women into disrepute. You can talk about plenty of other things.' The drunken Miller retorted, 'Dear old Oswald, when a man has no wife he's no cuckold. Not that I'm calling you one. There are heaps of virtuous wives— a thousand for every one that's bad—as you must know perfectly well yourself, unless you're cracked. Now, why get so worked up about my tale? Excuse me, I've a wife as well as you, yet not for my whole team of plough-oxen would I take it upon myself to think I was a cuckold unless I had to, and I'm pretty sure I'm not. A man shouldn't poke too closely into God's secrets, or his wife's.

So long as he finds God's plenty in her he has no call to be in-quisitive about the leavings.'

I can only say that the Miller would not curb his tongue for anyone, but told his low-bred tale in his own style. I fear I must reproduce it here: but I beg all persons of refinement for heaven's sake not to imagine I do so from any bad motive, but only because I must either report all their tales, good and bad, or else falsify part of my material. So let anyone who does not want to hear it turn over the page and choose another story—you'll find plenty of stories of all kinds which touch on manners, morality, and piety. Don't blame me if you choose wrong—as you should know by now, the Miller was a roughneck, and so was the Reeve and many of the others, and both of them told bawdy tales. Think it over and don't lay the blame on me. Besides it's all in fun and not to be taken seriously.

THE MILLER'S TALE

t one time
there was a rich old swindler who lived at Oxford. He was a
carpenter by trade, and took in lodgers. Living with him was a
poor scholar who was learned in the liberal arts but had an over-
riding passion for the study of astrology. And he could calculate
answers to certain problems—if you asked him when the stars
foretold drought or rain, for instance, or to forecast events of one
kind and another; I can't list them all.

This scholar was called Fly* Nicholas. Though demure as a
girl to look at, he had a knack—and he was both ingenious and
discreet at it—for surreptitious love-affairs and solacing women.
In his lodgings he had a room of his own, prettily furnished with
delicious herbs—and he himself was as delectable as root-licorice
or valerian. His *Almagest,* and other astrological text-books great
and small, and the astrolabe and calculating counters which he
needed for this science, were arranged on shelves at the head of
his bed. A coarse red cloth covered his clothes-press, and right on
top of it lay a gay psalter which he played nightly, filling the room
with pleasant melodies; he used to sing 'The Virgin's Angelus',
following it up with 'The King's Tune'; and people often praised
his cheerful voice. And so this engaging scholar spent his time,
with the help of what income he had and what his friends pro-
vided.

Now the carpenter had newly married a wife of eighteen: she
was dearer to him than life itself. As she was young and skittish
and he was old, jealousy drove him to keep her closely caged; he
already thought of himself as a cuckold. With his sketchy learning,
he had never come across Cato's advice that a man should marry
somebody like himself. Men ought to marry women appropriate
to their position and time of life, since youth and age are generally
at loggerheads. But having fallen into the trap he had to put up
with his troubles like other folk.

* i.e. artful, knowing. The M.E. word is 'hende' (courteous, pleasant);
Chaucer's repeated application of it to Nicholas is ironic.

She was a pretty young woman with a body as lithe and supple as a weasel. Round her loins she wore a milk-white flared apron, a girdle of striped silk, and a white smock with a collar embroidered all round with coal-black silk inside and out. She had a white cap with ribbons matching the collar, with a broad silk headband set high. And beneath her arched eyebrows, plucked thin and black as sloes, her eye was frankly lascivious. She was more delicious to look at than a pear in bloom and softer than fleece to the touch. A leather purse with silk tassels and round metal buttons hung from her girdle. You'd have to go a long way before you found anyone who could dream up a girl like that, or a prettier poppet. Her colour shone brighter than a gold coin newly-minted in the Tower; she sang as brisk and clear as a swallow perching on a barn; she would skip and frolic like a kid or a calf running after its dam; her mouth was sweet as honey or mead, or a store of apples laid in hay; she was skittish as a colt, tall as a mast and straight as an arrow. Low on her collar she wore a brooch as big as the boss of a shield, while her shoes were laced high up her legs. She was a daisy, a peach fit for a prince to lay in his bed, or for any good yeoman to marry.

Now, gentlemen, it so happened that one day when her husband was at Oseney, Fly Nicholas—these clerks are strange artful fellows—began romping and larking with this young woman. He slyly caught hold of her cunt, saying, 'Sweetheart, if you don't let me have my way, I'll perish for love!' And he went on, holding her tight round the haunches, 'For God's sake, sweetheart, let's make love this minute, or I'll die.' She bucked like a colt being shod and wrenched her head away. 'Let go! I won't kiss you! Let go, Nicholas, or I'll scream for help! Take your hands off! Is this the way to behave?'

But Nicholas began to plead; he made so good a case for himself that she surrendered at last and swore by St Thomas of Canterbury to be his as soon as she could find the opportunity. 'My husband's so eaten up with jealousy that unless you wait patiently and watch your step I'm quite sure it will be the end of me,' she said. 'So keep it dark.' 'Don't worry about that,' said Nicholas. 'If a scholar can't get the better of a carpenter he's been wasting his time.' So, as I've said, they agreed to watch for an opportunity. This settled, Nicholas gave her thighs a good petting, then

kissed her sweetly and took down his psalter and strummed a
lively tune.

But it so happened that one saint's day this good woman laid
her housework aside. She washed her face till it shone, and went
to the parish church to make her devotions. Now in that church
there was a parish clerk called Absolon. His curly hair glistened
like gold and spread out like a great fan from its parting, straight
down the middle. He had a rosy complexion, goose-grey eyes, and
dressed stylishly in scarlet stockings and shoes as fantastically
patterned as the rose-window in St Paul's. On top of this he had
a neat well-fitting light-blue jacket with magnificent tagged laces,
while over it he wore a gay surplice white as a spray of blossom.
My oath, he was a lad. For he could barber and let blood, and
draw up legal documents; dance in twenty different styles (but in
the Oxford vogue of those days, with legs flying in every direc-
tion); sing in a loud falsetto, accompanying himself on a two-
stringed fiddle; and also play the guitar. There was no inn or
tavern in the town he hadn't enlivened with a visit, especially the
ones with frisky barmaids. But in fact he was a bit squeamish of
farting, and prim in his talk.

On this particular saint's day Absolon was in high fettle when
he took the censer round. While censing the women of the parish
he made sheeps' eyes at them, especially the carpenter's wife: she
was so neat, sweet, and luscious he felt as if he could spend a
lifetime of happiness gazing at her. And had she been a mouse
and Absolon a cat, I swear he would have pounced at once. So
smitten was the waggish parish clerk that he took no offerings
from the women at the collection—good manners forbade it, he
said.

That night the moon shone bright when Absolon picked up his
guitar to go a-wooing. Full of ardour he jauntily set off, till he
reached the carpenter's house soon after cock-crow, and took his
stand near a casement-window that projected from the wall. Then
he sang in a low, soft voice, well-tuned to his guitar:

> *Dearest lady, hear my prayer,*
> *Show me pity if you care.*

The carpenter woke up and heard him. 'Alison,' he said to his
wife. 'Can't you hear Absolon singing under our chamber wall?'

She answered, 'Yes, John; goodness knows I can hear every note.'

Things went on as you might expect. Gay Absolon wooed her daily, until he became quite woebegone, unable to sleep either night or day. He combed his thick locks and spruced himself; he wooed her by proxy, sending go-betweens to swear he was her slave; he trilled to her like a nightingale, and sent her wine and mead and spiced ale and cakes piping hot from the oven; he offered her money, for she lived in a town where there are things to buy. Some may be won with riches, others with blows, and yet others with kindness.

Once, to display his talent and versatility, he played Herod upon the stage. But what was the use? So much did she love Fly Nicholas that Absolon might go jump in the river; he only got jeered at for his pains. And so she made a monkey out of Absolon and turned his devotion into a joke. There's a very true proverb which goes: 'Be nigh and sly if you'd advance/An absent lover stands no chance.'

Absolon might rant and rave; but because he was out of her sight Nicholas cut him out simply by being on the spot.

Now, Fly Nicholas, show your mettle and leave Absolon to his whimpering! For one Saturday it happened that the carpenter went to Oseney. Nicholas and Alison agreed he should cook up some scheme to delude the poor jealous husband, so that if all went well she could sleep all night in his arms as they both desired. Without another word Nicholas, who could wait no longer, quietly carried up into his room enough food and drink to last him a day or two. Then he told Alison that when her husband asked after him she was to say she hadn't set eyes on him all day and didn't know where he was; but thought he might have been taken ill because when the maid went to call him he wouldn't give any answer whatever, no matter how loudly she shouted.

So all that Saturday Nicholas kept quietly to his room, eating or sleeping or doing whatever he felt like, till nightfall on Sunday. The poor carpenter began to wonder what on earth was the matter with Nicholas. 'By St Thomas, I'm beginning to be afraid all is not well with Nicholas! I hope to God he hasn't died all of a sudden! It's an uncertain world, to be sure: today I saw them carrying to church the corpse of a man I saw at work only last Monday.' Then he said to his serving-lad, 'Run up and shout at his door, or bang on it with a stone. See what's up and tell me straight out what it is.'

The boy went boldly upstairs and bawled and hammered outside the chamber door. 'Hey! What are you doing, master Nicholas? How can you sleep all day long?' But it was all for nothing. There was no answer. However in one of the bottom panels he found a hole the cat used to creep under, and took a good look through it. At length he caught a glimpse of Nicholas sitting bolt upright, with mouth agape as if moonstruck; so he ran down and immediately told his master of the state he had found him in.

The carpenter began to cross himself, saying, 'Help us, St Frideswide! Who can tell what's in store for anybody! The fellow has been taken with some kind of fit or seizure with that astroboly of his. I knew very well how it would turn out! People shouldn't poke into God's secrets. Blessed be the plain man who knows no more than his Creed! This is just the kind of thing which happened to that other student of astroboly who went walking in the fields, star-gazing and trying to divine the future. He fell into a marl-pit—something he didn't foresee. Still, by St Thomas, I'm sorry for poor Nicholas! By Christ in heaven, he's going to be rated for his studying, if I've got anything to do with it! Get me a staff, Robin; I'll lever the door up while you heave—that will put an end to his studying, I reckon!'

And he addressed himself to the chamber door. His boy was certainly a strong lad, and had it off by the hasp in a moment. The door fell to the floor. There sat Nicholas as if petrified, his mouth gaping up in the air. Supposing him to be in a trance of despair, the carpenter gripped him powerfully by the shoulders and shook hard, yelling, 'Hey, Nicholas! Hey! Look down! Wake up! Remember Christ's passion! The sign of the cross defend you from hobgoblins and sprites!' And thereupon he began to gabble a charm over each of the four corners of the house and the threshold of the door outside:

> *Jesus Christ, Saint Benedict,*
> *Evil spirits interdict:*
> *Nighthags fly this Paternoster!*
> *What happened to St Peter's sister?*

At length Fly Nicholas sighed heavily and said: 'Alas! Must the world end so soon?' The carpenter answered, 'What are you talking about? Trust in God, like the rest of us working-men.' Then Nicholas replied, 'Fetch me a drink and I'll tell you—in the strictest confidence mind—about a certain matter that concerns us both. I'm telling no one else, for sure.'

The carpenter went down and came back with a huge quart of strong ale. Then when each had drunk his share Nicholas shut fast the door and sat the carpenter down beside him. Said he, 'Dear, John, dear host, you must swear to me here and now upon your honour never to betray this secret to anyone, for it's Christ's secret I'm telling you, and you are lost if you tell it to a soul. For this will be the punishment if you betray me—you'll go stark mad.' 'Christ and His Holy Blood forbid it!' replied the simple fellow. 'I'm no babbler, and though I say it I'm not one for chattering. You can talk freely—as Christ harrowed hell, I'll not repeat it to man, woman, or child.'

'Now, John,' said Nicholas, 'this is no lie: through my study of astrology and my observations of the moon in its bright period, I have discovered that on the night of Monday next at about nine there is to be a deluge of rain, so torrential and stupendous that Noah's flood won't be in it. So terrific will be the downpour,' he continued, 'the whole world will be drowned in less than an hour, and mankind shall perish.'

At this the carpenter exclaimed, 'My poor wife! Must she drown? Alas, poor Alison!' He was so overcome that he almost collapsed. 'Can nothing be done?' he asked.

'Why, of course yes,' said Nicholas, 'but only if you will be guided by expert advice instead of following bright ideas of your own. As Solomon says so truly, "Do nothing without advice, and you'll be glad of it." Now if you will act according to my good counsel I'll undertake to save the three of us, even without mast or sail. Haven't you heard how Noah was saved when the Lord warned him in advance that the whole world would perish beneath the waters?'

'Yes,' said the carpenter, 'a long, long time ago.'

'Haven't you also heard,' Nicholas went on, 'of all the trouble Noah and the rest of them had before he could get his wife aboard the Ark? I daresay that at the time he'd have given anything for her to have a boat all to herself. Do you know what we'd better do? This calls for speed, and in an emergency there's no time for speechifying or delay.

'Hurry off at once and bring into the house a kneading-trough or large shallow tub for each of us—and make sure they're big enough to use as boats. And put a day's food in them—we shan't need more, for the waters will abate and go by about nine the next morning. But your boy Robin mustn't know about it. I can't save the maid Gillian either—don't ask why, for even if you did I wouldn't reveal God's secrets. Unless you're crazy it should be enough for you to be as greatly favoured as Noah himself. Don't worry: I'll save your wife all right. Now off you go and look sharp about it. But when you've got the three kneading-tubs—one for her, one for me, and one for you—you must hang them high up in the roof so that nobody notices our preparations. And when you've done what I've told you and stowed our provisions away in them, not forgetting an axe to cut the rope so that we can cast off when the water comes, you must break a hole high up in the garden side of the gable-end above the stables: then we can pass through when the deluge has stopped. And I'll bet you'll paddle about as gaily as a white duck after its mate: I'll shout "Hi, Alison! Hi, John! Cheer up, the floods will be down", and you'll reply, "Hullo, Master Nicholas! Good morning, I see you plain, for it is day." And then we'll be lords of creation for the rest of our lives, just like Noah and his wife.

'But of one thing I must seriously warn you, when we embark that night: take care none of us says a single word, or calls or cries out, but prays instead; for that's the Lord's command.

'You and your wife must hang as far apart as possible because there must be no sin between you, not even a glance, much less the act. Those are your orders. Be off, and good luck! Tomorrow night when everyone is asleep, we'll crawl into our tubs and sit there, trusting God to deliver us. Now off with you: I haven't time to argue further about this. People say, "Send a wise man and save breath" but you're so intelligent you don't need to be taught. Go and save our lives, I entreat you.'

The simple carpenter went off lamenting and confided the secret to his wife, who already knew the purpose behind the whole fantastic scheme much better than he did. Nonetheless she pretended to be frightened to death. 'Alas!' she exclaimed, 'hurry up and help us escape, or we'll all be killed! I am your true and lawful wedded wife; and so, dear husband, go and help save our lives.'

How potent is the fancy! People are so impressionable, they can die of imagination. The poor carpenter began to quake; he really thought he was going to see Noah's flood come tumbling in like the sea to drown his honey-pet Alison. He sighed shudderingly, wept, lamented and looked thoroughly miserable. Then, having gone and got hold of a kneading-trough and a couple of large tubs and conveyed them surreptitiously into the house, he secretly hung them up. With his own hands he made the rungs and uprights for three ladders to climb into the tubs hanging in the rafters. Next he provisioned both the trough and the two tubs with bread and cheese and a jug of good ale, quite enough to last a day. But before completing these arrangements he packed off his serving lad, and the maid as well, to London on an errand. And on the Monday, when it drew towards night, he shut the door without lighting the candles and made sure that everything was in order. A moment later all three of them clambered up into the tubs and sat there motionless for a good few minutes.

'Now say the Lord's Prayer,' said Nicholas, 'hush!' 'Hush,' said John, and 'Hush,' said Alison. The carpenter said his devotions and sat quietly, then prayed again, listening for the rain.

After his busy and tiring day the carpenter fell dead asleep at about curfew time, or perhaps a little later. Nightmares set him loudly groaning, and because his head was resting uncomfortably he began to snore. Nicholas tiptoed down the ladder while Alison quietly slipped down, and without another word they went to bed where the carpenter used to sleep. All was fun and frolic as Alison and Nicholas lay there, busy with delight and bliss, until the bell rang for lauds and the friars began to sing in the chancel.

That Monday the parish-clerk, the lovelorn Absolon, woebegone with love as usual, was amusing himself at Oseney with a party of friends when he chanced to ask one of the residents of the cloister about John the carpenter. The man drew him aside out of the church and said, 'I don't know—I haven't seen him working here since Saturday. I expect he's gone to fetch some timber for the

Abbot—he often goes to fetch timber and stays at the Grange for a day or two. Or else he must be at home. I can't really say where he is.'

The delighted Absolon thought happily to himself, 'Now's the night to stay awake: I swear I haven't seen him stir from his door since daybreak.

'Trust me, I'm going to tap quietly upon the low window in his bedroom wall at cockcrow, and tell Alison all my love-longing; I expect I'll kiss her at least—at any rate I swear I'll get some satisfaction. My mouth has itched all day—an omen of kissing if not more. And I dreamed all night that I was at a banquet. So I'll take a nap for an hour or two. Tonight I'll stay awake and have a bit of fun.'

Then at the first cockcrow this jaunty lover arose and dressed himself to kill. Before combing his hair he chewed cardamom and licorice to make his breath sweet, and put a leaf of true-love under his tongue, thinking it would make him attractive. Then he sauntered to the carpenter's house and quietly took his stand under the casement window (which was so low that it reached to his chest) and gave a half-suppressed cough: 'Where are you, sweet Alison, honeycomb, pretty chick, sweet cinnamon Alison? Awake, sweetheart, speak to me! You give little thought to my unhappiness, yet I'm sweating for your love wherever I go; though it's no wonder I should sweat and languish, when I yearn for you like a lamb for the teat. Truly, sweetheart, I'm so much in love that I yearn like a turtle-dove and eat less than a girl.'

'Go away from the window, you jackanapes,' she said. 'So help me God, there's going to be no kiss-me-quick for you: I love someone else—and I'd be to blame if I didn't—a much better man than you, Absolon, for Jesus' sake! In the devil's name, run off and let me sleep or I'll throw a stone at you.'

'Alas and alack!' returned Absolon, 'that true love was ever so badly received. Anyway, kiss me, since I may hope nothing better, for Jesus' love and for love of me.'

'Then will you promise to be off?' said she.

'Yes, of course, sweetheart,' answered Absolon.

'Then get ready,' she replied. 'I'll come in a moment.'

And she whispered to Nicholas, 'Shush now, and you'll have a good laugh.'

Then Absolon went down upon his knees and said, 'In every way I'm well off, for there'll be more to come after this, I hope. Sweetheart, be kind, sweet chick, be kind to me.'

Hastily she unfastened the window. 'Come on and get it over,' she said: 'Be quick about it in case any of the neighbours see you.'

Absolon began to wipe his mouth dry. The night was pitch dark, black as coal, when she put her arsehole out of the window. As luck would have it Absolon gave her bare arse a smacking kiss before he knew what it was. Back he started—there was something wrong, for he felt a rough and hairy thing, and he knew women don't have beards. 'Foo! What have I done?' he exclaimed. 'Ha ha,' she laughed and clapped the window to. Absolon was left to take himself off in sorry case.

'A beard! A beard!' cried Fly Nicholas. 'By God, that's a good one!'

Poor Absolon heard every word, and bit his lip with rage. He said to himself, 'I'll pay you out for this!'

How Absolon rubbed and scrubbed his lips with dust, and sand, and straw, and cloth, and shavings! 'May the Devil take me, but I'd rather avenge this insult than own the town,' he kept repeating. 'Alas!' he continued, 'if I'd only steered clear!' His burning love was quenched and cold. From the moment he kissed her arse his malady was cured. He didn't give a damn for fancy women. He began a tirade of denunciation against them, weeping like a spanked child. Slowly he crossed the street to visit a smith called Master Gervase, who made plough-fittings at his forge. He was busy sharpening shares and coulters when Absolon knocked casually and said, 'Open up, Gervase, and be quick about it.' 'What! Who's there?' 'It's me, Absolon.' 'What, Absolon! Why are you up so early, for Christ's sake? Eh? Lord bless us, what's up with you? Some young trollop, I bet, leading you a dance. By St Neot! you know what I mean all right.'

Absolon didn't give a bean for his chaff and made no reply to it because he had more fish to fry than Gervase knew. He said, 'See that hot ploughshare in the chimney over there, old man? Please lend it me, for I've got a job for it. I'll bring it back in a minute.'

Gervase answered, 'Of course! As I'm an honest smith you could have it were it gold, or a whole bagful of sovereigns. But in Christ's name, what do you want it for?'

'Never you mind,' returned Absolon, 'I'll tell you all about it one day,' and picked up the ploughshare by its handle, which was cool. Very quietly he stole out of the door and went to the wall of the carpenter's house. First he coughed, then tapped upon the window exactly as before.

Alison answered, 'Who's there, knocking like that? I'm sure it's a thief.'

'Why, no,' he said. 'Heaven knows, my sweet chick, it's your own Absolon, my darling. I've brought you a gold ring,' he went on. 'God help me, my mother gave it me: it's a fine one, beautifully engraved. I'll give it to you if you'll kiss me.'

Nicholas had got up to piss and thought he would improve upon the joke by making Absolon kiss his behind before he escaped. He opened the window quickly, and quietly stuck his arse right out, the whole haunch, buttocks and all. Upon this Absolon the clerk said, 'Speak, sweet chick, I don't know where you are.'

Then Nicholas let off a great fart like a thunderclap. Absolon, almost blinded with the blast, had his hot iron ready and smote Nicholas plumb on the bum. The hot ploughshare seared his backside till the skin flew off for a handsbreadth round about. Nicholas thought the agony would kill him and in his anguish yelled like frenzy, 'Help! Water! Water! For God's sake, help!'

The carpenter started out of his sleep. Hearing someone crying 'Water!' as if demented, he thought, 'Alas, here comes Noel's flood!' and without another word he sat up and hacked the rope in two with his axe. Down came everything with a run to the floorboards and he lay there stunned.

Up leapt Alison and Nicholas and ran out into the street crying 'Help! Murder!' All the neighbours came running in to stare at the carpenter where he still lay pale and stunned. For he had broken his arm with the fall. But his troubles were not over. As soon as he could speak he was at once overborne by Fly Nicholas and Alison. They told everybody he was raving, being so terrified of a fancied 'Noel's Flood' that in his folly he had bought three kneading-tubs and hung them up in the rafters, even begging them for the love of God to sit there with him and bear him company.

Then they all began laughing at his delusion, staring and gaping at the roof and making a joke of his ordeal. No matter what the carpenter might say, it was no use; nobody would take him seriously. They beat him down with great oaths till the whole town thought him crazy. Learned scholars unhesitatingly agreed with one another: 'The man's a crackpot' and everyone laughed at the affair. And that's how, in spite of all his jealousy and precaution, the carpenter's wife was screwed; how Absolon kissed her bottom eye, and Nicholas got his bum scorched. This story's finished, and God save all of us!

When people had stopped laughing at this absurd affair of Absolon and Fly Nicholas, they made various comments but chuckled with amusement for the most part. So far as I could see, nobody took offence at the story except Oswald the Reeve—it left a spark of resentment in his heart, for he was a carpenter by trade. He began to carp at it a bit, grumbling: 'Happen I could pay you back properly with a tale of a swaggering miller who got his eye wiped, if I wanted to talk smut. But I'm old, too old for that game; grass-time's over, it's winter-fodder for me now; this white poll writes me down an old man. And my heart's just as mildewed as my hair—I might as well be a splitarse or medlar, and that's a fruit that gets mouldier and mouldier till it's rotten and laid up in muck or straw. Us old men are like that, more's the pity: never ripe till rotten. So long as the world pipes we'll keep on dancing; for there's always this snag—we'd like a white head and a green tail like a leek; even though our strength be gone we love folly just the same. And when we can't do it we'll talk about it; there's a spark yet in our raked-up ashes.

I'll show you four live coals—greed, lying, anger and boasting—four embers that belong to old age. Though we can scarcely move our old limbs, desire never fails, and 'ats the truth on it. As for me, there's life in the old dog yet, though it's many a year since my tap of life began to run. For surely, when I was born Death turned on the tap of life and let it flow; and it's run ever since, till the cask's almost empty. Now my life-stream's no more than a few drops on the barrel-edge. My poor old tongue may well ring and chime of the follies of long ago—there's nothing left but dotage for the old!'

Having listened to this homily, our Host exclaimed magisterially, 'What's the good of all this wisdom? Must we spend all day Bible-thumping? The devil made a preacher out of a reeve; and the devil made a sailor, or a sawbones, out of a cobbler. Tell your tale and don't waste time. See, there's Deptford, and it's half-past seven already! And Greenwich full of blackguards over there. It's high time you began your tale.'

'Well, gentlemen,' said Oswald the Reeve, 'I hope you'll none of you take offence if I answer by pulling his leg a bit—tit for tat's only fair. This drunken Miller has just told us how a carpenter was made a fool of—perhaps to make fun of me, because I'm one myself—and if you don't mind I mean to pay him out: I'll talk in his own bumpkin language. I wish to God he'd break his neck— he can see a mote in my eye but not the beam in his own.'

THE REEVE'S TALE

At Trumpington, not far from Cambridge, runs a stream with a bridge over it, and on this stream there stands a mill where—and it's the truth I'm telling you—a miller dwelt many a year. He was proud and gay as any peacock; he could play the bagpipes, fish, mend nets, turn wooden cups on a lathe, wrestle and shoot. A long cutlass and a keen-bladed sword always hung from his belt, while in his pouch he carried a natty little dirk—it was as much as a man's life was worth to go near him. And he kept a Sheffield knife in his stocking. Bald as a monkey, with a round pug-nosed face, he was a thorough-going market-bully. Nobody dared lay a finger on him —he swore he'd make them pay for it pretty soon if they did. In fact he was a crook, and a sly one at that, a habitual pilferer of corn and meal. His nickname was Swagger Simkin. He had a wife who came from a noble family—her father was the town priest.* He'd had to give a large dowry of brassware along with her to get Simkin to make the alliance. She had been brought up in a nunnery; for Simkin, to keep up his yeoman status, said he wouldn't take a wife if she wasn't well-brought-up and a virgin. And she was proud and pert as a magpie. The two of them were something to see on Sundays when he strutted in front of her with his hood wrapped about his head and she followed in a red get-up matching Simkin's stockings. No one dared call her anything but 'Madam' or had the nerve to make a pass at her in the street unless he wanted Simkin to slaughter him with cutlass, knife, or dagger —jealous people are always dangerous customers, or at any rate that's what they want their wives to think. As her reputation was a bit smirched she kept people at a distance—ditchwater does as much—with her supercilious disdain. She felt there was consideration owed her on account of her family and because of her good upbringing at the nunnery.

Between them they'd produced a daughter, twenty years old, but no others except a six-months-old child, a bouncing boy still in the cradle. The girl was well-grown and plump, with a snub nose,

* i.e. she was a bastard, as priests were celibate.

grey eyes, broad buttocks, high round breasts, and I must admit really pretty hair. And because she was pretty the town priest intended to make her the heiress of his house and land, and was being difficult about her marrying because he wanted her to marry well, into some worthy family of ancient lineage. The goods of Holy Church ought to be spent on blood descended from Holy Church; so he was going to honour his holy blood, even if he had to devour Holy Church in the process.

Be sure this miller levied a huge toll on the wheat and malt of the country round; and in particular there was a great college at Cambridge called Solar Hall, whose wheat and malt was ground by him. Now one day it happened that its manciple fell ill with some malady, and it was thought he was sure to die. As a consequence the miller began to steal a hundred times more meal and corn than before. Up till then he had been content with a polite pilfering, but now he was a barefaced robber. The Warden was annoyed about it and made a great to-do, but the miller didn't give a straw; he blustered and denied it point-blank.

Now at the college I speak of there were two young students, headstrong fellows game for anything. Just for the fun of it they pestered the Warden to give them a short leave to go to the mill and see their corn ground. They were ready to wager their necks the miller wouldn't be able to rob them, by force or fraud, of so much as a half-peck of corn. And in the end the Warden gave them leave. One was called John and the other Alan; both were born in the same town, a place called Strother somewhere in the far north.

Alan collected all his gear and slung a sack of corn over the horse. Then Alan and John set out, each with a good sword and buckler at his side. They didn't need a guide—John knew the way —and when they reached the mill he threw down the sack.

Alan spoke first: 'Howdo! Well, Simon, how's thi wife and lass?'

'Welcome, Alan,' said Simkin. 'And on my life, here's John as well! How's things? What brings you here?'

'Christ Almighty, Simon, need knows no law,' said John, "it behoves him that has no help to help hissen, or you're daft, as the learned say. Our manciple's near dying with toothache in his head; and so I've come with Alan to grind our corn and bring it home. You'll hurry it up for us, I hope.'

'I'll do that, trust me,' said Simkin, 'but what will you do while
I've the job in hand?'

'I sal stand right next the hopper, by God,' said Alan, 'and see
how the corn goes in. I've never seen yon hopper swingin' abaht in
my born days.'

'Do that, John,' answered Alan, 'then you can bet I'll be under-
neath to watch how the meal falls down into yon trough; I sal
play that game all reyt. For sure, me and you's the same sort,
John; I'm as bad a miller as you.'

The miller grinned at their fatuity and thought, 'This is all just
a ruse; they think nobody can diddle them; but as I'm a miller I'll
hoodwink them yet, for all their clever philosophy. The more
smart tricks they try the more I'll steal in the end. I'll give them
bran for flour still! As the mare said to the wolf one day, "The
most learned aren't always the wisest." I don't give a bean for all
their book-learning.'

When he saw his chance he stole quietly out of the door and
looked around until he found the students' horse standing tethered
under an arbour behind the mill. He went boldly up to the horse
and stripped it of its bridle on the spot. Once loosed, the horse
turned towards the fen where wild mares were running free; with
a whinny it raced off through thick and through thin. The miller
returned and said not a word, but went on with his job and joked
with the two students until their corn was well and truly ground.
But when the meal was sacked and tied John went out and found
their horse missing. 'Help! Help!' he cried. 'Our horse is lost!
God's bones, Alan, stir thi stumps—come out, man, at once! We've
lost warden's palfrey.' Alan forgot meal and corn and all, and the
need for keeping an eye on things went clean out of his mind.
'What? Where's he bahn?' he cried.

The miller's wife came running in: 'Alas! your horse is off to
the wild mares in the fen as fast as he can gallop—no thanks to
the hand that tied him up—you ought to have knotted the rein
better!'

'Alas!' cried John, 'Alan, for Christ's sake take thi sword off;
I'll do the same. God knows I'm wick as a roe—Christ Almighty,
he'll not escape the both of us! Why didn't you put the nag in
yon barn? Devil take it, you're daft, Alan, by God!'

And those two silly students ran off as hard as they could to-
wards the fen. When the miller saw they'd gone he took half a

bushel of their flour and told his wife to knead it into a cake. 'I bet those students have had a fright,' said he. 'Still, a miller can singe a scholar's beard, for all his book-learning. Let them run along! Just watch them go! Well, let the children play—they aren't going to catch him that easily, or I'll eat my hat.'

The poor students ran up and down crying, 'Watch out! Woa, woa! Hey up there! Watch out behind! You go whistle: I'll head him off!' In short, no matter how hard they tried the horse ran so fast they failed to catch it till nightfall; but they finally cornered it in a ditch.

Poor John and Alan came back wet and weary as cattle in the rain. Said John, 'I wish I'd never been born! We've been fooled, made a laughing-stock; our corn's stolen, and they'll all call us fools—the Warden and our mates and the miller worst of all!'

Thus grumbled John as he made his way to the mill leading his Bayard by the rein. He found the miller sitting by the fire, for it was night and they could go no further; so they begged him for God's sake to give them lodging and shelter for their money.

Said the miller, 'If there is any you shall have your share of it, such as it is. My house is pretty cramped, but you've been educated —you'll know how to argy-bargy and make out that a twenty-foot space is a mile across. Now let's see if this place will do—you can always make it bigger by talking, as is the way of you learned folk.'

'Now, Simon,' said John, 'there you have us—you'll have your joke, by St Cuthbert! But as the saying is, "A man sal take ane of twa things: sic as he finds or sic as he brings." Good host, let me beg you to get us some food and drink and make us welcome: we'll pay you on the nail. You can't catch a hawk with an empty hand. Look, here's our brass, ready to spend.'

The miller roasted them a goose and sent his daughter to town for bread and ale; he tethered their horse so that it wouldn't run loose again, and made up a fine bed spread with sheets and blankets for them in his room, not a dozen feet from his own bed. Near by, in the very same room, his daughter had a bed all to herself. This was the best they could do for the simple reason there was nowhere else in the place to sleep. They supped, talked, and made merry and drank any amount of strong ale, then at about midnight went to bed.

The miller got himself properly plastered; he wasn't flushed, but quite pallid with drink; he hiccupped and talked through his nose as if he'd asthma or a cold in the head. Off to bed he went, his wife with him; she was as merry as a grig, for she'd wet her whistle well and truly. The cradle was set at the foot of the bed, that she might rock it or give the child suck. And when they'd drained the jug the daughter went straight to bed, followed by Alan and John; there wasn't a drop left, and they'd no need of a sleeping-draught. The miller had certainly had a skinful, for he snorted like a horse in his sleep, honking at both ends—and his wife joined in the chorus with a will. People could hear them wheezing away a quarter of a mile off. And the girl snored with them for company's sake.

After listening to this melody Alan poked John and said, 'Are you asleep? Did ever you hear such a warbling before? Talk about evening prayers—the itch fall on them! It's the weirdest thing you ever heard. They're going to come to the worst of bad ends. There'll be no rest for me this long neet. But ne'er mind; it'll be all for the best. For, John,' said he, 'you can take it from me I sal swink with yon girl if I can. The law allows us some compensation, John; there's a law says if a man's harmed in one way he's to be relieved in another. There's no denying our corn was stolen—we've had bad luck all day; and since I'll get no amends against my loss I sal take compensation. Christ Almighty, that's how it sal be.'

'Watch your step, Alan!' answered John. 'Yon miller's a dangerous customer, and if he wakes up suddenly he might do both of us a mischief.'

'I count him less than a fly,' answered Alan, and got up and crept over to the girl. She was fast asleep on her back; by the time she saw him he was so close it was too late to cry out—in short, they were soon at one. Now I'll leave Alan to his fun and speak of John.

John lay quietly where he was for a few minutes, then began lamenting to himself. 'This isn't much of a joke!' said he. 'I can only say I've been made a monkey of, while my mate's had something for his pains—he's got the miller's daughter in his arms. He took a chance and got his oats, while I'm lying in bed like a sack of rubbish. And when this jape is told one day, I'll look a clahthead, daft as a brush! I'll get up and chance it—it's muck or nettles now, as the saying is.' So up he got and went softly over to the cradle, picked it up and quietly carried it to the foot of his own bed.

Soon afterwards the miller's wife stopped snoring and woke up. She went out to piss, came back, and missed the cradle; here and there she groped, but couldn't find it at all. 'Oh dear,' said she, 'I nearly went wrong and almost got into the students' bed. Bless us! I'd have found myself in bad trouble!' And she moved on until she found the cradle. She kept groping further and further with her hands until she found the bed, thinking all was well because the cradle stood next to it. Not knowing where she was in the dark, she fairly crawled in beside the student. She lay still and would have fallen asleep, but in a little while John came to life and threw himself upon this good woman. It was the best bout she'd had in years—he thrust away like a madman, hard and deep. And so the two students had the time of their lives till it was nearly dawn.

In the morning Alan began to tire after toiling all night long, and whispered, 'Goodbye, sweet Molly, the day is here, I can't stay no longer. But as I live and breathe, I'll always be thi own true lad, wherever I am.'

'Then go, sweetheart, and goodbye,' said she, 'but I'll tell you one thing before you go—when you're on your way home past the mill, just behind the entrance of the door you'll find a half-bushel cake made of your own flour, which I helped my father steal. God save and keep you, sweetheart.' And saying this she nearly began to weep.

Alan got up and thought, 'I'll slip in beside my friend before day breaks.' And soon his hand found the cradle. 'By God,' thought he, 'I'm up shit creek. My head's in a whirl from tonight's work, that's why I can't go right. I can tell by the cradle I'm off course—this is where the miller and his wife are kipping.' And as the devil would have it he passed on to the bed where the miller lay. Thinking to creep in beside his friend John, he crawled in beside the miller, threw his arm around his neck and whispered, 'You John, you pig's-head, wake up for Christ's sake and listen to a rare joke—for by St James, tonight I've screwed the miller's daughter three times upon her back, while you've been shivering, flade to death.'

'Have you, you blackguard!' cried the miller. 'By God, I'll kill you, you treacherous jackanapes! How dare you dishonour my daughter—so nobly born and all!' And he caught Alan by his Adam's apple, who in turn seized him furiously and belted him on the nose with his fist. A stream of blood poured down his chest, and they plunged about on the floor with bleeding mouths and noses, like two pigs in a poke; up and down they had it, until the miller tripped himself on a stone and fell backwards on his wife, who knew nothing about this silly brawl. She had just fallen asleep with John, who had kept her up all night; but the fall shocked her out of sleep. 'Help, holy cross of Bromeholme!' she cried. 'Into Thy Hands, O Lord! To Thee I call! Wake up, Simon! The fiend's upon me! My heart's bursting! Help, I'm dying! There's somebody lying on my stomach, and on my head! Help, Simkin! Those wretched boys are fighting!'

John leapt out of bed as fast as he could and groped along the wall to find a stick. And the miller's wife got up also; knowing the room better than John, she soon found a stick leaning against the wall. She saw a light glimmering where the moon shone brightly in through a hole, and by this light made out the pair of them, but couldn't tell who was who, till she caught a glimpse of something white: and when she saw this white thing she supposed that one of the students must be wearing a nightcap, so crept closer with her stick, meaning to hit Alan a good thwack; and instead smote the miller on his bald pate. Down he went, yelling, 'Help! I'm killed!' The students gave him a good beating and left him lying: then they threw on their clothes, collected their horse and meal and were off. But they stopped at the mill to pick up the cake baked from their half-bushel of flour.

And so that swaggering miller took a good beating, lost his fee for grinding the corn, and paid for every penny of Alan's and John's supper, who belaboured him into the bargain. His wife was screwed, so was his daughter—that's what comes of being a miller and a cheat! So it's a true proverb that says 'Do as you would be done by.' Swindlers always get themselves swindled in the end. Now may God who sits in majesty on high save everyone in this company! And so I've paid out the Miller in my tale.

While the Reeve was telling his story the Cook looked as pleased as if his back were being scratched. 'Ha ha,' he laughed. 'By Christ, the Miller got a tart answer to his argument about lodgings! Solomon had something there when he said, "Bring not every man into thy house." It's a risky business, taking people in for the night. A man can't be too careful who he takes into his home. May God send me sorrow and grief if ever since I was called Hodge of Ware I heard of a miller so thoroughly done—that was a wicked joke they played him in the dark! But God forbid we should leave off there: and if you'd like to listen to a story by a poor fellow like me I'll tell you as best I can of a little joke that happened in our city.'

Our Host answered, 'You've my consent. Tell away, Roger, and mind it's good, for many's the stale pasty with no gravy in it and twice-warmed-up Jack-of-Dover pie that you've sold, and many's the time pilgrims have called down Christ's damnation on you when they were the worse for the parsley stuffing they ate with your stubble-fed goose: for your cookshop's full of flies. Now tell on, good Roger, your good name's at stake! But for heaven's sake please don't mind me pulling your leg: many a true word's spoken in jest.'

'My word, that's true enough,' said Roger, 'but as the Flemings say, "a true joke's no joke"—and so, Harry Bailly, swear you won't take offence if I tell a tale about an innkeeper before we've finished. Nevertheless I shan't tell it yet—but I bet you'll be paid in full before we part.' And with that he laughed and cheered up. Then he told his story as you shall hear.

THE COOK'S TALE

Aprentice once lived in our city who worked in the victualling trade. He was merry as a goldfinch in the greenwood, a short handsome lad as brown as a berry with black hair elegantly combed; and he danced so well and merrily that they called him Perkin Reveller. Any girl who met with him was in luck, for he was as full of love and lechery as a hive is of honey. He danced and sang at all the weddings and was fonder of the tavern than the shop; for whenever there was a procession in Cheapside he would shoot out of the shop to run after it, and never come back till he'd danced his fill and seen all there was to see. He gathered a gang of his own sort about him, for dancing, singing, and like diversions. They rendezvoused in such and such a street to play dice: for there was no prentice in the town who threw dice better than Perkin; and moreover he was a free spender on the sly. This his master discovered to his cost, for many a time he found the till empty. For you may be sure that when a prentice is always living it up with dicing, gaming, and women, his master pays for it with his shop though he gets no share of the fun. Though the prentice may play the fiddle and guitar, his fun and games are the same as theft. As you can see, honesty and high living are always at loggerheads in the case of the poor.

Though scolded night and day, and sometimes hauled off with fanfares to Newgate jail,* this merry prentice stayed with his master until his apprenticeship was nearly completed. But one day his master, looking around for his indentures, finally recalled the proverb that says, 'Better throw the rotten apple out than let it rot the others.' It's the same with a riotous servant: it's less harmful to let him go than keep him to spoil all the other servants in the place. So his master gave him his release and bade him depart, with curses on his head. And so the merry prentice got his freedom; now he could revel all night long—or else give it up. And

* 'When disorderly persons were carried to prison, they were preceded *by minstrels,* in order to call public attention to their disgrace.' (Skeat.)

—because there's no thief without a hanger-on to help him to loot and swindle those he robs or sponges, Perkin immediately sent his bed and gear to one of his boon companions who was just as fond of dice, revelry, and dissipation, whose wife kept a shop for appearance's sake but screwed for her living.

[Chaucer left this tale unfinished. D.W.]

Our Host perceived that the bright sun had completed a quarter—plus half an hour or so—of the arc it travels between its rising and setting; and though not deeply learned in the art, he knew it was the eighteenth day of April, harbinger of May; and he observed that the shadow of each tree was the same length as the vertical body casting it. From the shadow he could estimate that Phoebus, shining so bright and clear, had climbed to a height of forty-five degrees; and thus, taking the date and latitude into consideration, concluded it was ten o'clock. Suddenly he turned his horse round.

'Sirs,' said he, 'I warn you, all of you, a fourth part of the day has already gone. Now for the love of God and St John let's waste no more time if we can help it. Gentlemen, Time wastes away day and night; what with our private slumbers and negligence when awake, it steals away like the unreturning stream that descends from the mountain to the plain. Well may Seneca and the philosophers lament the loss of Time more than a chestful of gold; for as he said, "Lost wealth may be recovered but lost time confounds us." You may be sure it won't come back, any more than wanton Molly's lost maidenhead. So let's not moulder away in idleness like this.

'Now Master Sergeant-at-Law,' he went on, 'as you hope for heaven, tell us a tale according to our bargain. You freely promised to stand by my decision in this matter. Now keep your promise; then, at least, you'll have done your duty.'

'Good Host,' he replied, 'I swear I'm perfectly willing; I've no intention of backing out. A promise is a promise and I'll gladly keep mine: I can't say fairer than that. By rights "they that make laws should not break them" as the saying is; but nevertheless I'm pretty sure that I can't tell any worthwhile story on the spur of the moment that hasn't already been told long ago, as most people know, by Chaucer (unskilful as he is with rhyme and metre) in such English as he commands. And if he hasn't related them in one book, my dear fellow, it's because he's told them in another; for he has recounted stories about all sorts of lovers,

more than Ovid mentioned in those old Epistles of his. Why should I repeat them when they've already been told?

'In youth he wrote of Ceix and Halcyon: since when he has celebrated every one of these noble ladies and their lovers—anyone who pleases can look out that huge tome of his called The Legend of Good Women. *There* you may read about the wide and gaping wounds of Lucrece, of Thisbe of Babylon: Dido dying by her sword for false Aeneas; Phyllis hanging from a tree because of Demophon; the lament of Dejanira, of Hermione, of Ariadne, and of Hypsipyle; the barren island standing in the sea; Leander drowned for his Hero; the tears of Helen, the grief of Briseis and of Laodamia; the cruelty of Queen Medea with her little children hanged by the neck because Jason was false! And Hypermnestra, Penelope, Alcestis—he celebrated their womanhood with the best of them! But he wrote not a single word concerning that disgraceful affair of Canace and her sinful love for her brother— shame upon such accursed stories, I say! Nor did he draw from Apollonius of Tyre that story of the criminal King Antiochus who bereft his daughter of her maidenhead. That tale is too horrible to read, especially the part where he throws her on the pavement. Advisedly, therefore, Chaucer would never write of such unnatural abominations in any of his dissertations: nor will I repeat any, if you don't mind.

But what shall I do for my tale today? You may be sure I shouldn't care to be likened to those would-be Muses known as the Pierides (you'll find them in Ovid's Metamorphoses) but all the same I don't give a bean if, coming after him, my offering seems like baked crabapples. I talk in prose, and I'll leave poetry to him.'

And with these words he gravely began to tell the following story.

Direst of misfortunes is the condition of poverty; confounded by thirst, cold, and hunger, you are shamed to the heart to ask for help, yet so badly hit that if you ask none, sheer necessity uncovers your hidden wound. In spite of all you can do, indigence forces you to steal, beg, or borrow your keep. You lay the blame on Christ, bitterly observing that He misapportions worldly riches; or sinfully blame your neighbour, saying he has everything and yourself too little. You swear he'll pay for it one day when he finds his tail burning in the fiery coals because he refused to help the needy in their distress.

Hear what the wise have said: 'Death is better than indigence, when your own neighbour will despise you. If you are poor you lose all respect.' And here's another sage observation: 'All the days of the poor are evil.' So take care you are not driven to this pass. For if you are poor your brother hates you and all your friends shun you.

O you rich merchants, O you worthy, prudent folk, the luck's with you in this case; your bags aren't stuffed with double aces but fives and sixes* and runs of luck; you can dance gaily at Christmas time when poor men freeze. You scour land and sea for your profits and like wise men keep yourselves informed concerning the condition of different countries; you are a fount of news and of tales of peace and war. Were it not for a merchant who taught me a tale many years ago I would be quite out of stories to tell. And now you shall hear it.

* Losing and winning throws respectively at Hazard (a game of dice).

THE
SERGEANT-AT-LAW'S
TALE

here was in Syria
at one time a rich company of merchants, sober and honest men
who exported their spices, cloth of gold, richly coloured satins far
and wide. So novel and cheap was their merchandise that every-
one was eager to sell goods and do business with them. Now it
chanced some of these merchants decided to go to Rome, either
on business or pleasure—in any case, instead of sending repre-
sentatives they themselves went to Rome, where they took lodg-
ings in the quarter that seemed to suit their purposes best.

For some time these merchants sojourned at their pleasure in
the town. And as it happened, detailed reports of the excellent
renown of the Emperor's daughter, Lady Constance, came each
day to the ears of these Syrian merchants, as I shall tell. Thus ran
the common report: 'Our Emperor of Rome—may God protect
him!—has a daughter; and if you reckon up her goodness with
her beauty there has been none like her since the world began.
May God sustain her in honour: she deserves to be queen of all
Europe. In her is great beauty, without vanity; youth, without
wantoness or folly; virtue guides her every action; in her humility
has put an end to all arrogance; she is the mirror of courtesy,
her heart a very shrine of holiness, and her hand a liberal instru-
ment of alms!'

And all this report was true as God is true. But to return to the
story. The merchants finished loading their ships, and when they
had seen this blessed maiden they returned contentedly home to
Syria and pursued their business as before. I can tell you no more
than that they lived prosperously ever after.

Now these merchants happened to stand well with the Sultan
of Syria: for whenever they returned from any strange country he
used to entertain them with generous hospitality and diligently
inquire after the news of various lands in order to keep himself
informed of any wonders they might have seen or heard. And
among other things the merchants spoke particularly to him of the
Lady Constance, giving a circumstantial account of her great

worth with such earnestness that the thought of her captured the Sultan's imagination and wholly obsessed him till his one desire was to love her to the end of his days.

Perhaps at his birth it was written in the stars—in that great book men call the sky—that he would be unlucky and die for love. For in the stars, clearer than glass, is written each man's death, could men but read it. Years before they were born the deaths of Hector, Achilles, Pompey, and Julius Caesar, the war of Thebes and the deaths of Samson, Turnus, and Socrates were set down in the stars; but men's wits are so dull that nobody can interpret them fully.

The Sultan sent for his privy council. In short, he told them what was in his mind, and said he would die for certain unless he had the luck to win Constance very soon. So he charged them to make haste and devise some means of saving his life. Various counsellors made various suggestions. They argued and debated back and forth, bringing forward any number of subtle lines of argument.They talked of magic and conjuration; but in the end concluded they could see no advantage in these means, or in any others except marriage. And in this, owing to the arguments against it, they foresaw great difficulties. Because of the difference between the faiths of the two countries they said they believed no Christian prince would willingly permit his daughter to be wed according to the cherished laws taught them by their prophet Mahomet.

But he replied, 'Be sure I will be baptized rather than lose Constance. I must be hers: I have no other choice. Kindly leave off arguing. Try to save my life by seeing to it that you obtain the lady who holds my life in her hands, for I cannot live much longer in this anguish.'

There's no need to expatiate further. I'll only say that by dint of treaties, embassies, and the mediation of the Pope backed by the entire church and nobility, they agreed to the abolition of idolatry and the spread of Christ's blessed law. Each party swore to keep the following bargain: the Sultan, his nobles, and all his subjects were to be baptized in return for Constance's hand in marriage, together with a certain sum of gold (I don't know how much), sufficient surety of this to be provided. And now, fair Constance, may Almighty God be your guide!

Now I suppose some people will expect me to describe all the preparations that the Emperor in his magnificence made for his daughter Lady Constance: but you know perfectly well it is impossible to recount in a few words the elaborate arrangements for an occasion so important. Bishops, lords, ladies, famous knights and plenty of other folk—the list is endless—were appointed to go with her. Everyone in the city was ordered to pray devoutly to Christ that He should bless the marriage and grant a prosperous voyage.

The day came for her departure: a fatal, melancholy day. There could be no more tarrying now, for one and all were ready to embark. Pale and overcome with sorrow, Constance rose and prepared herself to go, for she could see plainly there was no alternative. What wonder is it if she wept at being sent away from her friends who had cared for her so tenderly, to a strange people; to be bound in subjection to a man whose character she knew nothing of? As wives know, all husbands are good and always have been; I dare not say more.

'Father,' said she, 'and you, my mother, my greatest joy above all things except Christ in heaven, your wretched child Constance, the daughter whom you so tenderly reared, commends herself once more to your hearts. For I must go to Syria, never again to see you with these eyes. Alas! since you wish it, I must go to the people of Barbary; may Christ Who died for our salvation give me the strength to obey His commands! It doesn't matter if I perish, wretched woman that I am! Women are born to suffering and bondage, to live under the domination of men.'

I'd say that not even at Troy when Pyrrhus broke down the wall, before the burning of Ilium, nor at the city of Thebes, nor in Rome harried by Hannibal who three times vanquished the Romans, was heard so heartbroken a weeping as in that room where she took her departure. But weeping or not she had to go.

Now, at the beginning of this terrible voyage, the Primum Mobile* (that unpitying sphere whose diurnal motion presses

* According to the astronomy of Chaucer's day there were nine spheres revolving round the earth, which was supposed to be in the centre and stationary. Each of the seven innermost spheres carried with it one of the seven planets—the Moon, Venus, Mercury, the Sun, Mars, Jupiter and Saturn. The eighth sphere carried the fixed stars and had a slow motion from west to east along the signs of the Zodiac. The ninth, outermost

against all things, hurtling from east to west what would naturally go in the opposite direction) crowded the heavens into such a disposition that Mars' cruel planet must destroy the marriage. For the sign of Aries, ascending obliquely, presaged misfortune; while cadent Mars, its ruler, thrust helplessly from his angle into Scorpio the darkest house, was here a malign influence, with the moon feebly placed (for having been moved from a favourable position the moon now stood in an unfavourable conjunction). That imprudent Emperor of Rome! Was there no astrologer in his whole city?

In cases of this kind, is it a matter of indifference what time is set for departure? Is there no choice of astrologically suitable times for starting a voyage—especially when persons of high rank are concerned, and the hour of their birth is known? Slackness and ignorance is the trouble.

With pomp and circumstance the beautiful and unhappy girl was conducted to the ship. 'Now Jesus Christ be with you all!' she said; and they replied, 'Farewell, fair Constance!' and that was all. She did her best to compose her features. Now I shall leave her to sail away while I pick up the threads of my story.

That well of evil, the Sultan's mother, perceiving her son's evident purpose to forsake their ancient sacrificial customs, immediately summoned her advisers. When these people had come and assembled together to hear what she had in mind, she took her seat and said:

'My lords, you all know that my son is on the point of renouncing the holy laws of our Alkoran given by Mahomet the messenger of God. But I make one vow to Almighty God: the life shall quit my breast before the law of Mahomet is torn from my heart. What can this new faith bring us except suffering and bondage for our bodies, and after that to be dragged down to hell because we renounced our belief in Mahomet? But, my lords, will you swear to do as I say and agree to follow my advice—and I shall make us safe for ever?'

They swore: every man of them promised to stand by her in

---

sphere, was called the Primum Mobile—the sphere of the first motion—and had a daily revolution from east to west, carrying everything with it, in the opposite direction to the 'natural' motion of the Sun advancing along the signs of the Zodiac.

life and death; and each, as best he could, rallied his friends to her support. Then she began the enterprise I shall describe, and addressed them in this manner:

'First we must pretend to become Christians—cold water won't hurt us much! And I'll prepare such a banquet as will settle accounts with the Sultan. Let his wife be baptized never so white, she'll need water by the font-ful to wash away the blood!'

Sultaness! Root of iniquity! Virago! Second Semiramis! Serpent in female shape, like the serpent fettered in nethermost hell! Treacherous woman, malignant nest of every vice, in whom breeds all that may confound virtue and innocence! O Satan, envious since the day you were chased from your heritage, you know the old road to women only too well! You made Eve bring us to bondage; now you are about to destroy this Christian marriage. When you wish to mislead us you make women your instrument, more's the pity.

The subject of my curses, the Sultaness, secretly dismissed her advisers. Why prolong the story? One day she rode over to see the Sultan, saying she would renounce her faith and receive baptism at the hands of a priest. She said that she repented having remained a heathen for so long, and besought him to grant her the honour of inviting the Christians to a banquet. 'I'll do my best to please them,' said she. To this the Sultan replied, 'It shall be as you ask.' He knelt and thanked her for her request, so pleased that he hardly knew what to say. She kissed her son and rode off home.

ii

The Christians arrived and landed in Syria with a large and illustrious company. The Sultan speedily sent a message to announce his wife's arrival, first to his mother and then to all the country round. For the honour of the kingdom he begged the Sultaness to ride to meet his queen.

The Syrians and Romans met together in a great and splendidly-arrayed congregation. Richly dressed and gay, the Sultan's mother received Constance as fondly as any mother her daughter. They slowly rode in state to the city near by. I don't suppose that the triumph of Julius Caesar, of which Lucan boasts so much, could have been more magnificent or elaborate than the assembly of that smiling multitude; yet for all her blandishments this malignant ghoul, this scorpion of a Sultaness, was preparing to deliver a mortal sting. Soon afterwards the Sultan arrived in marvellous pomp and welcomed Constance with every mark of happiness and delight. Here I will leave them to their rejoicing: I am only concerned to tell the outcome of the affair. In due course they thought it proper to end the revels and take their rest. And the time came when the Sultaness fixed the day for the banquet I spoke of. All the Christians, young and old, made themselves ready for the feast. It was a magnificent spectacle, and they feasted upon more dainties than I can describe; but they had to pay for it all too dearly before they rose from the table.

Sudden sorrow always succeeds earthly felicity, which is shot through with bitterness: for grief, the outcome of our delight in all our earthly striving, lives at the back of our happiness. Listen to my advice if you want to be on the safe side: in the day of happiness remember the unexpected sorrow or calamity coming from behind. For in one word, the Sultan and every one of the Christians with the single exception of the Lady Constance was stabbed and hacked to pieces at the table. This accursed deed was done by that damnable old crone, the Sultaness, with the aid of her friends. She wanted to rule the country herself. Not one of the converted Syrians in the Sultan's confidence but was hacked to shreds before he could start to his feet. Hastily they seized Constance and put her aboard a rudderless ship, telling her she could learn to sail home to Italy from Syria. They gave her a certain amount of the treasure she had brought with her and (to do them justice) a great plenty of provisions; she had clothes also. Thus she set sail upon the salt sea. O Constance, full of loving-kindness, the Emperor's beloved young daughter, may He who is the Lord of Fortune be your guide! Crossing herself, she prayed with piteous voice to the cross of Christ:

'O bright and blessed altar, holy cross, red with the compassionate blood of the Lamb that washes away the ancient iniquity of the world, save me from the fiend and his claws upon the day that I shall drown in the deep sea! Victorious tree, protection of the faithful, that alone was worthy to bear the newly-wounded King of Heaven, the white Lamb pierced by the spear! Thou hast power to expel demons from the man or woman over whom thy blessed arms extend. Guard me, and grant me strength to amend my life.'

For many a year, for many a day she floated over the Grecian seas till chance brought her to the Strait of Morocco; many a scant and meagre meal did she eat, and many times look for death, before the wild waves cast her up at the place where she was destined to arrive.

People may ask why she was not slain with the others at the banquet: who was there to save her? To that question I reply: who saved Daniel in the fearsome den where everyone but he—master and slave together—was devoured by lions before they could escape? None but God, whom he carried in his heart. Through her, God chose to show His miraculous power, that we should see His mighty works. The philosophers know that Christ (Who is the sure remedy for all evil) employs chosen instruments for purposes obscure to human understanding; our ignorance cannot grasp His wise providence. Yet, as she was not slain at the banquet, who saved her from drowning in the waves? Who saved Jonah in the fish's maw till he was spouted up at Nineveh? As you well know, none other than He who saved the Hebrew people from drowning when they passed with dry feet through the sea. And who commanded the four spirits of the storm that have power to vex the whole earth: 'North, south, west, and east, vex not a leaf, nor sea, nor land'? Surely He who gave that command kept this woman, sleeping or awake, safe from the tempest. Where might she find food and drink, and how did her provisions last three years and more? Who fed Mary of Egypt in the desert and the cave? Surely none but Christ. It was as great a miracle as when He fed five thousand people with five loaves and two fishes. God sent His plenty to her in her need.

She was driven forth into the fierce seas of our ocean, till in the end the waves cast her up under a castle whose name is unknown to me, far in Northumberland. For the whole of a tide her ship stuck fast in the sand, it being Christ's will that she should there remain. The Constable of the castle came down to see the wreck. He made a thorough search of the vessel and found the woman exhausted with her troubles; and also discovered the treasure she had brought. In her own tongue she besought his mercy, begging him to take her life and put her out of her misery. Her speech was a kind of corrupt Latin, but she could be understood nonetheless. When the Constable had seen enough he brought the poor woman ashore. She thanked God upon her knees for His aid; but nothing would induce her, for good or ill, to tell anyone who she was. Her wits, she said, had been so mazed in the sea that she had lost her memory. The Constable and his wife felt such great compassion for her that they wept for pity. And she was so diligent and unwearied in serving and pleasing everyone there that she was loved by all who looked upon her face.

The Constable and his wife, Lady Hermengyld, were pagans, like everyone else in the land; yet Hermengyld came to love Constance dearly. Constance remained there for a long time, giving herself to weeping and prayer, till through the grace of Jesus Christ the Constable's wife was converted. Throughout the land no Christian dared meet for worship—all the Christian folk had fled from that country because pagans had conquered by land and sea all the regions of the north. Christianity had fled with the Britons (the old inhabitants of this island) to Wales where they had taken refuge for the time being. Yet the Christian Britons had not been so totally banished that there were not some remaining who deceived the heathen and secretly worshipped Christ. Three such dwelt near the castle. One was blind and could not see except with those eyes of the mind with which the blind are able to espy.

The sun shone bright the summer's day when Constance together with the Constable and his wife took the direct path to the sea, meaning to amuse themselves and stroll to and fro for a half mile or so. But on their walk they met this old man, blind and bent, with his eyes shut fast.

'Lady Hermengyld!' cried the old Briton, 'in the name of Christ, give me back my sight!' Hearing this the lady grew terrified, fearing her husband would slay her for her love of Jesus Christ. But Constance gave her courage, telling her to perform Christ's will as one of the daughters of His church.

Disconcerted by the sight the Constable exclaimed, 'What's all this about?' Constance replied, 'Sir, it is the power of Christ that saves people from the snare of the fiend.' And she began to expound the faith with such effect that before evening she had converted the Constable and made him believe in Christ. Now, this Constable was by no means the ruler of the place I mentioned, where he found Constance; he had held it for many years under Alla, king of all Northumberland, who was as you know that astute king who curbed the Scots with a hand of iron. But let me return to my story.

Satan, who is always lying in wait to entrap us, saw the perfection of Constance and cast about to find a means of making her pay for it. He caused a young knight living in the town to fall hotly in love with her, with such lustful passion that he really believed he must perish unless he could have his way with her sooner or later. But when he wooed her it got him nowhere; she was not to be tempted. In his fury he schemed to make her die a death of shame. Waiting until the Constable was away, one night he crept secretly into Hermengyld's chamber while she was asleep.

Both Constance and Hermengyld were sleeping, weary and tired out with prayer and vigil. Tempted by Satan, the knight stole up to the bed and cut Hermengyld's throat in two. He laid the bloody knife beside Lady Constance and made off—may God curse him!

Soon afterwards the Constable returned home with Alla, the king of that country, and found his wife cruelly murdered. At this he wept and wrung his hands; and there in the bed beside Lady Constance he discovered the bloodstained knife. Alas, what could she say, driven out of her wits with grief?

King Alla was informed of this catastrophe; and also the time and place and all the circumstances in which Lady Constance had been found in the ship, of which you have already heard. The king's heart was shaken with pity at the sight of so good and gentle a creature in such distress and tribulation. Like a lamb led to the slaughter this innocent stood before the king, while the dishonest knight who had committed the crime falsely maintained she had done it. Nevertheless there was a great outcry from the people, who declared they could not imagine her capable of so monstrous an act; for they had seen how consistently good she was and how dearly she loved Hermengyld. To this everyone in the house bore witness save the man who had slain Hermengyld with his knife. Yet this witness gave the good king a clue that made him think he should inquire more deeply into the matter to discover the truth.

Now Constance has no champion, neither can she defend her-

self: but He who perished for our redemption and bound Satan
—who yet lies where he fell—shall this day be her stout champion.
Unless Christ performs an open miracle, though innocent she
must immediately be slain. She went down upon her knees and
prayed: 'Immortal God, who saved Susanna from false accusa-
tion, and thou, O merciful Virgin, Mary daughter of Saint Anne,
before whose Child the angels sing Hosanna, be my succour if
I am guiltless of this crime; else I must die.'

Who has not seen at some time a pale face among a crowd, the
face of one led to his death after being refused pardon? Such
is its colour, you can single out that face beset with peril from all
the faces in the mob. So Constance looked as she gazed about her.

All you queens, duchesses, and ladies that dwell in prosperity,
take pity upon her adversity! An emperor's daughter stands alone
with none to whom she may turn for sympathy. It is royal blood
that stands in jeopardy, its friends far away in its hour of need.

But King Alla, since noble hearts are always compassionate,
took such pity on her that the tears rained down from his eyes.

'Quickly fetch a book,' said he, 'and if this knight will swear
that she slew this woman, we will consider our sentence.'

A British book inscribed with the Gospels was brought. He
immediately swore upon this book that she was guilty: and sud-
denly, in full view of everyone there, a hand smote him upon
the neckbone; down he fell like a stone, both his eyes bursting
out of his face. All heard a voice speak: 'You have slandered
an innocent daughter of Holy Church in the presence of the
king. You have done this, and shall I hold my peace?' At this
wonder the crowd was terrified, and all except Constance stood
as if stunned, fearing vengeance.

Those who wrongly suspected the saintly, innocent Constance
were penitent and afraid. Because of the miracle, and Constance's
mediation, in the end the king and many others there present
were converted, thanks be to Christ's grace.

Alla sentenced the dishonest knight to be slain immediately
for his perjury; yet Constance greatly pitied his death. Then,
in His mercy, Jesus caused Alla to wed this beautiful and saintly
maiden with solemn ceremonial. Thus Christ made Constance
a queen.

But who, to tell the truth, was grieved at this marriage? None
other than Donegild, the king's tyrannic old mother. She was

so opposed to her son's act she felt her accursed heart must break in two. That he should take such a foreign creature for his mate seemed to her a dishonour.

I don't wish to spend more time on the chaff and straw of my story than on the grain: why should I tell of the marriage pomp, the order of the courses, who blew the horn, and who the trumpet? It all boils down to this: they ate, drank, danced, sang, and enjoyed themselves. They went to bed, as was right and proper. Wives may be saintly creatures but at night they must patiently put up with those necessary acts which give pleasure to the people who marry them with rings, and for the time being lay aside their saintliness a little; these things can't be helped.

In time he begot upon her a male child. But when he had to go to hunt down his foes in Scotland, he entrusted his wife to the care of his Constable and a bishop. The mild and gentle Constance, being far gone with child, kept quietly to her room and awaited the will of Christ. In due course she bore a boy whom they baptized Mauricius. The Constable summoned a messenger and wrote to King Alla to give him this good news with other urgent tidings. The messenger took the letter and set off. But, in the hope of advancing his own interests, he rode swiftly to the king's mother. Courteously saluting her in his own tongue he said, 'Madam, you may rejoice and be glad, and give thanks to God a hundred thousand times over. My lady the queen has borne a child, to the undoubted delight and joy of the whole country round. See, these are sealed letters with the news, which I must carry with all haste. I am your servant at all times if you wish to say anything to the king your son.' 'Not just now,' replied Donegild; 'but I would like you to rest here for the night. Tomorrow I will tell you what I wish.' The messenger drank deeply of ale and wine. While he was sleeping like a pig his letters were secretly stolen from his box and another missive concerning the matter, ingeniously forged, addressed to the king as from his Constable, was wickedly contrived. This letter said that the queen had been delivered of a fiendlike creature so horrible that nobody in the castle dared remain there any longer; that the mother was some witch sent by fate or spells or sorcery; that everyone hated her presence.

When he read this letter, the king was grief-stricken. Yet he told no one of his heavy sorrow. Instead he wrote a reply in his own hand, 'Let whatever Christ sends be always welcome to me now that I have been taught His doctrine. Lord, let Thy will and pleasure be welcome. I place my desires wholly at Thy disposal. Keep the child—whether it be a monster or no—and my wife also, until my homecoming. When He wills, Christ may send me an heir more to my liking than this one.' Hiding his tears, he sealed the letter which was immediately handed to the messenger, who set off without further ado.

That messenger! Sodden with drink, with stinking breath, limbs staggering, wits astray, face distorted, and chattering like a jay, he was ready to betray any confidence. In any company where drunkenness is the rule you may be sure no secret can be kept hidden. As for Donegild, I have no English to do justice to her malice and cruelty, and so I resign her to the Devil; let him celebrate her treachery. That unwomanly—by God, I lie, that fiendlike spirit! For I swear that though she walked upon earth her soul was in hell.

Returning again from the king, the messenger arrived at the court of Donegild, who made much of him and entertained him in every way she could. He drank, stuffed his girdle well with wine, then slept as usual, snoring away the night till sunrise. Again all his letters were stolen and forged ones substituted which ran: 'The king commands his Constable, upon pain of judgement and death, not to suffer Constance on any account to remain in his kingdom for more than three days and a quarter of a tide. He is to put her and her young son and all her gear in the same vessel that he found her in, and thrust her from the land, charging her never to return.' Well might the soul of Constance be afraid and her sleep filled with nightmares while Donegild contrived this order!

When the messenger awoke next morning he took the shortest way to the castle and delivered the letter to the Constable, who exclaimed over and over again with dismay as he read the grievous missive. 'Lord Christ,' said he, 'how may the world survive when there is so much wickedness in its creatures? Almighty God, if it is Thy will, how is it—since Thou art a righteous Judge—that Thou wilt suffer the innocent to perish

and the wicked to reign in prosperity? How unhappy I am, good
Constance, that I must either be your executioner or die a shame-
ful death: there's no alternative.'

Everybody in the place, young and old, wept at the damnable
letter sent by the king. On the fourth day, her face deadly and
pale, Constance went towards the ship. Nevertheless she meekly
accepted the will of Christ. Kneeling upon the shore she said,
'Lord, let me always welcome what Thou sendest! He who saved
me from false accusation while I was among you on the land
can keep me from harm and also from shame upon the salt sea,
even if I do not see how; but He is as mighty to save as He
has ever been. In Him I trust, and in His dear Mother, my sail
and rudder both.'

Her little child lay weeping in her arms. Still kneeling, she said
to him tenderly, 'Hush, little son, I shall do you no harm,' and
then, drawing the kerchief from her head, she laid it over his
little eyes and lulled him in her arms. She cast up her eyes towards
heaven and said, 'Mary, bright Maid and Mother, it is true that
through a woman's incitement mankind was lost and condemned
to eternal death, for which your child was racked upon a cross.
Your blessed eyes saw all His agony; and so there can be no
comparison between your grief and any that man sustains. You
saw your child slain before your eyes, yet my little child lives
still. Bright Lady, to whom the sorrowful make their cry, glory
of womanhood, fair virgin, haven of refuge, bright star of day,
who in your gentleness take pity on the pitiable in their distress,
take pity on my child!

'O little child, who never yet sinned, what is your guilt? Why
does your hard father want you killed? Have mercy, Constable,'
she said, 'only let my baby stay here with you; or if you dare not
save him for fear of blame, kiss him just once for his father's
sake.'

Then she looked backward to the land and said, 'Pitiless hus-
band, farewell!' She rose and walked along the strand towards
the ship, hushing her baby all the while, with the whole crowd
following her. Then she took her leave. Devoutly she crossed
herself and went aboard the ship. Have no fear but that it was
abundantly provisioned to last her a long time; and praise be

to God, she had enough of whatever other necessaries she might require. May Almighty God temper the wind and weather and bring her home! Over the sea she drove: I can say no more.

iii

Soon after this King Alla came home to his castle and asked where his wife and child might be. The Constable's heart grew cold, but he told him plainly all the circumstances you have already heard, and which I've related as best I can. He showed the king his seal and letter, saying, 'Sir, I have done exactly as you commanded me upon pain of death.' The messenger was tortured until he had named the places where he had slept each night, and confessed everything from beginning to end. Thus, by skilful questioning and inference, they guessed the source of the mischief. I'm not sure how it was done, but the hand that wrote the letter was discovered, and all the venom of this accursed deed. In the upshot, as you may read elsewhere, Alla slew his mother for her treachery. Thus Donegild came to a bad end, and good riddance.

No tongue can tell the sorrow that consumed Alla night and day for his wife and child. But now I'll turn to Constance who (so Christ willed) drifted upon the sea in privation and distress for five years and more before her ship drew near to land. In the end the sea cast up Constance and her child near a heathen castle whose name I cannot find in my authorities. May Almighty God who saved mankind remember Constance and her child, once more fallen into the hands of the heathen and once more —as you will soon hear—at the point of death! Many came down from the castle to gape upon Constance and the ship. In short, one night the steward of the castle (a felon and a renegade, God's curse on him) came alone to the ship and told her he was going to be her lover whether she would or no.

The wretched woman was now in the greatest distress. Her child began crying; she herself burst into piteous tears—but the blessed Mary came swiftly to her aid, for in their fierce struggle he suddenly pitched overboard, where retribution overtook him and he drowned in the sea. Thus Christ kept Constance without spot.

See the effect of the loathsome vice of lechery, which not only debilitates the mind but actually destroys the body. Misery is its outcome, and that of its blind desires. How many one sees either killed or destroyed, not by the act but the intention to commit this sin!

How could this feeble woman find the strength to defend herself from that renegade? There was Goliath with his immeasurable height: how could David pull him down? So young and scantly armed, how dared he look upon that fearsome countenance? Only through the grace of God, it is evident. Who gave Judith courage and hardihood to slay Holofernes in his tent and thus deliver God's chosen people from their misery? My point is that just as God gave them strength and saved them from disaster, so did He give Constance strength and vigour.

Her ship passed through the narrow strait between Gibraltar and Ceuta, always driving on, sometimes west, sometimes north, south, or east, for many a weary day, until Christ's Mother (may she be blessed eternally!) in her neverfailing goodness contrived to bring the sorrows of Constance to an end.

Now let us leave Constance for a while, and speak of the Roman Emperor. He had been informed by letters from Syria of the massacre of the Christians and the dishonour done to his daughter by that snake in the grass—in other words that damnable wicked Sultaness who had had them slain one and all at the banquet. For this the Emperor despatched his Senator with a great number of other lords, splendidly equipped, to take full vengeance on the Syrians. For many a day they burned and slew and wrought havoc. But in the end they set their course homewards; and according to the story were sailing in princely style on their victorious return to Rome when they met the ship driving along with the forlorn Constance on board. The Senator had no idea who she was or how she came to be in such a state; nor would Constance for the life of her say anything about her rank and condition. He brought her to Rome and handed her and her young son over to his wife; and so she lived with the Senator. Thus did our Lady deliver Constance (like many others) out of trouble. There she was destined to live for a long time, occupied always with good works. And though the Senator's wife was her aunt, for all that she was no better able to recognize Constance. I will not linger over this but leave Constance in the care of the Senator while I return to King Alla, who was still sorrowing for his wife.

To cut a long story short, one day King Alla felt such great remorse for killing his mother that he came to Rome to submit himself to whatever penance the Pope might impose and beseech Christ's forgiveness for the evil he had done. The couriers that went ahead of him brought the news (which soon spread throughout the town of Rome) that King Alla was coming upon a pilgrimage. Upon this the Senator, as was the custom, rode to meet him with many of his family, as much to impress him with his great magnificance as to show respect to a king. The noble Senator and King Alla exchanged courtesies and entertained one another with great hospitality. A day or two later it so happened that the Senator went to a banquet given by the king. If I am not mistaken, Constance's son was among his party. Some say the Senator brought the child along to the banquet at Constance's request. All these details are beyond my scope: but be that as it may, at any rate he was there. For the truth is that by his mother's wish the child stood in the presence of Alla and looked upon the face of the king while they dined. Seeing the child, the king was struck with wonder, and later remarked to the Senator: 'Whose is that handsome child standing over there?' 'By God and St John, I've no idea,' replied the Senator. 'He has a mother, but no father that I know of.' But after a moment or two he told Alla how the child had been found. 'And God knows,' added the Senator, 'of all earthly women, married or virgin, I never saw or heard of one more virtuous than she in all my life. For I dare venture she would sooner have a knife through her breast than be a sinful woman; there is no man who could tempt her to that pass.'

Now this child was as like Constance as it is possible for a creature to be. The face of Constance was fixed in Alla's memory; he began to wonder if by any chance the child's mother might be his wife. With a secret sigh he left the table as quickly as he could. 'By heaven,' he thought, 'I am imagining things; by all reasonable standards I should believe my wife is at the bottom of the sea.' But a moment later he argued, 'How do I know but that Christ may have brought my wife hither across the sea, just as He brought her to my own land from whence she came?' And in the afternoon Alla went home with the Senator to see if this miraculous chance might be so. The Senator paid him

every honour and sent in haste for Constance. When she under-
stood why she had been sent for, you may easily believe that she
was in no mood to dance—indeed she could scarcely stand upon
her feet.

When Alla saw his wife he greeted her courteously, and then
broke down. For with his first glance he knew it was really she.
And for her part, sorrow rooted her to the spot as dumb as a
tree, her heart shut up in her pain as she remembered his unkind-
ness. Twice she fainted before his eyes while he wept and tried
to explain in broken tones: 'May God and all his glorious saints
have mercy on my soul,' said he, 'for I am as guiltless of all the
harm done to you as Maurice, my son, whose face is the image
of yours—else let the fiend seize me where I stand!'

Their tears and anguish did not soon subside and it was long
before their sad hearts found relief. It was heartbreaking to hear
them weep, and weeping increased their sorrow. But I must
ask you to release me from my task, for I haven't got all day
to depict their grief, and I am getting tired of describing these
melancholy scenes. But when in the end the truth was known,
that Alla was guiltless of her sufferings, I suppose they kissed a
hundred times over: and between them was a happiness such as
no creature has ever seen since the world began, save only that
joy which is eternal. Then she humbly begged her husband as
a repayment for her long and grievous sufferings to make a
special invitation to her father, asking him to vouchsafe to do
him the honour to come to dine. And she begged him not on any
account to say a word to her father about her.

Some would claim that the child Maurice delivered this mes-
sage to the Emperor. But I imagine Alla was not so foolish as
to send a child to one of such sovereign honour as he, the glory
of Christendom. It seems better to suppose that he went himself.
The Emperor courteously consented to come to dine as he was
asked. And I have read that he looked intently upon the child
and thought of his daughter. Then Alla returned to his lodging,
and as was proper made all arrangements he could think of in
preparation for the banquet.

When the day came Alla and his wife made themselves ready
and rode joyfully forth to meet the Emperor. Then Constance
saw her father in the street. She alighted, throwing herself at his

feet and exclaiming, 'Father, have you clean forgot your young child? I am your daughter Constance, whom you sent to Syria long ago. Father, it is I, who was thrust alone upon the salt sea and doomed to perish. Now, dear father, I cry you mercy: do not again send me to the heathen, but thank my husband here for his kindness.'

Who could describe the affecting joy between the three of them at this meeting? But I must make an end of my tale; the day is quickly passing and I'll delay no longer. These happy people set themselves down to the banquet, where I shall leave them in joy and delight, a thousandfold happier than I can tell.

Their child Maurice was afterwards made Emperor by the Pope. He led a Christian life and brought great glory to the Church. But I'll let his story go by default, as my tale deals only with Constance. You can find Maurice's life in the old Roman histories; for myself, I've forgotten it.

King Alla chose his time and returned to England by the quickest way, taking with him his sweet and saintly wife Constance; and there they lived in happiness and peace. But, I promise you, earthly happiness lasts only a short while: time will not stay but changes like the tide, turning from day to night.

Who ever lived for a single day in complete happiness, unmoved by either conscience, anger, desire, envy, pride, passion, injury or fear of some sort? I only say this to point out that Alla's bliss with Constance lasted only a little while in joy and content; for Death who takes toll of high and low snatched King Alla out of this world after about a year had passed. Constance mourned him deeply—may God bless his soul! To wind up the story, she made her way to Rome, where this saintly creature found her friends sound and well. Her adventures were over. And when she encountered her father, she fell upon her knees on the ground weeping tender tears, yet with happiness in her heart, giving praise to God a hundred thousand times. They lived in virtue, dispensing holy alms, and never again parted. Thus they lived until death divided them. Now farewell; my tale is ended. May Jesus Christ who has the power to send joy after grief keep us in His grace, and guard all who are here!

Then our Host stood up in his stirrup and exclaimed, 'Listen, all of you! That was a tale worth hearing at any rate. God's bones, Master Parish Priest,' said he, 'tell us a story as you promised earlier! I can see you educated folk know a heap of good things.'

'Bless us,' replied the Parson, 'what makes the man swear so sinfully?' 'Johnny, are ye there?' returned the Host. 'Listen to me, fellows: I smell a Lollard in the wind. Just you wait: by God's holy passion, we'll have a sermon next. This Lollard here means to preach a bit.'

'No, by my father's soul, that he shall not,' said the Sea-Captain. 'He shan't preach here; I'll have none of his gospel-thumping and commentaries. All of us believe in God Almighty,' continued the Sea-Captain, 'but he'd only sow debate and scatter weeds among our good corn. And so I give you warning, Host, my jolly self shall tell a tale that will ring the bell and wake you all up. But it won't be about philosophy or phisoboly or lawyer's mumbo-jumbo—there isn't much Latin in my gob.'

THE
SEA-CAPTAIN'S
TALE

t St Denis
there once lived a merchant, who was rich and therefore ac-
counted shrewd. His wife was a great beauty, but sociable and
fond of parties—a thing which causes more expense than all the
regard and attention men pay them at feasts and dances is worth.
Those polite expressions and salutations pass like a shadow on a
wall—but I pity him who has to pay for it! It's always the poor
husband who has to fork out; for his own credit's sake he must
adorn us women* in the dresses and finery we dance so gaily in
—and if it turns out that he can't or won't put up with the expense
but thinks it an extravagant waste, why then, somebody else must
foot the bill, or lend us money—and there lies the danger.

This excellent merchant kept a splendid establishment. You'd
wonder at the numbers who resorted there all day because of his
hospitality and the beauty of his wife—but let me get on with my
story. Among his other guests—they came from all ranks—was a
monk, a bold handsome fellow about thirty years of age by my
guess, who was always visiting the house. This handsome young
monk had become so familiar with the good man since they were
first acquainted that he was as intimate in the house as a friend
can possibly be.

Seeing that both the merchant and the monk had been born in
the same village, the monk claimed kinship; which in his turn the
merchant never once denied, for it gave his heart pleasure and
made him as happy as a bird in the spring. Thus they were linked
by an eternal friendship, and swore to one another to be brothers
as long as they lived.

This monk, Brother John, was a free spender when he stayed in
the house. He took great care to be generous and make himself
pleasant, never forgetting to tip even the meanest page in the
place. Whenever he came he gave his host and each of the servants
some suitable gift according to their standing. So they were as

* Chaucer's slip: probably this Tale was originally intended for the
Wife of Bath.

glad of his coming as birds are of dawn. But enough of that for the present.

Now it happened one day that the merchant made arrangements to go to the town of Bruges to buy a quantity of merchandise; whereupon he sent a messenger to Brother John in Paris asking him to come and spend a few days' holiday with him and his wife at St Denis before he left for Bruges as he had fixed.

This excellent monk I speak of was in a position of trust and authority, and thus had permission from his Abbot to ride off to inspect their distant barns and granges whenever he wished. He soon arrived at St Denis. Who was more welcome than milord Brother John, our most dear and urbane cousin? As usual he brought with him a cask of malmsey, and another of sweet Italian wine, besides a present of game. And now I'll leave the merchant and the monk to eat, drink and enjoy themselves for a day or two.

But on the third day the merchant arose and began to give serious attention to his affairs. Up he went into his counting-house, most likely to reckon how things stood with him for that year, and to calculate his expenditure and work out whether or no he'd made a profit. So he spread out his books and money-bags upon the counting-board in front of him, and (since his treasure was great) shut fast the counting-house door, having given orders that in the meantime no one was to disturb him at his accounts. Thus he remained till it was past nine in the morning.

Brother John had also risen with the dawn and was walking to and fro in the garden devoutly reciting his office. As he paced sedately up and down the good wife stole quietly into the garden and greeted him as she had often done before. With her she had a little girl who was under her authority and still subject to the rod.

'Dear cousin, Brother John,' said she, 'why are you up so early? Is anything the matter?'

'Niece,' he replied, 'five hours' sleep a night should be enough, except for some worn-out old fellow like one of these married men who lie cowering like a hare in its form after being hunted half to death by the hounds. But why so pale, dear niece? I'm pretty sure our good friend has been at work upon you since nightfall. Hadn't you better go and have a good rest?' With that he gave a merry laugh, and reddened at his own thought.

But the pretty wife shook her head. 'Yes, God knows every-thing,' said she. 'No, cousin, it isn't like that at all, for by the God who gave me my body and soul, there's not a woman in the entire kingdom of France has less pleasure from that sorry sport. Oh, I can sing

Alas and woe is me
That ever I should be

but I daren't tell a soul how things stand with me. Indeed I'm so frightened and worried that I'm thinking of leaving the country or making an end of myself.'

The monk stared at her. 'Alas, niece,' said he, 'God forbid that any fear or grief should make you do away with yourself. But tell me what the trouble is—perhaps I can advise or help you in your difficulty. So tell me all your worries; and it won't go any further. See, I swear upon this prayer-book that nothing will ever make me betray your confidence as long as I live, for good or ill.'

'I say the same to you,' she said. 'I swear by God and by this prayer-book that though I were to be torn to pieces I'll never breathe a word of anything you tell me, even if I have to go to hell for it—and not because we are cousins, but only because of my love and trust.'

Having sworn this they kissed and began to speak their minds freely to each other.

'Cousin,' she said, 'if I had the time, which I haven't, especially in this place, I'd tell you a story of a life of martyrdom—every-thing I've suffered from my husband since I became a wife, even though he's your cousin—'

'No!' cried the monk. 'By God and St Martin, he's no more my cousin than this leaf hanging on the tree! By St Denis of France, I only call him that to have more excuse to see you, for I most certainly love you above all other women—I swear it on my monkhood! Tell me what your trouble is; be quick in case he comes down—then you can go.'

'My dear love,' she began, 'O my dearest Brother John, I'd much rather keep all this to myself, but it must out; I can't stand any more. As far as I'm concerned, my husband is the worst man that ever lived since the beginning of the world. As a wife it ill befits me to tell a soul of our private affairs, in bed or elsewhere:

God forbid I should say anything of them! I know a wife ought
never to say anything in the least discreditable about her husband,
but to you alone I'll say this much: so help me God, he's not
worth the price of a fly one way or another. But what upsets me
most is his stinginess. You know perfectly well that women—I for
one—naturally desire six things: they want their husbands to be
brave, intelligent, rich, and generous too; considerate to their
wives and lively in bed. And now, by the Lord that shed His
blood for us, by next Sunday I've got to pay—only for dresses I
must wear if I'm to do him credit—a hundred francs or be ruined.
I'd rather I'd never been born than endure a scandal and disgrace
—besides if my husband ever finds out, I'm as good as finished—so
I must beg you to lend me the amount, else I must die. Brother
John, I pray you lend me these hundred francs and if you'll only
do what I ask I swear I'll not disappoint you with my thanks! I'll
pay you back on the day, and if there's anything you want, any
pleasure, any service I can do you—if I don't may God punish me
worse than the traitor Ganelon of France.'*

The good monk replied as follows. 'My dearest, I feel truly sorry
for you; and I give you my word of honour that when your hus-
band has gone to Flanders I'll help you out of this little trouble.
I'll bring you a hundred francs.' Then catching her round the
flanks he squeezed her tight and kissed her again and again.

'Be off now,' said he, 'as quietly as you can; and let's dine as
soon as you can manage it—for by my pocket dial it is nine in the
morning. Go now, and be as true to me as I to you.'

'God forbid I should be anything else,' said she, setting off as
gay as a lark to tell the cooks to hurry so that they might dine
without delay. Then up she went to her husband and boldly
knocked upon the counting-house door.

'Who's there?' said he. 'By St Peter, it's me,' she answered.
'When are you going to eat? How long will you be at your sums
and calculations and ledgers and stuff? The devil take accounts!
Hasn't God given you enough, for heaven's sake? Come on down
and let your moneybags alone. Aren't you ashamed to leave
Brother John miserably fasting all morning? Let's hear Mass, then
go and dine.'

* Ganelon was the traitor who betrayed Charlemagne's army at Ronces-
valles, for which he was torn apart by wild horses.

'Dear wife,' said the merchant, 'how little you understand the intricacies of business. By God and St Ive, scarcely two out of a dozen merchants ever make a steady profit in the whole of their working lives. We've got to put a good face on things, keep up appearances, live our life as best we can and keep our business affairs secret till we're dead; there's nothing else for it, except taking a holiday and going on pilgrimage to stay out of the way of creditors. And therefore it's most necessary I should keep an eye on this queer world, for in business we're always at the mercy of chance and circumstance.

'I'm going to Flanders at daybreak tomorrow, but I'll be home as soon as I can. And so, dear wife, please be polite and obliging to everyone. Take great care of our goods and see the house is properly run, for you've everything a good household can possibly want. You've no lack of clothes and stores, and there's plenty of money in your purse.' And saying this he shut the counting-house door and came downstairs without more delay. Mass was quickly said, the tables promptly laid, and they hurried in to dinner, where the merchant gave the monk a splendid meal.

Soon after dinner Brother John put on a serious air and took the merchant aside for a word in private. 'Cousin, I see you are off to Bruges. Godspeed, and may St Augustine be your guide! Take care of yourself when riding, cousin; and be temperate in your diet, especially in this heat. There's no need for ceremony between us, so goodbye, cousin, and God keep you from harm! And if there should ever be anything whatever you'd like to ask of me that lies in my power to perform, it shall be done exactly as you wish.

'Before you go, there's one thing I'd like to entreat of you if I may: could you lend me a hundred francs for a week or two? It's for some cattle I have to buy to stock one of our farms—Lord save us, I wish it were yours! Be sure I shan't fail to repay it on the day—even if it were a thousand francs I wouldn't keep you waiting a quarter of an hour. Only I must beg of you to keep it secret, for I have still to buy the cattle tonight. And now farewell, my dearest cousin: a thousand thanks for your hospitality and kindness.'

The good merchant gently answered, 'Brother John, my dear cousin, this is really a very small thing to ask. My money's yours whenever you want it, and not only my money but my goods. Take what you please: God forbid you should be sparing!

'But I don't have to tell you there's one thing about us merchants—money is our plough. We can get credit as long as our name is good—but it's no joke being out of cash. Pay me back when it's convenient; I'm happy to oblige you so far as I'm able.'

Then he fetched these hundred francs and quietly handed them over to Brother John. Apart from Brother John and the merchant, no one at all knew of the loan. Then for a while they drank, talked, and strolled about at their ease till Brother John rode back to his abbey.

Next morning the merchant set out to ride to Flanders. His apprentice proved a good guide and they arrived in Bruges in fine fettle. Then the merchant went busily about his affairs, buying and borrowing. But he neither diced nor danced; in short, he behaved like a merchant, and so I leave him.

The Sunday following the merchant's departure Brother John arrived at St Denis with a new tonsure and freshly-shaven beard. The entire household down to the smallest serving-lad was delighted that 'milord Brother John' had returned. But to the point: the pretty wife made a bargain with Brother John; in short, she agreed to lie all night in his arms in return for the hundred francs. This agreement was duly acted upon; they spent a merry night busily employed till daybreak, when Brother John again set off after bidding farewell to the staff. None of them had the slightest suspicion of the monk, nor had anyone in the town. He rode off home to his abbey or somewhere; I'll say no more about him for the present.

When the fair was over, the merchant returned to St Denis, where he feasted and made merry with his wife. But he told her he had paid so high a price for his merchandise he would have to negotiate a loan, since he was bound by a recognizance to pay twenty thousand crowns within a very short time. So, taking some of the money with him, he set out for Paris to borrow the remainder from amongst his friends. When he arrived in the town, first of all he paid a friendly visit to Brother John because of his great fondness and affection for him—not to ask or borrow money, but to see how he was and discuss his business deals, as friends do when they are met. Brother John made much of him and gave him a hearty welcome. On his part the merchant told him in detail of the good bargains that—God be thanked—he had made buying merchandise; the snag being that he had somehow to raise a loan before he could relax in comfort.

Brother John replied, 'I'm truly delighted that you've come home safe and sound. Lord save us, if only I were rich you wouldn't be short of twenty thousand crowns, for you so kindly lent me money the other day. I don't know how to thank you enough, by God and St James! However, I returned the money to your good lady and put it on your table at home; she's sure to know about it by certain tokens I can tell her of—and now, if you'll excuse me, I can't stay longer, for our abbot is on the point of leaving town and I must join his party. Give my regards to your good lady, my own sweet niece! And farewell, cousin, till we meet again!'

The merchant, a shrewd and sensible man, borrowed on credit and then paid the money into the hands of certain Lombard bankers in Paris who gave him back his bond. Then off he went home, merry as a grig, for he knew that over and above his outlay he stood to make a thousand francs on the trip.

His wife stood ready at the gate to meet him as she always used to do, and they spent the night rejoicing: for he was rich and clear of debt. Then in the morning the merchant embraced his wife all over again, kissing her face—and up he went, stiff and strong. 'Stop,' she cried, 'you've had enough, for goodness' sake!' And she turned wantonly to him till at last the merchant said, 'Really, I'm a little annoyed with you, my dear, much as it grieves me— and do you know why? Upon my word, so far as I can make out you've caused a certain coolness between me and my cousin. You should have warned me before I left that he's paid you a hundred francs by ready tokens—he thought it poor thanks when I talked to him about borrowing money, or so it seemed by the look on his face. But, Heaven be my witness, I never thought to ask him for anything. Please don't do it again, my dear; always tell me before I go away if any debtor has repaid you in my absence, lest through your carelessness I ask him for something he has already paid back.'

His wife, neither frightened nor dismayed, boldly retorted, 'A fig for that lying monk, Brother John! What do I care for his tokens? He brought me a sum of money—I know that—bad luck to his monk's snout! The Lord knows I was perfectly sure he had given it to me for your sake, to spend on making myself look smart, because he's our cousin and because of all the hospitality he's had here. But I see I'm in an awkward position, so I'll give you a short answer. You've many worse debtors than me! I'll pay you promptly and in full, a little every day, and if I let you down, why, I'm your wife—charge it up! I'll pay as soon as ever I can. On my word of honour I've not wasted it but spent every penny on dress—and because I've laid it out so well and all to look a credit to you, for goodness' sake don't be angry I say, let's laugh and be happy instead. There's my pretty body for your pledge! I'll not pay you back except in bed! So, dearest, forgive me; turn round and see if it doesn't cheer you up!'

The merchant saw there was no help for it; it was senseless to scold when things were past mending. 'I'll let you off, my dear,' said he. 'But don't you dare make so free again! And take better care of my goods: that's an order.'

So my tale ends: and while we live may God give us tail in plenty!

What the Host said to the Sea-Captain and the Lady Prioress

'Corpus dominus, well said!' exclaimed the Host. 'Long may you sail the coast, good master mariner! God send the monk bad luck in cartloads! Oho, boys, watch out for such tricks! That monk made a monkey of the fellow, and his wife too, by St Augustine! Never bring monks into the house!

'But let's get on and see who'll be next in our party to tell another tale.' With that, speaking as politely as any young lady, he said, 'Excuse me, my lady Prioress, if only I were sure it wouldn't put you out, I'd say it was your turn to tell a story if you would. Dear lady, will you condescend?' 'Gladly,' said she, and began as follows.

'O Lord, our Lord, how marvellously is Thy name spread abroad
in the world!' she began. 'For not only is Thy excelling praise
rendered up by men of mark, but the mouths of children utter
Thy bounty and sometimes even those who suck the breast declare
Thy praise. Wherefore I shall endeavour as best I may to tell a
story in honour of Thee and of the white lily flower that bore
Thee while remaining a virgin; not that I can increase her honour,
for she herself is honour and next her Son the help of souls and
source of all goodness. Mother and Maid! Maid and Mother! O
unburned bush that burned in Moses' sight! Help me tell it to
thy glory, O thou whose humility drew down from God the
Spirit that alighted in thee, and by whose power, when He had
lit thy heart, the Word was made Flesh! Lady, no tongue has art
to express thy bounty, thy magnificence, thy power, and thy great
humility. For sometimes, Lady, before we pray to thee in thy
benignity thou anticipatest us, bringing by thy prayers the light
that guides us to thy dear Son. So feeble is my skill, O blessed
Queen, that I cannot sustain the burden of declaring thy great
worth; I am like a child of twelve months or less, hardly able to
express a word; and so I pray thee guide the song I shall sing of
thee.'

THE PRIORESS'S TALE

here was in Asia
a great Christian city in which stood a Ghetto. It was protected
by the ruler of the land because of the filthy lucre gained by the
Jews' usury, abhorred by Christ and those who follow Him; and
people could go freely through it, since the street was unbarri-
caded and open at either end. Down by the farther side stood a
little Christian school where a great flock of children from Chris-
tian families received instruction year by year in the usual kind
of things small children are taught in infancy, such as reading and
singing. Among these children was a widow's son, a little boy of
seven, a chorister, who used to go to school daily; he used also to
kneel down and say an *Ave Maria* as he had been taught, when-
ever he saw the image of Christ's Mother in the street. For the
widow taught her little son always to revere our Blessed Lady
thus, and he did not forget, for an innocent child always learns
quickly. But every time I think of this, St Nicholas comes into
my mind; for he also reverenced Christ at the same tender age.

As this little child sat in school with his primer learning his little
book, he heard *Alma redemptoris* being sung by children practis-
ing their anthem-books. He crept nearer and nearer till he was as
close as he dared, and listened to the words and music until he
knew the first verse by heart. Because of his tender years he had
no idea what the Latin meant, but one day began asking a com-
panion to explain the meaning in his native tongue and tell him
why it was sung. Many times he went down on his bare knees to
beg his friend to translate and explain the song, till at last his elder
companion made him this answer: 'I have heard say that the song
was made to greet our gracious blessed Lady and to beseech her to
be our help and succour when we die. That's all I can tell you
about it—I'm learning singing, but I don't know much grammar.'

'And is this song made in honour of Christ's Mother?' said the
innocent. 'Then I shall try my hardest to learn all of it before
Christmas, even if I am scolded for not knowing my primer and
beaten three times an hour. I shall learn it for the honour of Our

Lady.' And so his friend taught him in secret on their way home each day until he knew it by heart, and could sing it confidently word for word in tune with the music. And twice a day the song passed through his throat, once on the way to school, and once on the way home; for his whole heart was set upon the Mother of Our Lord.

As I have said, this little child was always merrily singing *O Alma Redemptoris* as he came and went through the Ghetto, for the sweetness of Christ's Mother had so pierced his heart he could not stop singing her praise upon his way. But our first enemy—the serpent Satan who has built his wasp's nest in every Jewish heart—swelled up in wrath and cried: 'Alas, O people of the Jews! Does it seem right to you that a boy like this should wander where he likes and show you his contempt by singing songs which insult your faith?' And from then on the Jews conspired together to hunt the innocent child out of this world. For this they hired a murderer, a man who had a secret hide-out in an alley. As the child passed by, this vile Jew seized firm hold of him, cut his throat and threw him in a pit. Yes, they threw him in a cesspit where the Jews purged their bowels. Yet what may your malice profit you, O you damnable race of new Herods? Murder will out, that's certain; and especially where the glory of God shall be increased. The blood cries out upon your fiendish crime.

O martyr espoused to virginity! (cried the Prioress) now mayest thou ever follow, singing, the white celestial Lamb of whom St John the great evangelist wrote in Patmos, saying that those who go before the Lamb singing a new song have never known the bodies of women.

All night the widow watched for her little child, but he never came. As soon as it was daylight she went looking for him in the school and everywhere else, with anxious heart and face pale with dread, till in the end she found out this much: he had last been seen in the Ghetto. Her heart bursting with a mother's pity, half out of her mind, she went everywhere she fancied there was any likehood of finding her little child; all the while calling upon the meek and gentle Mother of Christ. At last she came to seek him among the Jews. Piteously she besought and entreated every Jew that lived in the Ghetto to tell her if her child had passed by; but they said no. Then after a time Jesus in His mercy put it into her head to call her son while she was near the pit into which he had been thrown.

Almighty God, whose praise is made known by the mouths of innocents, lo Thy power is here displayed! As he lay with his throat slit, this gem and emerald of chastity, this bright ruby of martyrdom, began singing *Alma Redemptoris* so loud the whole place rang.

Christians who were passing by in the street crowded in to marvel. They made haste to send for the Provost. He same at once without delay and when he had given praise to Christ the King of Heaven and His Mother the glory of mankind, he ordered the Jews to be bound. With piteous lamentations they lifted up the child, still singing his song, and carried him in solemn procession to an abbey close by. His mother lay fainting beside the bier, a second Rachel; and the people there could scarcely part her from it.

Thereupon the Provost caused each of the Jews who had been concerned in the murder to be tortured and put to a shameful death, for he would not tolerate such abominable wickedness. 'Evil must have its due reward.' So he had them torn apart by wild horses and then hanged according to law.

All the while the innocent child lay upon his bier before the high altar as Mass was sung. Then the Abbot and his monks hastened to give him burial. But when they sprinkled the holy water and it fell on the child, he still sang *O Alma Redemptoris Mater*. Now, the Abbot was a holy man, as monks are or ought to be; so he began to question the child, saying, 'My dear child, I conjure you by the Holy Trinity to tell me how it is that you can sing when seemingly your throat is cut in two?'

'My throat is cut to my neckbone,' answered the child, 'and by all the laws of nature I should have died long ago, were it not that Jesus Christ has willed, as you may read in Holy Writ, that His glory shall be remembered and endure; and so for the honour of His dear Mother I am able still to sing *O Alma* loud and clear. So far as in me lay I have always loved that well of mercy, Christ's sweet Mother; and when I had to render up my life she came to me and bade me sing this anthem even in death, just as you have heard. And when I sang it seemed to me she laid a pearl upon my tongue. Therefore I sing, as I must always sing, in honour of that blessed gracious Maid until the pearl is taken away; for she said to me, "My little child, I will come to fetch you when the pearl is taken from your tongue; don't be afraid, for I shall not forsake you.'

Then this holy man—that is to say the Abbot—pulled out his tongue and removed the pearl, when the child gently gave up the ghost. At this miracle the Abbot's salt tears trickled down like rain and he fell flat upon his face on the ground, and there lay motionless as though chained to the spot; while the monks also prostrated themselves upon the pavement, weeping and giving praise to Christ's dear Mother. Then they arose and took the martyr from his bier. They enclosed his tender little body in a tomb of clear marble. God grant we meet him where he now is!

O young Hugh of Lincoln, slain also by the vile Jews, as is well known (for it happened only a little while ago) pray also for us weak and sinful folk; that in His grace merciful God may multiply His great mercy upon us, for the sake of His Mother Mary.

What the Host said to Chaucer

*When the story of this miracle had been told everyone fell
strangely silent, till at last our Host again began to crack his
jokes. For the first time his eye fell upon me. 'What kind of man
are you?' said he, 'for I see you staring upon the ground all the
time, as if you were looking for a sixpence. Come over here,
look up and smile! Make way, sirs, and give this man room—
he's as well-made around the waist as I! What a poppet for a
pretty girl to cuddle in her arms! His face looks elfish, for he
speaks to nobody. Now tell us something, since the others have;
tell us some cheerful tale and look sharp.'*

*'Host,' I replied, 'don't be put out, but the fact is I don't know
any other tale but a ballad I learned a long time ago.'*

*'That's all right,' said he. 'Now we'll hear something choice,
to judge from his looks.'*

SIR TOPAZ

The First Fit

Listen, sirs, with right good will,
And believe me I shall tell
   Of the merry capers
Of that knight with so much mettle
Whether for tournament or battle
   Whose name was Sir Topaz.

He was born in a far country,
In Flanders far beyond the sea,
   And Poperinghe was the place.
His father was of high degree,
For he was lord of that country,
   Thanks be to Heaven's grace.

A stalwart swain Sir Topaz grew;
White was his face as whitest dough,
   His lips as red as rose;
And like a scarlet dye his hue,
And it's the truth I'm telling you,
   He had a handsome nose.

And saffron was his beard and hair
That to his girdle fell so fair,
   Of Spanish hide his shoes;
His brown hose came from Bruges Fair,
His silken gown beyond compare
   Had cost him many sous.

A huntsman he of savage deer,
And he'd ride hawking by the river
   A goshawk on his wrist;

At that he was a good archer,
At wrestling you'd not find his peer,
  He always won his bets.

Many a maiden in her bower
Had sighed for him with wild desire
  ('Twere better she had slept);
But he was chaste and no lecher
And sweeter than the bramble flower
  That bears a scarlet fruit.

Of a verity I say
It so befell upon a day
  Sir Topaz out would ride;
He clambered on his steed so grey,
And lance in hand he rode away,
  A long sword at his side.

He galloped through a fair forest
Filled with many a savage beast,
  Aye, both buck and hare;
And as he galloped east and west
I shall relate how he almost
  Fell to a grievous snare.

There flourished herbs of every sort,
Like licorice and ginger-root
  And cloves and many more;
And nutmegs which you put in ale
Whether it be dark or pale,
  Or put away in store.

And birds were singing, I must say!
The sparrowhawk and popinjay,
  Till it was joy to hear;
The throstlecock piped up his lay,
And the wood-dove upon the spray
  Piped up both loud and clear.

And when he heard the throstle sing,
The knight was filled with love-longing,
    And spurred away like mad;
His good steed kept on galloping
Wet as a rag, so much 'twas sweating,
    With sides all drenched in blood.

Then Sir Topaz so weary was
From galloping over the tender grass,
    So fiery was his courage,
That he alighted there and then
To give his horse a breather, when
    He also gave it forage.

'O Saint Mary, Heaven bless me!
Why must this love so distress me
    And bind me with its rope?
All last night I dreamed, dear me,
An Elf-Queen should my sweetheart be,
    And sleep beneath my cloak.

I'll only love a Fairy Queen;
No woman I have ever seen
    Is fit to be my mate
        In town;
    All other women I forsake,
I'll follow in the Elf-Queen's track
    Over dale and down!'

Then he climbed into his saddle,
Galloped over stile and puddle,
    A Fairy Queen to find;
He rode so long at gallop and trot
Till at last he found, in a secret spot,
    The country of Fairyland
        So wild;
For in that country there was none
That dared to show his face to him,
    Neither wife nor child;

Until there came a burly giant,
His name it was Sir Elephant,
    A dangerous man indeed.
He said, 'Sir Knight, by Fee Fo Fum!
I live round here, so gallop home
    Or I will slay your steed
                With mace!
For it is here the Fairy Queen
With harp and flute and tambourine
    Has made her dwelling place.'

The knight said, 'Sir, believe you me,
Tomorrow I shall meet with thee,
    When I've my armour on;
And on my word, if I've the chance,
You'll pay for it with this stout lance,
    And sing another song.
                Your gob
Shall be run through from cheek to chine
Before it's fully half-past nine,
    And here I'll do the job.'

Sir Topaz beat a quick retreat;
This giant pelted him thereat
    With stones from a terrible sling;
But he escaped, did Childe Topaz,
And it was all through Heaven's grace
    And his own noble bearing.

Yet listen, masters, to my tale
Merrier than the nightingale,
    And I shall make it known
How Sir Topaz of the slender shanks
Galloping over braes and banks
    Is come again to town.

His merry men commanded he
To make mirth and revelry
    For he had got to fight

A monstrous giant whose heads were three,
All for the love and levity
   Of one that shone so bright.

'Call hither, call hither my minstrels all,'
He said, 'and bid them tell some tale,
   The while I gird my armour on;
Some romance that is really royal
Of Bishop, Pope and Cardinal,
   And also of a lover lorn.'

First they brought him delicate wine,
Mead in bowls of maple and pine,
   All sorts of royal spices,
And gingerbread as fine as fine,
And licorice and sweet cummin,
   And sugar that so nice is.

He put on next his ivory skin
Breeches of the purest linen,
   He also donned a shirt.
And next his shirt he did not fail
To have wadding and a coat of mail
   For to protect his heart.

And over that a fine hauberk
—It was a most expensive work,
   Made of the stoutest steel;
And over that his coat-armour
Whiter than the lily flower,
   In which to take the field.

His shield was of the gold so red
Emblazoned with a great boar's head,
   And a carbuncle beside;
And then he swore by beer and bread,
That giant shortly would be dead,
   Betide what may betide!

His greaves were of tough leather; he
Sheathed his sword in ivory,
    And wore a helm of brass;
A whalebone saddle he sat on,
And like the sun his bridle shone,
    Or like the moon and stars.

His spear was of the best cypress,
'Twas meant for war, and not for peace,
    So sharp its tip was ground;
His charger was a dapple-grey
It went an amble all the way
    And gently paced around
                    The land.
Well, gentlemen, that's the first fit!
If you want any more of it,
    I'll see what comes to hand.

The Second Fit

Now hush your mouth, for charity,
Each gentle knight and fair lady,
    And listen to my tale
Of battle and of chivalry,
Of courtship and of courtesy
    That I'm about to tell.

They talk about those grand old stories
Of Horn and of Sir Ypotis,
    Of Bevis and Sir Guy;
Of Libeaus and Sir Pleyndamour,
But Sir Topaz bears away the flower
    Of royal chivalry!

He bestrode his noble grey
And forth he glided on his way
    Like a spark from flame;
Upon his crest he bore a tower

Wherein was stuck a lily flower,
　God shield him from all shame!

　This knight was so adventurous
He never slept in any house,
　But wrapped him in his hood;
His pillow was his shining helm,
While his charger grazes by him
　On herbs so fresh and good.

　And he drank water from the well
As did the knight Sir Percival
　Whose armour was so fine;
Till on a day—

'No more of this, for Christ's dear sake!' cried our Host, 'you're wearing me out with this sheer drivel, till as God's my witness it makes my ears ache to listen to the rubbish you spout. Devil take such jingles! It's what they call doggerel, I suppose.'

'Why?' said I. 'Why interrupt my tale rather than another's, when it's the best ballad I know?'

'God Almighty!' he returned, 'in short, if you must know, your shithouse rhyming's not worth a turd! You're doing nothing but waste time. In one word, sir, no more rhyming from you! Let's see if you can relate one of those old romances, or at least something in prose that's edifying or amusing.'

'Gladly,' I replied. 'By the Lord, I'll tell you a little thing in prose which ought to please you, I should think, or else you must be pretty hard to satisfy. It's a very edifying tale, with a moral—though I should explain it's sometimes been told differently by different people. For instance, you know that when the Evangelists describe the Passion of Christ they don't all put things in the same way as one another; yet each tells the truth, and all agree in their general meaning, though in the telling there may be differences. Some of them tell more, and some less, when they—that is, Matthew, Mark, Luke and John—describe His piteous Passion; but there's no doubt their meaning is the same. Therefore, gentlemen, I beg you not to blame me if you think I've introduced changes into the story, if for example I put in more proverbs than usual into this little discourse to strengthen the effect, or if I don't tell it in the same words you've heard before—for you won't find any difference between my general drift and that of the little treatise from which I drew this capital tale. So listen to what I'm going to say, and this time please let me finish my story.'

THE TALE OF MELIBEUS

[The 'little thing in prose' which Chaucer related to the Pilgrims after the Host had put a stop to 'Sir Topaz', his burlesque parody of the metrical romances of the day, turned out to be an immensely long example of the didactic allegories that were so popular in the Middle Ages. *The Tale of Melibeus* is a close translation of the French *Livre de Melibée et de Dame Prudence,* which was in turn a paraphrase of the *Liber Consolationis et Consilli* by Albertanus of Brescia. It is not so much a story as a debate on the subject of the horrors of war and a plea for conciliation and agreement among enemies, and it bristles with maxims and quotations from recognized authorities. As the general reader would undoubtedly find *The Tale of Melibeus* wearisome I have omitted it. But W. W. Lawrence has pointed out that it has an important place in the scheme of *The Canterbury Tales,* for from it derives the discussion on marriage—whether the wife or the husband should have the authority—which is the theme round which the tales of the Nun's Priest, the Wife of Bath, the Scholar, and the Merchant and centred, and which is resolved in *The Franklin's Tale.*

Here is a brief summary of the story. A rich young man called Melibeus and his wife Prudence had a daughter called Sophie. While Melibeus was away from home three of his enemies broke into his house and beat up his wife and daughter, leaving the latter for dead. On his return his wife advised him to have patience and consult what he should do with his friends and relatives. Melibeus did so; and some advised vengeance, but others recommended caution. Prudence herself enjoined him not to be overhasty, but Melibeus said he would not be guided by her because of the danger of following female advice, and because if he followed her counsel it would seem he had yielded his authority to her; whereupon Prudence defended the excellence of women's advice, quoting numberless authorities in support, till Melibeus gave in and agreed to do as she counselled. After this she gave him a good deal more advice and finally sent for his enemies and persuaded them to give Melibeus satisfaction if he wished; but in the end Melibeus forgave them completely. D.W.]

When my tale of Melibeus and of Prudence and her magna-nimity was over, our Host exclaimed, 'By holy corpus Madrian, as I'm a Christian I'd give a barrel of ale to have my dear wife hear that story! She's nothing like as patient as this wife of Melibeus! God's bones, when I beat my serving-lads she fetches out great clubbed staves and yells, "Murder every one of the swine! Break every bone in their bodies!" And if some neighbour of mine fails to bow to her in church or has the cheek to offend her, when we come home she flies at my face screaming, "Miser-able coward, avenge your wife! Corpus bones, give me your knife, take my distaff and go spin!" She carries on like that night and day. "Alas!" she says, "it was my fate to marry a milksop, a cowardly ape who lets himself be put upon by everyone! You haven't the guts to stand up for your wife's rights!"

'So it goes on, unless I fight; and then I've got to put on my coat to go outside; my life's not worth living unless I'm reck-less as a raging lion. Some day I'm pretty sure she'll make me murder one of the neighbours, then I'll have to run for it—for even if I daren't stand up to her I'm a dangerous man with a knife. For you can take it from me, she has pretty hefty biceps, as anybody who crosses or contradicts her will soon find out! But let's drop the subject.

'My lord Monk,' said he, 'cheer up, for indeed you must tell a story. Look, we're almost at Rochester! Ride forward, my lord: don't spoil our fun. Yet upon my honour I don't know your name—whether to call you milord Brother John, or Brother Thomas, or perhaps Brother Alban? Tell me straight—what's your monastery? You've a fair and delicate skin, I swear to God! There's good grazing where you come from: you don't look like a penitent, nor no ghost either. My faith, you must be some sort of supervisor—a sacristan or a cellarer perhaps? By my father's soul, I'd say you're someone in authority when you're at home— no poor novice or cloisterer, but some wise shrewd administrator, and a brawny, well-set-up man at that! May God confound

whoever first brought you into Holy Orders! You'd have been a rare cock with the hens. If you'd as much freedom as you've manhood to make love as you'd like, you'd have plenty of offspring. A pity you wear the cope! God damn me, were I Pope, not only you but every stout fellow, tonsured or no, should have a wife. The world's like to perish because religion's got hold of the best stallions, and we laymen are mere shrimps. You get miserable shoots from weak trees. This makes our sons so feeble and scrawny they can scarcely make love; it's why our wives want to try out clerics, because you make a better payment to Venus than we can—and, God knows, in no counterfeit coin! But don't take offence, my lord, at my jokes—I've heard many a true word spoken in jest.'

The good Monk bore it all with patience and replied: 'I'll do my best to tell you a tale or two as far as is consistent with decency. And if you care to listen I'll tell you the life of Edward the Confessor—or first I'll recount a few Tragedies—I've a hundred of them in my monastery.

'As the ancient authorities remind us, Tragedy means a certain kind of story about those who once lived in great prosperity, and fell from their high estate into misfortune and came to a miserable end. They are usually versified in lines of six feet called hexameters. Many have also been composed in prose as well as in a number of varying metres. This definition should suffice.

'Now listen, if you would like to hear a few examples—but first I beg of you to excuse my ignorance if I do not tell these stories, whether they're of popes, emperors, or kings, in chronological order as you find them in books, but put some before and some behind just as they come into my head.'

THE MONK'S TALE

In the Tragic Mode
I shall lament the misfortunes of those who fell from high estate
into irremediable adversity. For it is certain that when Fortune
makes up her mind to flee no man can withhold her from her
course. Let none put his trust in blind prosperity but take warning
from these old and true instances.

LUCIFER

I'll begin with Lucifer, although he was not a man but an angel:
for though Fortune cannot harm angels, yet it was owing to his
sin that he fell from his high station down into Hell where he yet
remains. Lucifer, brightest of the angels, is now Satan and shall
never escape from the misery into which he has fallen.

ADAM

Take Adam, not begotten of unclean human sperm but fashioned
by the very finger of God in the field where Damascus now stands.
He ruled all Paradise but for one tree. No earthly man was ever
better off than Adam till his misbehaviour drove him from his
great prosperity to labour, misery, and Hell.

SAMSON

Take Samson, whose coming was announced by an angel long
before his birth; who was consecrated to Almighty God and stood
in the high honour until he lost his sight. There was never such
another for strength and the courage that goes with it; but he told
his wife his secret, and so slew himself in his misery. Samson, that
great and mighty champion, slew a lion as he walked along the
road going to his wedding, tearing it completely apart with no
weapon but his two hands. But his treacherous wife coaxed and
pleaded till she knew his secret; when the traitress betrayed it to
his enemies and forsook him for a new husband.

In his rage Samson took three hundred foxes, and tied their
tails together and set them on fire, having attached a firebrand

to each tail. And they burned all the crops in the land, including the vines and olives. And he also slew, single-handed, a thousand men with no other weapon than the jawbone of an ass. Having slain them he was so athirst he was like to perish, and so he prayed God to take pity upon his distress and send him drink lest he die. Then from one of the molars of that dry ass's jaw there sprang a well from which he drank his fill. Thus God came to his help, as it says in the Book of Judges.

One night at Gaza, despite the Philistines in the city, he plucked up the town gates by main force and carried them on his back to the top of a hill where all might see. Had the great, all-powerful Samson, so honoured and beloved, not told his secret to women, the world would never have beheld his peer!

By command of the angelic messenger he touched no wine or strong drink, nor allowed razor or shears to come near his head; for all his strength lay in his hair. But he who ruled Israel throughout twenty winters was soon to shed tears in plenty—women were to bring him to ruin! He told his sweetheart Delilah that all his strength was in his hair, whereupon she treacherously sold him to his foes. For one day while he slept in her bosom she had his hair clipped and shorn, and let his enemies discover his secret. When he was in this state they found him, bound him tightly, and put out his eyes. Before his hair was clipped and shaven no bonds might bind him; now he was imprisoned in a cave where they made him grind a hand-mill.

Now may the great Samson, strongest of men, sometime a Judge of Israel living in wealth and splendour, weep with blind eyes, cast from happiness into misery!

This was the end of the wretched captive. One day his enemies prepared a feast and made him perform before them as their butt. This happened in a crowded temple. But at the last he made terror and havoc, shaking two pillars till they fell, when temple and all crashed down; and thus he slew himself together with his foes—that is to say, all the princes as well as three thousand people were slain there by the fall of the great temple of stone. I shall say no more of Samson. But take warning by this old and simple tale: let no man tell his wife anything he truly wishes to keep secret, particularly if it touches safety of life and limb.

HERCULES

His labours sing the laud and high renown of Hercules greatest of conquerors; for in his day he was a paragon of strength. He slew the Nemean lion and took its skin; humbled the pride of the Centaurs; slew the Harpies, those fell and cruel birds; seized the golden apples of the Dragon; drove out Cerberus, the hound of Hell; slew the cruel tyrant Busirus and made his horse devour him, flesh and bone; slew the fiery poisonous Hydra; broke one of the two horns of Achelous; slew Cacus in his stone cave, and that mighty giant, Antaeus; slew the formidable Erymanthian boar; and for a time carried the sky upon his shoulder.

No man ever killed as many monsters as he since the beginning of time. His name ran throughout the wide world for strength and magnanimity; he visited all its kingdoms, and according to Trophee set up a pillar at each end of the world to mark its limits.

This noble hero had a lover called Dejanira, fresh as the month of May. Scholars say that she sent him a fine new shirt—a fatal shirt alas! for it had been so cunningly poisoned that before he had worn it half a day all his flesh began to fall from his bones. Nevertheless there are learned men who exonerate her and blame one Nessus who made the shirt. Be that as it may, I shall not accuse her—still, Hercules wore this shirt upon his naked back until the poison blackened his flesh. And when he saw there was no remedy he disdained to die from poison, but raked hot coals about himself.

Thus perished Hercules, mighty and famous. Now who can trust Fortune for a moment? Those who follow the ways of this turbulent world are frequently laid low before they know where they are. He is wise who knows himself. Be on your guard, for when Fortune wishes to beguile, she bides her time and overthrows her man in the way he least expects.

NEBUCHADNEZZAR

What tongue can properly describe the mighty throne, the precious treasure, the glorious sceptre and royal majesty of King Nebuchadnezzar, who twice conquered the city of Jerusalem and bore off the vessels of the Temple? His regal seat was at Babylon, his glory and delight. He castrated the handsomest children of the royal house of Israel and made them all slaves. Among others Daniel was one; of all these children he was the wisest, for he expounded the king's dreams when there was no Chaldean sage who knew their proper interpretations. This vainglorious king ordered a statue of gold sixty cubits in height and seven in breadth to be made. He commanded old and young to bow down and revere this image; those who refused to obey would be burned in a fiery furnace. But neither Daniel nor his two young companions would consent to this act.

Proud and uplifted, this king of kings imagined that God who sits in majesty might never deprive him of his great position; yet he suddenly lost his sceptre, became like a beast and roamed for some time with wild animals, eating hay like an ox and lodging in the open and in the rain. His hair grew like an eagle's feathers and his nails like the claws of a bird, till after some years God released him and gave him back his reason. Then he thanked God, the tears pouring down his face; and for the rest of his life feared to sin or to trespass further. To the day he was laid upon his bier he knew God to be filled with power and grace.

BELSHAZZAR

His son Belshazzar ruled the kingdom after his father's day, yet would not be warned by his fate, but was proud of heart, lived in pomp and magnificence, and moreover a confirmed idolater. His great position assured him in his pride, yet Fortune cast him down and suddenly divided his kingdom.

One day he held a feast for his nobles. Bidding them make merry, he called to his officers, 'Go and fetch all those vessels which my father carried off from the temple in Jerusalem in the days of his triumph, and let us give thanks to the gods above for the honour our ancestors left us.' His wife, his nobles, and his concubines drank their fill of various wines from these holy vessels. And the king glanced upon the wall and saw a hand without an arm write swiftly upon it. At this he shook with terror and gave a great sigh, while the hand that so affrighted him wrote 'Mene, Tekel, Pares' and no more. No magician in the whole land could interpret the meaning of the writing, but Daniel soon expounded it, saying, 'O King, God sent your father glory, honour, kingdom, treasure, revenue; but he was proud and had no fear of God at all, therefore God exacted a great vengeance and took from him his kingdom. He was cast from the company of men to dwell among asses and eat grass like an animal in the sun and rain until he understood through grace and reason that the God of heaven has dominion over all creatures and kingdoms. Then God took compassion upon him and restored him his kingdom and his former shape. Now you, his son, know all this to be true, yet are proud like him; you rebel against God and are His enemy; moreover, you have had the audacity to drink from His vessels, and from the same vessels your wife and also your harlots have sinfully drunk various wines; and you wickedly worship false gods. Therefore great sufferings are in store for you. Believe me, the hand that wrote "Mene, Tekel, Pares" on the wall was sent from God: your rule is over, you have been weighed and found wanting; your kingdom is divided and shall be given to the Medes and the Persians.' That same night the king was slain and his throne occupied by Darius, though he had no lawful claim to it.

Sirs, the moral of this is, there is no security in power. When Fortune means to forsake a man she will take away his kingdom, his wealth, and his friends both high and low. Those friends a man makes through good fortune will turn to enemies in bad, I imagine—a proverb that is both true and generally applicable.

ZENOBIA

Of the fame of Zenobia Queen of Palmyra, the Persians write that she was so bold and accomplished in arms no man surpassed her in hardihood or in lineage and other noble attributes. She was descended from the blood of Persian kings. I won't say she was the most beautiful of women, but her figure was without flaw. I find that from childhood she avoided all women's work and would go off to the woods, where with her broad hunting-arrows she shed the blood of many a wild deer. She was so fleet she could even catch them; and when she grew older she would kill lions, leopards, and bears by tearing them apart, and do what she liked with them with her bare hands. She would boldly seek out the lairs of wild beasts and roam all night in the mountains, sleeping in the open. And she could wrestle with any youth, no matter how nimble, and subdue him by main force—in her arms nothing could resist. She kept her maidenhood inviolate, scorning to be tied to any man.

Yet in the end her friends married her, despite her long delays and procrastinations, to Odenathus, a prince of Palmyra. You must understand he shared her tastes and ideas. Nevertheless, once they were joined together they lived in joy and felicity, for each loved the other dearly, one thing excepted: on no account would she ever permit him to lie with her more than once at a time, for her sole object was to bear a child that the world might increase and multiply. If, after the act, she saw that she was not with child, then she would suffer him to have his will once again, and only once; and if this time she found herself pregnant, that sport was denied him till forty clear weeks were past, when she would again allow him to repeat the act. Odenathus might rage or plead, but he got no more out of her. For she would say it was shame and lechery on a wife's part if her husband made love for any other reason.

By Odenathus she had two sons whom she brought up in virtue and learning. But to return to our story: I say that nowhere in the world was there to be found a living creature more wise and honourable, generous yet not extravagant, more courteous, more resolute and indefatigable in war. It is impossible to describe the magnificence of her plate and apparel. She was entirely clad in gold and precious gems; her hunting did not stop her from finding time to obtain a sound knowledge of various languages —her greatest delight was in learning from books how to lead a virtuous life.

But to cut short the tale, she and her husband were both formidable warriors who conquered and held with a strong hand many great kingdoms of the East, and many a splendid city belonging to the imperial majesty of Rome. Their enemies could never put them to flight while Odenathus was alive. But those who wish to read of her battles against King Shapur and others, and how all these events came about, why she made her conquests and what title she had to them, of her later misfortune and grief, and how she was besieged and captured, should turn to my master Petrarch; I assure you he wrote enough upon the subject. When Odenathus died she held the kingdoms with her own hand and fought her enemies in person with such savagery, there was no prince or emperor in the land who did not count himself lucky if she did not make war on his country. They made formal alliances with her that they might live in peace, and let her ride or hunt as she pleased. Neither Claudius, the Emperor of Rome, nor Gallienus before him, nor any Armenian, Egyptian, Syrian, or Arabian ever summoned the courage to take the field against her lest she slay them with her own hands or put them to flight with her army. Her two sons were royally clad as befitted the heirs to their father's kingdom. Their names were Hermano and Thymalao, according to the Persians. But Fortune always mixes gall with her honey. This powerful queen was not to endure for long. Fortune made her fall from her throne to misery and ruin.

When the government of Rome came into the hands of Aurelian he planned to take vengeance upon the queen and marched against Zenobia with his legions—in short, he put her to flight and captured her at last. He fettered Zenobia and her two children, conquered the country and returned to Rome. Among the other things captured by that great Roman, Aurelian, was her jewelled golden chariot which he brought back with him that it might be seen by the people. She walked before him at his triumph, crowned as a queen, with gold chains around her neck and her clothes encrusted with gems.

Alas, Fortune! She who was once the bane of emperors and kings is now gaped upon by the mob; she who in stern onslaughts wore the helm and stormed the strongest citadels must now wear a woman's cap upon her head; she who bore the flowering sceptre must carry a distaff and earn her keep.

OF PEDRO KING OF SPAIN

Noble and honourable Pedro, glory of Spain, whom fortune sustained in such great splendour, we have every cause to lament your pitiable death. Your brother drove you out of your own land; later, at a siege, you were betrayed by a trick and led into a tent where he slew you with his own hand, thus succeeding to your kingdom and revenues. Who contrived this villainy and sin? A black eagle upon a field of snow, caught in a limed twig red as burning coal.* Who helped the assassin in his need? A nest of evil.† No Charlemagne's Oliver, ever scrupulous of loyalty and honour, but a Genilon-Oliver, corrupted by bribery, brought this noble king into the trap.

OF PETER KING OF CYPRUS

You also, O noble Peter, King of Cyprus, whose generalship won the city of Alexandria. Many and many a heathen did you bring to grief; and for this your own liegemen became envious and assassinated you one morning in your bed, for no other reason than your knightly prowess. Thus Fortune rules and guides her wheel, bringing men from joy to sorrow.

OF BERNABO OF LOMBARDY

Why should I not recount your ill fortune, great Bernabo, Viscount of Milan, god of pleasure and scourge of Lombardy, since you climbed so high a pinnacle? Your brother's son—doubly bound in loyalty to you, being your nephew and son-in-law— caused your death in his prison; why or how I do not know; only that you were slain.

OF UGOLINO COUNT OF PISA

For pity no tongue may describe the slow starvation of Count Ugolino of Pisa. A little way out of Pisa stands the tower in which he was put in prison with his three small children, the eldest scarcely five years old. O Fortune, how cruel it was to put such birds in such a cage! In that prison he was condemned to die. Roger, bishop of Pisa, had laid a false charge against him, whereupon the people rose and imprisoned him as I have described. The little food and drink he was given was barely enough, besides being poor and bad. One day, about the time his food used to be brought in, the jailer shut the gates of the tower. He heard it plainly but said nothing, yet in his heart he thought they

---

* The arms of Bertrand du Guesclin, who lured Pedro into the tent where he was murdered.

† Sir Oliver Mauny (Old French *mau ni* = wicked nest).

meant to starve him to death. 'Alas that I was born!' he cried, and tears fell from his eyes.

His youngest son, three years of age, said to him, 'Father, why are you weeping? When will the jailer bring our broth? Have you no morsel of bread saved up? I am so hungry I cannot sleep. Would to God I might sleep for ever, then hunger could not creep into my belly. There's nothing I want so much as bread.'

Thus day by day the child cried out, till he lay down in his father's bosom, saying, 'Goodbye, Father, I must die.' He kissed his father and died the same day. When the heart-broken father saw he was dead he bit upon his arms in his agony, crying, 'O Fortune! I may lay the blame for all my grief upon your treacherous wheel!' Thinking he bit his arms from hunger instead of grief, his children said, 'O father, don't do that! Rather eat of our flesh, the flesh you gave us; take it and eat.' These were their very words; and a day or two after that they lay down in his lap and died.

He himself despaired, and also perished of hunger. Such was the end of the mighty Count of Pisa, whom Fortune cut down from his high estate. Enough of this tragic story: whoever wishes to hear a longer version must read the great poet of Italy, for he describes it all from beginning to end, leaving no word out: his name is Dante.

NERO

Though Nero was vicious as any fiend in the lowermost pit of hell, yet as Suetonius tells us he held the four quarters of the world in subjection. He delighted in jewellery and his clothes were embroidered from head to foot with rubies, sapphires, and white pearls. No emperor was more sumptuous in dress than he, or more vain and fastidious. Once he had worn a robe he never looked at it again. He kept a store of nets made of gold thread for fishing in the Tiber when he had a mind to amuse himself. His wish was law, and Fortune obeyed him as if she were his friend.

He burned Rome for his amusement; and slew his senators one day to hear them weep and scream; he slew his brother, and lay with his sister. He made a pitiable spectacle of his mother: he slit open her womb to see where he had been conceived. Alas that he should have so little feeling for his own mother! Not a tear dropped from his eyes at the sight; he merely remarked, 'She was a fine-looking woman.' Well may you wonder how he could bring himself to sit in judgement upon her dead beauty. He commanded wine to be brought, which he immediately drank, but showed no other sign of grief. When power is conjoined with cruelty the poison goes too deep.

In youth this emperor had a tutor who—unless the books lie—was the pattern of moral wisdom in his time, who taught him learning and manners. He was intelligent and tractable while this tutor had him in his charge, and it was long before despotism or any other vice dared invade his heart. Nero stood in great awe of this Seneca of whom I speak because he used to rebuke him circumspectly for his vices with words rather than blows, saying, 'Sir, an emperor should be virtuous and detest oppression.' For this Nero caused him to bleed to death in a bath after opening the veins of his arms. In youth Nero had been accustomed to rise in the presence of his tutor; which later appeared a grievance to him, so he caused his death. Nonetheless the wise Seneca chose to die like this in a bath rather than brave other torments. Thus Nero slew his beloved tutor.

The time came when Fortune would no longer nourish Nero's enormous arrogance. Though he was strong, yet she was stronger. 'For God's sake, I must be mad,' thought she, 'to place a man so crammed with vice in a position so high and call him emperor—by God I'll topple him out of his seat; he'll fall just when he least expects it.'

One night the people rose against him because of his crimes. Seeing this he slipped out of his palace gates alone and hammered upon a door where he expected to find help; but the more he cried out the faster they barred the doors against him, till he realized he had deluded himself. Not daring to call out any longer he went away. Everywhere the people cried and shouted round about; with his own ears he heard them yell, 'Where's that damned tyrant Nero?' He almost went out of his wits for fear and prayed piteously to his gods for succour, but it never came. Half dead with terror he ran into a garden to hide himself. In this garden he found a couple of peasants sitting beside a roaring fire. He begged these two yokels to strike off his head so that no ignominy might be done his body after his death to dishonour him. Not knowing what else to do, he slew himself; and Fortune laughed at her joke.

OF HOLOFERNES

In his day no king's captain ever subjugated more kingdoms, was more omnipotent in the field, or more magnificent in his arrogance than Holofernes, whom Fortune lovingly embraced and led by the nose till before he knew it his head was off. Not only did all men hold him in awe for fear of losing their liberty or riches: he forced them to renounce their faith besides. 'Nebuchadnezzar was God,' he declared, 'no other god is to be worshipped.' None dared dispute his edict save in the strong city of Bethulia where Eliakim was priest. Now mark the death of Holofernes: one night he lay drunk in his tent, which was the size of a barn, in the midst of his army; yet for all his power and splendour a woman, Judith, smote off his head as he lay asleep. Undetected by them all she stole away, bearing his head to her city.

OF THE ILLUSTRIOUS KING ANTIOCHUS

What need to recount the royal majesty of King Antiochus, his huge arrogance and poisonous crimes? There never was another like him. Read what he was, in Maccabees: read the proud boasts he made, why he fell from the height of prosperity, and how miserably he perished upon a hillside. Fortune had so exalted his pride that he really believed he might reach to the stars, weigh each mountain in the balance, and hold back the floods of the sea! Most of all he hated God's people. Supposing that God could never subdue his pride, he used to put them to death in torment and agony. And because they had inflicted a crushing defeat upon Nichanor and Timothy, he conceived such hatred for the Jews that he ordered his chariot to be made ready in all haste, savagely swearing to set out at once for Jerusalem and wreak his rage upon it with the utmost cruelty. But his plan was soon thwarted. God smote him grievously for these threats with an invisible and incurable wound that cut and bit into his guts till the pain was not to be borne; a just punishment indeed, as he had tortured the guts of so many others. Despite his torment he would not give up his wicked damnable purpose, but ordered his army to make ready forthwith; when suddenly, before he knew it, God subdued all his boasting and arrogance, for he fell heavily from his chariot, lacerating his limbs and flesh so that he could neither walk nor ride but had to be carried about in a chair because of his bruised back and sides. Evil worms crawled in his body, so grievously did God's vengeance smite him; he stank so horribly none of the personal attendants that guarded him sleeping and waking might bear the stench. In this torment he wept and lamented, and knew God to be Lord of creation. The stink of his carrion was nauseous to himself and his whole army; none might carry him. In this stench and horrible agony he perished miserably upon a mountain. And so, that criminal murderer who had brought tears and lamentation to so many received the due reward of arrogance.

OF ALEXANDER

The story of Alexander is so generally known that all persons of discernment have heard some or all of his fortunes. In short, he conquered the wide world by main force, except in the case of those who were glad to sue him for peace on account of his formidable reputation. Wherever he went he humbled the pride of man and beast from one end of the world to the other. No comparison could ever be made between him and any other conquerer; the whole world quaked in terror before him. He was the pattern of chivalry and magnanimity; Fortune made him heir to all her honours. So filled was he with lionlike courage that nothing, save women and wine, could blunt his ambitious undertaking of vast labours and great deeds of arms. What praise would it be to him were I to tell you of Darius and a hundred thousand other brave kings, princes, dukes and earls whom he conquered and brought to ruin? What more can I say than that the length and breadth of the world was his? Were I to talk for ever about his knightly prowess it still would not suffice. According to Maccabees, he reigned twelve years. He was the son of Philip of Macedon, the first king of the land of Greece. O noble and excellent Alexander, that it should ever have befallen you to be poisoned by your own people! Dicing with Fortune, she turned your six into an ace and never shed a tear.

Who will give me tears to lament the death of that nobleness and generosity which ruled the world as a kingdom, yet thought it not enough, so filled was his spirit with high ambition? Who will help me cry out upon treacherous Fortune and indict Poison, both of whom I blame for all this woe?

OF JULIUS CAESAR

Through wisdom, valour, and immense labour the conqueror Julius raised himself from a humble station to royal majesty, gaining the whole Occident, land and sea, by diplomacy or force of arms, and making it tributary to Rome, of which he later became Emperor: till Fortune turned against him. In Thessaly great Caesar fought his father-in-law Pompey, who had at his command the whole chivalry of the East as far as the rising of the sun! By his prowess he slew or took prisoner all except a few who fled with Pompey. Thus he overawed the whole Orient. For this he could thank Fortune that served him well.

Let me for a while lament Pompey, that noble ruler of Rome who fled after this battle. One of his men, a base traitor, cut off his head and brought it to Julius in the hope of winning his favour. To such an end did Fortune bring the wretched Pompey, conqueror of the East!

Julius returned again to his triumph in Rome, crowned with laurels; but in time Brutus Cassius, who had always envied his great eminence, secretly wove a subtle conspiracy against Julius and (as I shall relate) chose the spot where he was to be killed with daggers. Julius went to the Capitol as usual one day, and there he was suddenly set upon by the treacherous Brutus and other of his enemies who stabbed him with their daggers and left him lying covered with wounds. Yet he groaned only at one of these blows, or at the most two, unless history is mistaken.

So noble was Julius' heart, and so much did he love honour and decorum, that in spite of the anguish of his deadly wounds he threw his mantle over his hips that none should see his private parts. As he lay dying, half-conscious, and knowing death was certain, he kept decorum in mind. For a full account I refer you to Lucan and Suetonius, and also Valerius, who have written the story from beginning to end—how Fortune was at first a friend and later an enemy to these two great conquerors. Let no man trust in her favour long but be ever on the watch—take all these mighty conquerors as an example.

CROESUS

The rich Croesus who was once king of Lydia, of whom Cyrus himself stood in awe, was seized in the midst of all his pride and led to the fire to be burned. But such a deluge poured down from the sky that it quenched the flames, thus allowing him to escape. Yet he had not the grace to take warning, till Fortune hung him gaping from a gibbet. For when he escaped he could not resist making a new war. Since Fortune had arranged the rain to enable him to escape, he was convinced his enemies could not kill him. Besides he had a dream one night which made him so pleased and proud he set his heart upon vengeance.

He dreamed he was up in a tree. There Jupiter washed his back and sides, while Phoebus brought him a fine towel to dry him with. So he was puffed up with pride and asked his daughter standing beside him to tell what it meant, for he knew she had great learning. She began to interpret his dream thus:

'The tree,' she explained, 'stands for a gallows; Jupiter betokens rain and snow; Phoebus with his clean towel stands for the rays of the sun. Father, you will be hanged for certain; you shall be washed by the rain and dried in the sun.' Thus his daughter, whose name was Phanye, gave him plain warning. And Croesus the proud king was hanged; his royal throne availed him nothing.

The burden of all tragedies is the same: that Fortune always assails proud kingdoms with unexpected strokes. For when men trust in her she fades away and covers her bright face as with a cloud.

'Stop!' *exclaimed the Knight,* 'no more of this, good sir! What you have said is true enough, certainly, and more than true; but for most folk, it seems to me, a little melancholy goes a long way. As for me I find it pretty depressing to hear about people living in wealth and ease, only to be told of their sudden ruin. On the other hand it delights me to hear of a man of low estate who climbs up and becomes fortunate and stays prosperous—that seems to me much pleasanter and the right sort of story to tell.'

'Yes,' *said our Host,* 'what you say is true, by St Paul's bell! This monk goes booming on about how Fortune covered something or other with a cloud, and about what Tragedy is, as you've just heard. For goodness' sake, it's no use whining and lamenting when what's done's done; and as you say, it's a penance to have to listen to these calamities. No more of them, Master Monk, God bless you! This stuff bores the whole company. That sort of talk's not worth a butterfly; there's neither fun nor enjoyment to be had from it. And so, Master Monk, or Brother Peter, if that's your name, I entreat you to tell us something else, for by the Lord in heaven, if it hadn't been for the clinking of those bells hanging all over your bridle I'd surely have gone to sleep and fallen off, though the mud were never so deep. Then you'd have told all your stories in vain, for certainly, as the scholars say, it's no use giving a lecture when there isn't any audience. And I'm a good listener to any story that's well told. Tell us something about hunting, sir, if you please.'

'No,' *returned the Monk.* 'I'm in no mood for frivolity. Now let someone else tell his story, as I have.' *Then our Host addressed the Nun's Priest in his rough hearty way:* 'Come nearer, you Priest, come over here, Brother John! Tell us something to keep our spirits up. Cheer up, never mind that miserable hack you're riding on. It doesn't matter a bean how gaunt and ugly a horse is so long as he serves. See you always keep a merry heart.'

'Yes, indeed,' *he replied.* 'Host, I swear you're right: if I don't give satisfaction I should certainly be blamed.' *And he broached his tale without delay. And this is what that genial priest, kindly Brother John, told us.*

THE NUN'S PRIEST'S TALE

A poor widow, somewhat advanced in age, once lived in a small cottage beside a clump of trees standing in a valley. This widow of whom I tell had led a very patient, simple life since the day she was last a wife, for she had little property or income. She kept herself and her two daughters by making do with what God sent her; she had three large sows, no more, three cows and a sheep called Moll. The hall and bower where she ate her scanty meals was thick with soot. No need had she for sharp sauces, for no dainties passed her lips; she only ate what she could afford. Thus she never fell ill through overeating; a temperate diet, exercise, and a contented heart were all her medicine. No gout stopped her from dancing, no apoplexy hurt her head; she drank no wine, either white or red. Most of the dishes served at her table were white and black—milk and brown bread, which she had no lack of, broiled bacon and sometimes an egg or two; for she was by way of being a dairy-woman.

She had a yard fenced round with palings and a dry ditch on the outside, in which she kept a cock called Chanticleer. For crowing he had no match in all the land. His voice was mellower than the mellow organ that's played in church on Mass-days. At home his crow kept better time than a clock or an abbey horologe. He knew by instinct each revolution of the equinoctial in that town; for every fifteen degrees, on the hour, he would crow to perfection. His comb was redder than the finest coral and embattled like a castle wall. His black bill shone like jet; his legs and toes were azure, with nails whiter than a lily, and his feathers the colour of burnished gold.

This noble cock had in his charge seven hens for his delectation; they were his sisters and mistresses, all remarkably like him in hue; and the one whose throat had the loveliest colours was called pretty Madame Pertelote. She was courteous, tactful, elegant and companionable, and had such pretty ways that Chanticleer's heart had been absolutely in her keeping and firmly locked with hers since she was a week old. How happy he was in his love! And at sunrise what a delight to hear them sing in sweet accord, 'My love is gone!' For in those days, I'm told, animals and birds could sing and talk.

Now it so happened that early one morning as Chanticleer sat among his wives next to pretty Pertelote on the perch in the kitchen, he began groaning like a man badly troubled in a dream. When Pertelote heard the racket he made she was terrified and exclaimed, 'Dear heart, what's the matter with you? Why are you groaning away like that? A fine sleeper you are—you ought to be ashamed of yourself.'

And Chanticleer replied, 'Please don't let it worry you, Madam. My goodness! I dreamed I was in such a fix just now—my heart's still fluttering with fright! May God render my dream propitious and save my carcass from some filthy dungeon! For I dreamed I was wandering up and down in our yard when I saw a creature like a dog making as if to grab hold of my body and do me to death. His colour was reddish-yellow, but his tail and ears were tipped with black, unlike the rest of his hair; he had a narrow snout with two burning eyes—I'm still half dead with fright at the looks of him—no wonder I was groaning.'

'Get along with you!' said she. 'Shame on you, faintheart! Alas, now you've lost my heart and my love, by the Lord in heaven! I swear I can't love a coward! For whatever women may say it's certain we all desire—if possible—husbands that are brave, wise, generous, and reliable; not skinflints, nor fools, nor scared of the sight of a weapon, and not braggarts either, for God's sake! How can you have the face to tell your sweetheart that anything could make you afraid? Haven't you a man's heart to go with that beard of yours? Alas! can you be scared of dreams? Lord knows dreams are nothing but foolishness. Dreams come from overeating; and sometimes from stomach-vapours and a mixture of overabundant humours. Excuse me, I'm certain the dream you had last night comes from the surplus of red bile in your blood, which makes people have terrifying dreams about arrows, red tongues of flame, huge red ravening beasts, of fighting, and of dogs all shapes and sizes; just as the black melancholy humour makes many cry out in their sleep for fear of black bears, or black bulls, or of being hauled off by black devils. I could tell you of other humours besides, which trouble plenty of people in their sleep, but I'll pass on

as quickly as I can. Look at Cato, who was a man of such wis-
dom: didn't he say, "Take no stock in dreams"?

'Now sir,' (she went on) 'when we fly down from the rafters, for
goodness' sake take some laxative. On my life and soul the best
advice I can give you is that you purge yourself of both these
humours, and that's the plain truth. To save time, as there's no
apothecary in town, I myself will instruct you in the herbs which
will help you to recover your health. In our own yard I'll find
those herbs whose natural properties will purge you from top to
bottom. Now for heaven's sake don't forget! You've a very choleric
temperament, so be careful the noonday sun doesn't find you filled
with hot humours, for if it does I'll lay sixpence you catch the
tertian fever, or an ague, and that'll be the death of you. You must
have a light diet of worms for a couple of days before you take
your laxatives: spurge-laurel, centaury, fumitory, hellebore (they
all grow here), catapuce, buckthorn berries, or the herb ivy that
grows in our nice garden. Peck them where they grow and eat
them up! Cheer up, husband, for gracious' sake! Don't be afraid
of any old dream, that's all.'

'Madam,' replied the cock, 'a thousand thanks for your informa-
tion. Nevertheless, as regards Cato who's so renowned for his
wisdom, though he laid it down that dreams are nothing to worry
about—by God, you'll find a contrary opinion in ancient books
written by many men of far greater authority, believe me, than
Cato! They have clearly shown from experience that dreams are
auguries of the joys and sorrows we undergo in this present life.
It needs no argument: experience provides the proof.

'One of our greatest authorities tells this story: One day two
friends embarked upon a pious pilgrimage, and they happened
to come to a town where there were such crowds of people and
such shortage of accommodation they couldn't find as much as a
single cottage where they might both put up. So of necessity they
had to part company for the night, each going to his inn and
taking whatever offered in the way of shelter. One was housed in
a stall of plough-oxen that stood far out in a yard; the other, as
luck or the fortune that governs us all would have it, found him-
self a good enough lodging.

'Now, long before daybreak, it happened that this man dreamed
as he lay in his bed that his friend was calling him, crying, "Alas!

I shall be murdered tonight in this oxstall where I lie. Come to my help, dear brother, or I die! Come in all haste!"

'The man started out of his sleep in panic but when he was fully awakened turned over and took no further notice, thinking his dream an absurdity. But he dreamed it twice again; and the third time it seemed to him his friend came and said, "Now I'm killed! Look at these gaping bloodstained wounds! Get up early in the morning, and at the west gate of the town you'll see a cart filled with dung in which they've secretly hidden my body: don't hesitate, but stop that cart. If you want to know the truth I was murdered for my gold." And with pale face and piteous looks he gave him the details of how he had been killed.

'Depend upon it, the man found his dream was absolutely true, for the next morning as soon as it was light he made his way to his friend's inn. When he reached the oxstall he began shouting for him, but the innkeeper quickly answered, "Your friend's gone, sir; he left the town at daybreak."

'Remembering his dreams, the man became suspicious and set off without delay to the west gate of the town, where he found a dungcart apparently on its way to dung a field, just as you heard the dead man describe. Then he called stoutly for vengeance and justice on the crime. "My friend's been murdered this very night! He's lying stiff and stark in that cart with his mouth gaping open! Fetch the magistrates whose job it is to keep order in the town! Help, hoa! Here's my friend lying dead!"

'What more need I add to the tale? The people came rushing out and threw the cart to the ground, and in the middle of the dung they found the newly-murdered man.

'See how our blessed Lord always unmasks murder, for He is just and true. "Murder will out"—we see it every day. Murder is so heinous and abominable to the justice and reason of God that He will not suffer it to be hidden, though it may stay secret two or three years. "Murder will out"—that's my opinion!

'Then the officers of the town seized the carter and the innkeeper. They tortured the one and put the other on the rack until they confessed their crime and were hanged by the neck.

'From this we may see that dreams should be treated with respect. Indeed, I find in the very next chapter of the same book —and believe me, I'm not exaggerating—the story of the two men who for some reason were about to cross the sea to a far country, had the wind not been contrary and kept them waiting in a city that stood pleasantly beside the harbour. One day, however, the wind changed towards evening and blew in the direction they desired. So they went joyfully to bed, planning to sail early the next day. But a wonderful thing befell one of the men as he lay asleep: before dawn he dreamed an extraordinary dream. It seemed to him a man stood by the side of his bed commanding him to remain, saying, "If you go tomorrow you will be drowned; that's all I can tell you." The man awoke, told his friend what he had dreamed, and begged him to abandon the voyage and stay where he was that day. But his friend, who slept beside his bed, laughed him to scorn. "No dream is going to scare me from attending to my affairs," he said. "I don't give a straw for your dreams. They're no more than a snare and a delusion: people are always dreaming of owls and apes and all sorts of things nobody can make head or tail of—things that never were or will be. But I see you mean to stay dawdling here and miss your tide. Well, Lord knows I'm sorry for it—but good day to you!" And so he took his leave and set sail. But before the voyage was half over (don't ask me why or what went wrong) the ship's bottom was rent asunder by some accident, and ship and man went down together in sight of the other vessels near them which had sailed at the same time. And so, my dearest Pertelote, you may gather from such time-honoured instances that nobody should be too heedless of dreams: for as I say there is no doubt whatever there are many dreams that are sorely to be dreaded.

'What about Kenelm's dream, which I read in the life of Saint Kenelm, the son of Kenalphus the great king of Mercia? One day, just before he was murdered, he had a vision of his assassination. His nurse interpreted every detail of his dream to him and warned him to guard himself against treason: but he was only seven years old and therefore took little account of dreams; he had such a saintly mind. By the Lord, I'd give my shirt to have you read his story, as I have. Dame Pertelote, I'm telling you the plain truth: Macrobius, who wrote about Scipio's dream in Africa, affirms their trustworthiness and says they give warning of future events. And moreover I beg you look at the Old Testament—see if Daniel thought dreams nonsense! Read about Joseph too, and there you'll find whether dreams are sometimes—I don't say always—warnings of things to come. Think of Pharaoh, the king of

Egypt, and his butler and his baker—did they find dreams of no effect? Anyone who inquires into the history of various kingdoms may read hundreds of extraordinary stories about dreams. What about Croesus the king of Lydia—didn't he dream he was sitting in a tree, which signified he would be hanged? And there's Hector's wife Andromache—the very night before Hector was to lose his life she dreamed he would perish if he went into battle that day. She warned him, but it was no use; he went out to fight just the same, and Achilles slew him. But that's much too long a story to tell; besides it's nearly dawn, and I must go. To wind up, let me say just this: that dream portends danger to me, and furthermore I tell you I take no stock in laxatives; they're poisonous, as I very well know—to hell with them, I can't stand them!

'Now let's drop the subject and speak of pleasanter matters. Madame Pertelote, in one thing, I swear, God has been merciful to me. Whenever I see the loveliness of your face, and those scarlet circles round your eyes, it kills all my fears. It's gospel truth that *"Mulier est hominis confusio"*.* (Madam, the meaning of the Latin is: "Woman is man's whole joy and happiness.") For at night when I feel your soft side next to mine—a pity they made our perch so narrow that I can't mount you—I'm so full of joy and content I defy all dreams and visions.'

Saying this he flew down from the rafters, for it was now day; and all his hens followed him. He clucked to call them, for he'd found a grain of corn lying in the yard. Royal he was and no longer fearful; he feathered Pertelote twenty times and trod her as often again before the day reached prime. Now he looks like a grim lion; up and down upon his toes he struts, disdaining to set foot on the ground; finding a grain of corn he clucks, and all his wives come running up. Here I'll leave Chanticleer feeding like a royal prince in his palace, and relate the adventure that befell him.

The month of March (in which the world began and God first created humankind) was complete and two and thirty days had passed since March began, when Chanticleer, walking in all his pride with his seven wives beside him, cast up his eyes to the sun (which stood twenty-one degrees and more in the sign of Taurus) and knew by sheer instinct that it was nine o'clock. He crowed with a merry note and remarked, 'The sun has climbed

* 'Woman is man's ruin.'

forty-one degrees and more in the heavens. Madame Pertelote, my heart's delight, hark at those happy birds—how they sing! See the flowers freshly springing! My heart's filled with joy and content!'

But the next moment he was in grievous trouble, for happiness is always followed by grief. The Lord knows earthly joys are soon spent; and a rhetorician skilled in writing elegant poetry might safely chronicle this as a notable truth. Now let all wise men listen to me: I guarantee this story is as true as the book of Lancelot de Lake, whom women hold in such great reverence. But to return to my theme.

Foreordained by almighty Providence, a sly, unprincipled coal-black fox that had lived for three years in the nearby copse had broken through the hedge that same night into the yard where proud Chanticleer was wont to repair with his wives. He lay crouching in a bed of cabbages until it was about midday, biding his time to fall on Chanticleer, just like these assassins who lie in wait to murder people.

O treacherous murderer, lurking in your den! O you second Iscariot, new Ganelon! False dissembler, O you second Sinon, that Greek who brought Troy to utter grief! Ah, Chanticleer, cursed be the day that you flew into the yard from the rafters! Your dream gave you good warning that for you it would be a day of peril. But according to the opinion of certain scholars, what God foresees must come to pass. Any accomplished scholar will tell you that on this subject there is great altercation and dispute in the schools, and that a hundred thousand have argued it. But I can't sift it to the bottom like that holy theologian St Augustine, or Boethius, or Bishop Bradwardine, and say whether God's divine foreknowledge of necessity constrains one to perform any particular act (by 'necessity' I mean 'simple necessity'); or whether one is granted free choice to do or not to do, even if God foreknows the act before it's performed; or whether His knowing does not constrain at all except by 'conditional necessity'. With such problems I'll have nothing to do. My tale, as you can hear, is only about a cock who took his wife's advice (with disastrous results) to go into the yard that same morning after the dream I told you about. Women's advice is generally fatal: woman's advice first brought us to grief and caused Adam to leave Paradise where he was so happy and comfortable. But let's pass that over, as I don't know whom I might offend if I disparage the advice of women—I'm only saying it in fun. Read those authors who treat of the subject and you'll hear what they have to say of women. I'm only giving you the cock's words, not my own—women are divinities and I can't imagine any harm coming from them.

Pertelote was happily taking a dustbath in the sand, and all her sisters sunning themselves near by, while Chanticleer was singing more gaily than a mermaid in the sea (Physiologus confirms they sing merrily and well) when his eye fell upon a butterfly among the cabbages and he became aware of the fox crouching low. He never felt less like crowing, but started up like a man panic-stricken, chattering 'cok-cok'. For an animal will instinctively wish to flee when he sees his natural enemy, even though he may never have set eyes on him before.

So when Chanticleer caught sight of him he would have fled had not the fox quickly exclaimed: 'Good sir, where are you off to? Alas, are you afraid of me, when I am your friend? Could I be such a monster as to do you any harm or mischief? I've not come to spy upon you—indeed, the only reason for my coming was to hear you sing. Indeed, indeed, you've a voice as beautiful as an angel's in heaven, besides more feeling for music than Boethius or any other singer. Your good father—God bless his soul!—and your mother too, used to be kind enough to visit my house, to my great contentment; and I'd love to be able to entertain you as well. For when it comes to singing, I'll say this—strike me blind if I ever heard anyone, except you, sing as your father did in the morning! Indeed, it came straight from the heart, everything he sang. And to reach the highest notes he'd strain himself till both his eyes were screwed tight, standing on tiptoes and stretching out his long slender neck—and then how loud was his cry! Besides, he was a man of great discernment and there wasn't anybody in the country round to surpass him in song or wisdom. I've read in *Burnel the Ass,* among other verses, of that famous cock whose leg was broken by a priest's son when he was young and foolish, and how he made the priest lose his benefice: but there's certainly no comparison to be made between the cleverness of that cock and your father's wisdom and discretion. Now sing, sir, for charity's sake—let's see if you can imitate you father!'

Chanticleer began to flap his wings, enchanted by his flattery and suspecting no treason.

You nobles, there are many lying sycophants and flatterers in your courts who please you far more, believe me, than those who tell you the truth. Read what Ecclesiastes says about flattery and beware its guile!

Chanticleer stood on the tips of his toes with his neck stretched out and his eyes screwed tight, and began to crow as loud as he could. And in a trice Master Russell the Fox leapt up, seized Chanticleer by the throat, slung him over his back and carried him off towards the copse, for as yet there was nobody to give him chase.

O ineluctable Fate! Alas that Chanticleer ever flew from the rafters! Alas that his wife paid no heed to dreams! And all this bad luck came on a Friday too. O Venus, goddess of pleasure, Chanticleer was your worshipper and served you with all his might, more for delight than to multiply his race—how then can you allow him to die on that day that belongs to you?

O dear sovereign master, Geoffrey de Vinsauf, you who movingly elegized the death of noble King Richard when he was slain by the arrow, would that I had your art and skill to rail at Friday as you did—for it was in fact upon a Friday that the king was slain. Then I'd show you how I'd rhapsodize the agony and terror of Chanticleer!

Surely the Trojan ladies never sent up such a cry of lamentation when (so the *Aeneid* tells us) Ilium fell and Pyrrhus with drawn sword seized King Priam by the beard and slew him, as did those hens in the chicken-run when they saw Chanticleer carried off. But Dame Pertelote shrieked the loudest of all—far louder than Hasdrubal's wife at her husband's death, when the Romans burned Carthage and, filled with frenzied anguish, she leapt of her own will into the flames and resolutely burned to death! Yes, those woebegone hens cried out just like the senators' wives when Nero burned the city of Rome and, slain by Nero, their guiltless husbands perished! Now I'll return to my story.

The poor widow, hearing the hens screeching and lamenting, ran out of the house with her two daughters in time to see the fox make for the woods bearing off the cock upon his back. 'Help! Help! Stop thief! A fox! A fox!' they cried, and ran after him, followed by a crowd of men with cudgels. They all came running —Coll the dog, Talbot, and Garland, with Malkin the maid still clutching her distaff; cows and calves and the very pigs came running fit to burst, terrified by the barking of the dogs and the shouting of the men and women. They yelled like fiends in hell. The ducks squawked as if about to be slaughtered; the geese flew over the trees in panic; even the bees came swarming out of their hive. I tell you Jack Straw and his mob never let out such hideous, ear-splitting shouts when they were out lynching the Flemings, as were heard on the day they chased the fox. They brought trumpets of brass and wood and horn and bone, and they blew and hooted and screamed and whooped till it seemed the skies would fall.

Now please listen, good sirs, and you'll see how Fortune suddenly overturns the hope and pride of her enemy!

The cock, slung over the fox's back, managed to address him in spite of his terror and said: 'Sir! So help me God, if I were you I'd shout, "Run home, you stuck-up yokels! Plague on you! Now I've reached the edge of the wood I'll keep the cock whatever you do —and trust me, I'll eat him up right now!"'

Replied the fox, 'I'll do just that'—and as he spoke, with great dexterity the cock suddenly broke away from his mouth and flew high up on a tree.

When the fox saw that the cock was gone, he cried, 'Ah, Chanticleer! I fear I behaved very badly to you just now when I scared you by snatching you out of the yard. But, sir, I meant no harm; come down, and I'll tell you what I intended—and so help me God I'll speak the truth!'

'Oh no,' returned the cock. 'Curses on both of us, and on me first and worst, if you trick me more than once! You're not going to flatter me into singing with my eyes shut again! Anybody who wilfully keeps his eyes closed when they ought to be wide open deserves to have God forsake him.'

'No,' said the fox, 'rather, God send bad luck to anyone with so little self-control as to chatter when he ought to keep his mouth shut.'

That's what comes of being heedless and careless, and believing in flattery.

Good people, if you think this tale is no more than a farce about a cock and a hen, remember the moral! St Paul says that everything that's written is written for our instruction. So take the corn and leave the chaff.

Now, gracious Father, if it be Thy will as Our Lord says, make us all good men and bring us to His heavenly bliss. Amen.

Then our Host said, 'Bless your breeches and balls, Master Nun's Priest! That was a splendid tale of Chanticleer. But on my word, were you a layman you'd be a rare cock with the hens—and if you would as you could, I imagine you'd have a need of hens—yes, seven times seventeen and more! See what muscles this good priest has—what a big neck, what a broad chest! His eyes are like a sparrowhawk's—he needs no dyes from Portugal or the Indies to touch up his complexion! Bless you for your tale!'

And then he turned cheerfully and spoke to another of us, as you shall hear.

THE DOCTOR OF MEDICINE'S TALE

There was once, according to Livy, a knight called Virginius: a man of much honour and distinction, rich in friends, and of great wealth.

The knight had a daughter by his wife: she was his only child. This lovely girl surpassed all others in the perfection of her beauty, for Nature had moulded her excellence with singular care, as if to say: 'See! This is how I, Nature, can shape and colour a living creature when I wish: who can imitate me? Not Pygmalion, were he to carve and paint and forge and hammer for ever; and I daresay Apelles and Zeuxis, did they presume to counterfeit me, would toil in vain at their hammering, forging, carving or painting. For He that is the prime Maker has made me His vicar-general to shape and colour earthly creatures exactly as I please. All things under the waxing or the waning moon are in my care: I ask nothing for my work, for my Master and I are in full accord. I made her for the worship of my Master, just as I do all my other creatures of whatever shape or colour.' This is what Nature seemed to me to wish to say.

The girl in whom Nature took such delight was fourteen years of age. And just as she paints the lily white and reddens the rose, so did she paint these colours in their proper places on the beautiful limbs of this noble creature before her birth; and Phoebus dyed her thick tresses to the colour of his burnished rays. If her beauty was perfect, she was a thousandfold more virtuous, and lacked no quality praised by the discerning. She was chaste in soul and body; and so her virginity flowered in all humility, abstinence, patience, temperance, modesty of dress and behaviour. It could be said she was as wise as Pallas, yet her replies were always circumspect, and her conversation simple and womanly, for she used no grandiloquent phrases to seem learned. When she spoke she put on no airs; everything she said declared her virtue and good breeding. She was shy with a maiden's shyness; her heart was steadfast; and she was always busy that she might keep herself from sloth and idleness. Drunken Bacchus held no sway over her mouth—for wine and youth augment venery like oil or fat thrown on the fire. Moved only by her native goodness, she very often pretended illness in order to avoid company where there was likelihood of foolishness such as feasts, revels, and dances, which are the occasion of flirtations. Such things, as you know, make children too forward and precocious. This has always been the great danger. For a girl becomes versed in boldness all too soon when she grows to womanhood.

Now take no offence at my words, you middle-aged ladies in charge of the daughters of gentlefolk; remember you have been put in charge of them for one of two reasons: either because you have kept your chastity, or else were frail and fell, and thus well acquainted with the game, and have entirely given up that sort of misconduct for ever. Therefore see to it you never cease to instruct them in virtue, for Our Lord's sake. A deerstealer who has forsworn his taste for his old trade makes a better gamekeeper than anyone else. Now guard your charges well, for if you will, you can; and see to it you never wink at vice of any description lest you be damned for your villainous connivance. Pay heed to what I am about to say: of all betrayals the most pestilent and most damnable is betrayal of innocence.

You fathers and mothers, if you have one or more children, remember that the responsibility of their supervision is yours so long as they owe you obedience. Take care lest they perish through the example you set, or through your neglect to chastise them—for if they do I daresay you will pay for it dearly. Many a sheep and lamb has been torn in pieces by the wolf because their shepherd was slack and lazy. But one instance is enough for the present; I must return to my theme.

The girl whose story I am about to relate was her own safeguard and needed no governess, for in her life others might read as in a book the words and actions that become a virtuous maiden. So good and prudent was she that the fame of both her beauty and her abundant goodness spread everywhere, till throughout the land all lovers of virtue sang her praises—only excepting Envy, which grieves at others' happiness and is cheered by their sorrows and misfortunes. (This characterization is St Augustine's.)

One day the girl went into the town with her dear mother, as is customary with young girls, to visit a temple. Now in that town there was then a judge, the governor of the district. It happened that his glance fell upon the girl as she came past where he stood and he took particular notice of her. At once he was so struck with her beauty that his heart turned over and his thoughts took a new direction. Under his breath he said to himself, 'That girl must be mine, no matter what.'

Then the fiend ran into his heart and in a trice showed him how he could win the girl for himself by a ruse. For he felt certain that neither force nor bribery would avail him, since she had powerful friends; moreover, as she had lived a blameless life for so long that he knew perfectly well he would never win her by inducing her to sin with her body. So after much deliberation he sent for one of his hangers-on in town, whom he knew for a bold, crafty fellow; and in strict confidence this judge told the man his story, making him swear never to repeat it on pain of losing his head. When the fellow had given his assent to the villainous plan, the delighted judge made a great fuss of him and gave him rich and expensive gifts.

Once their cunning conspiracy (which soon will be made clear to you) for the satisfaction of his lust had been worked out to the last detail, the fellow, whose name was Claudius, returned home. And the dishonest judge, Apius (such was his name, for this is no legend, but a well-known historical anecdote—there is no doubt but that it is in the main true) quickly set to work to do everything he could to speed the consummation of his desire. So, according to the story, one day soon afterwards, as the dishonest judge sat in court as usual delivering judgement on various cases, this perfidious fellow came hurrying in and said, 'So please you, my lord, do me justice upon this poor petition in which I make complaint against Virginius; and if he says it is not true I'll prove it and produce good witnesses to the truth of my petition.'

The judge replied, 'I cannot give a final judgement upon this in his absence. Have him summoned and I'll gladly hear the case. You shall have full justice here and no wrong.'

Virginius came to learn of the judge's decision, and the villainous petition was immediately read to him. Here is the gist of it:

'Sir Apius, dear my lord, on the showing of your poor servant Claudius, a knight named Virginius holds against law and equity and my express wish, my servant and legitimate bondslave, who was stolen from my house one night at a tender age. I can produce evidence, my lord, to prove this to your satisfaction. She is not his daughter, whatever he may say. Wherefore I pray you, my lord Judge, deliver me my bondslave if it please you.' Such was the substance of the petition.

Virginius stared at the fellow. But before he could give his own version and prove, on his word of honour as a knight as well as the evidence of many witnesses, that everything his adversary said was false, this infamous judge peremptorily refused to wait or even hear a word from Virginius; but delivered his verdict as follows:

'I rule that the man is to have his servant back at once. You are not to keep her in your house a moment longer. Go and fetch her and place her in our keeping. The man is to have his bondslave: that is my verdict.'

The good Virginius, forced by the verdict of the judge to give his beloved daughter up to Apius for the satisfaction of his lusts, made his way home. Taking his seat in the hall he commanded his daughter to be sent for. With ashen face he gazed at her meek countenance. A father's pity pierced his heart, yet could not deflect him from his resolve.

'My daughter,' said he, 'my Virginia! There are two alternatives you must suffer—either death or shame. Would I had never been born! For you have never done anything to deserve death by the knife or sword. O my dear daughter, ender of my life, whom I have taken such delight in bringing up, you have never been out of my thoughts. O my daughter, my life's last grief and last joy, O gem of chastity, accept your death in patience, for I have made up my mind. From love, not from hate, your death must come; my pitying hand must strike off your head. Alas that Apius ever set eyes upon you! This is the dishonest verdict he passed upon you today'—and here he explained the whole position to her. As you have already heard it I need not recapitulate.

'O my dear father, mercy!' cried the girl; and with these words she laid, as she always used to, her two arms round his neck. The tears burst from her eyes: 'Dear father, must I die?' she said. 'Is there no pardon, no remedy?'

'None whatever, my dearest daughter,' he replied.

'Then give me time, Father,' she said, 'to mourn my death for a little while, for indeed even Jephtha gave his daughter time to lament before he slew her—and God knows she had done no wrong except to run to be the first to meet her father to give him a proper welcome.' Saying this she fell fainting to the ground; but when the faintness passed she arose and said to her father: 'Blessed be God that I shall die a virgin! Give me my death before shame touches me. Do your will upon your child, in God's name!'

And having said that, she begged him again and again to strike gently with his sword; and as she said it she fell down in a faint. With sorrowful heart and will her father smote off her head, seized it by the hair and presented it to the judge as he sat in court passing sentence. According to the tale, when the judge saw it he ordered Virginius to be arrested and hanged on the spot. But on the instant thousands of people, filled with pity and compassion, burst in to save the knight, for the terrible crime had become known. The people had soon become suspicious of the matter; from the way in which the fellow had framed his accusation they guessed it was with the assent of Apius, for they knew all about his lecherousness. So they went to Apius and forthwith flung him into prison, where he slew himself. As for Apius' servant, Claudius, he was sentenced to be hanged from a tree; and had not Virginius out of compassion pleaded for him to be exiled instead he would certainly have perished. The rest of those who were parties to this infamous business were hanged, one and all.

Here you may see how sin is rewarded. And beware! for no man knows whom God will strike, nor how the worm of conscience may shudder at wicked behaviour even though it be so secret that none know of it but God and he. Layman or learned, he can never tell when the blow will fall. Therefore I recommend you to take this advice: Forsake sin before sin forsakes you.

What the Host said to the Doctor of Medicine and the Pardoner

*Our Host broke into a fit of swearing. 'The crooks!' cried he,
'Christ's nails and blood! What a lying rascal, what a scound-
relly judge! The most shameful death you can think of is too
good for these judges and their lawyers! And alas, the poor girl
was killed. Ah, she paid dear for her beauty! As I always say, it's
plain the gifts of Fortune and of Nature are fatal to many. One
might say her beauty was her death. Ah, how piteously was she
slain! Very often more harm than good comes from those sort of
gifts I just now spoke of. But my good sir, it was truly a most
affecting tale. But no matter; let's get on. Dear Doctor, I pray
God save and keep you, not forgetting your urinals and chamber-
pots and medicines and cordials and boxes of linctus—God and
our lady Saint Mary bless them all! You're a real man, or I'm a
Dutchman! By St Ronyan, you might be a bishop! That's right,
isn't it? I can't use learned terms, but I know you touch my heart
so much it's almost given me a heart attack. Corpus bones! Give
me a dose of tonic, or a draught of new malt ale, or hurry up and
tell me some cheerful story, else my heart will give out from pity
for that girl! Hey, friend Pardoner,' he continued, 'tell us a few
jokes, or something amusing, and look sharp!'*

*'I'll do that,' replied the Pardoner, 'by St Ronyan! But first,' he
went on, 'I'll have a drink and snack at this ale-house here.'*

*But the gentlefolk cried out at once: 'Don't let him tell us any-
thing bawdy! Tell us something moral that we can learn from,
and we'll be pleased to listen.'*

*'Granted,' said the Pardoner. 'But I'll have to have a drink
while I think up something decent.'*

'Gentlemen,' he began, 'when I preach in churches I take pains to cultivate a stately delivery and ring it out as round as a bell. For I have everything I say by rote. My text is always the same and always has been: Radix malorum est cupiditas.*

'First of all I announce where I've come from, then I produce every single one of my bulls and certificates. To begin with I show my patent with the bishop's seal for my own protection, so that nobody, whether priest or clerk, shall have the impudence to interrupt me in the holy work of Christ. Then after that I tell my stories; I show bulls and mandates from popes, cardinals, patriarchs, and bishops; then I speak a few Latin words to give colour to my sermon and stir them to devotion. Next I bring out my glass cases crammed full with rags and bones—these are relics, or so they all think. Then I've got the shoulderbone of one of Jacob's sheep set in brass, and I say,

'"Good sirs, listen carefully. Just dip this bone in a well, and if any cow, calf, sheep, or ox should sicken because they've eaten worms or been stung by them, take water from the well and wash its tongue, when it will at once be cured: and furthermore any sheep that drinks a draught of water from this well shall be healed of pox, scab, and sores of all kinds. Remember this too: if, once a week, before cock-crow, the farmer who owns the cattle drinks a draught from the well while fasting (as that sainted Jew taught our fathers), his cattle and goods shall increase and multiply.

'"And sirs, it also cures jealousy. Should a man fall in a jealous passion, make his broth with this water and he'll never mistrust his wife again even if he knows the truth about her lapses, though she should have had half a dozen priests!

'"And here's a glove, as you can see. Now whoever puts his hand into this glove shall find his grain multiply after sowing, be it wheat or oats—so long as he makes an offering of pence or silver.

'"But, good people, of one thing I must warn you: if there be

* The love of money is the root of evil.

any person now in this church who has committed any sin so hor-
rible that for shame he dare not confess it; if there be any woman,
young or old, who has made a cuckold of her husband; such per-
sons shall be accorded neither the power nor the grace to make
offerings to my relics here. But whosoever finds himself free of
guilt of that sort may come up and make his offering in God's
name, when I shall absolve him by authority granted me by papal
bull."

'*By this trick I've earned a hundred marks a year since I became*
a pardoner. I stand in the pulpit like a priest, and when the yokels
have settled down in their seats I preach what you've just heard;
and a hundred other taradiddles besides. I do my best to stretch
out my neck and bob right and left at the people like a dove
perching on a barn. My hands and tongue go so fast it's a joy to
watch! All my preaching is about avarice and like evils, so that
they'll give their pence freely—to me, that is. My only purpose is
gain—I'm not interested in correcting sin. When they're dead
their souls can go a-blackberrying for all I care. Take it from me,
most sermons are preached from gross motives as a rule—some to
please folk, flatter and gain advancement by hypocrisy; others
from vanity or malice. For if I daren't attack a man by other
means, then I'll sting him with my sharp tongue in some sermon
so that he won't escape slander and defamation if he has offended
me or any of my brethren. For even if I don't name him directly
everyone knows perfectly well by my hints and circumstantialities
that he's the one. That's how I pay back people who annoy us,
and spit venom under cover of holiness while professing truth and
piety.

'*But I'll tell you what I'm after, in five words: I preach only for*
money, and that's why my text is still Radix malorum est cupiditas
and always has been. Thus I know how to preach against the very
vice I practise, which is avarice. But though I'm guilty of the sin
myself, I know how to make other people turn away from it and
bitterly repent. Yet that's not my real object. I only preach for
money. But that's enough of the matter.

'*Next I tell them any number of moral tales, old stories of long-*
ago; for these bumpkins love old tales, as that's the kind of thing
they can best remember and repeat. What, do you suppose that
while I can preach, and win gold and silver with sermons, it's

likely I should deliberately choose to live in poverty? No, no! Take it from me it never once crossed my mind! I'll preach and beg wherever I go. I'll not labour with my hands, or make baskets for a living like St Paul, when begging pays so well! I'm not out to imitate the apostles. I must have money, wool, and cheese, and wheat, even if it's given by the poorest servant-boy or the poorest widow of a village—no matter if her children perish for hunger! No, I must drink the juice of the grape, and have a pretty girl in every town! But listen, ladies and gentlemen; in short, it's your wish I should tell a story, and by the Lord, now I've had a draught of malt ale I hope to tell you something you'll be bound to like! I may be vicious enough myself, yet I can tell a moral tale—the one I generally preach for money. Now be quiet! I'll begin my tale.

THE
PARDONER'S
TALE

In Flanders
there was once a band of youths who practised every kind of
dissipation: gaming, dicing, haunting brothels and taverns, where
night and day they diced and danced with harp, lute and guitar,
eating and drinking more than they could hold. Thus with their
abominable excesses they made the vilest sacrifices to the devil in
that devil's temple, the tavern. And it would make your flesh
creep to hear the terrible blasphemous oaths with which they
dismembered our blessed Lord's body, as if the Jews had not
mangled Him enough already. They laughed at one another's
wickedness—and in would come the pretty little dancing-girls, the
singers with harps, old bawds, and young women selling fruit and
confectionery—the last are real agents of the devil at kindling and
blowing the fires of Lust, which follows upon Greed. For Holy
Writ is my witness that lechery springs from wine and drunken-
ness.

"Think how, without knowing it, drunken Lot lay with his two
daughters, against nature: so drunk he didn't know what he was
doing. When Herod (as you'll find if you look it up in the his-
tories) was gorged with wine while banqueting at his own table,
he gave the order to slay the innocent John the Baptist. And
Seneca undoubtedly has a good point when he says he can find no
difference between a drunkard and a man that's out of his mind
—except that madness, when it overtakes a sinner, lasts longer
than drunkenness. Ah, infamous Greed, first cause of our undo-
ing, origin of our damnation—till Christ redeemed us with His
blood! In short, how dearly we have paid for that accursed vice!
The whole world was corrupted for the sake of Greed.

"No doubt of it, for that vice our father Adam and his wife
were driven from Paradise to labour and woe. As I see it, while
Adam fasted he remained in Paradise, but the moment he ate of
the forbidden fruit upon the tree he was cast out into misery and
pain. We have every reason to lament Greed! Ah, if a man only
knew how many maladies follow from gluttony and intemper-

ance, how much more moderate would he be in his diet when he sits down at table! O how the narrow throat and delicate mouth make men labour—east and west and north and south, in earth and air and water—all to bring the daintiest food and drink to a glutton! How well St Paul treats of this subject: *'Meats for the belly and the belly for meats: but God shall destroy both'*—thus says St Paul. On my soul it is a filthy thing to utter that word; yet the act is filthier, when through damnable intemperance a man drinks the white wine and the red till he turns his throat into a jakes!

"With tears in his eyes the apostle said, *'For many walk of whom I have told you often, and now tell you even weeping, that they are the enemies of the cross of Christ: whose end is destruction, whose god is their belly.'* Paunch! Belly! Stinking pouch crammed with dung and corruption, making filthy music at both ends! What a terrific labour and expense it is to keep you provided! How those cooks pound and strain and grind to make one dish taste like another, all to satisfy your lustful appetite! They beat the marrow out of the toughest bones, for they throw away nothing that will slip sweetly down the gullet; to give it a better appetite they make delicious sauces from mingled spices of leaf, root, and bark; yet certain it is that he who indulges in those pleasures is dead while he lives in those vices!

"Wine stirs up lust; drunkenness is filled with quarrelling and wretchedness. You sot, your face is blotched, your breath sour, your embraces disgust; through your drunken nose there seems to come a music as if you were saying 'Samson, Samson' over and over, though God knows Samson never touched wine. You fall down like a stuck pig; your tongue's gone and so has your self-respect—for drunkenness is a real graveyard of a man's intelligence and judgement. No one under the domination of drink can keep anything secret; that's a fact. So keep clear of wine, whether white or red, and especially from the white wine of Lepe that's sold in Fish Street and in Cheapside. For in some strange way this Spanish wine seems to find its way into other wines growing next to it; and from the blend rise fumes of such strength that after drinking three glasses a man who thinks he's at home in Cheapside finds himself in Spain—not in Rochelle or Bordeaux either but right in the town of Lepe,* snorting 'Samson, Samson!'

* A town near Cadiz famous for its strong wines.

"But listen, gentlemen, just one more word if you please! Let me point out that by the grace of the true God, who is omnipotent, all the most notable victories and achievements in the Old Testament were won in abstinence and prayer. Look at the Bible, and you'll see.

"Look at Attila, the great conqueror, who died in shame and dishonour, bleeding at the nose in his drunken slumber. A captain should keep sober! Above all you should give serious thought to the commandment given to Lemuel—not Samuel, but Lemuel, I say—read the Bible and see what it expressly lays down about giving wine to those who sit in judgement. But no more of this— I've said enough.

"Now, having dealt with Greed, I'll warn you against gambling. Gambling's the real mother of lies, deceit, damnable perjuries, blasphemies against Christ, manslaughter, as well as the squandering of time and money; furthermore, to be known as a common gambler is a slur and disgrace on a man's good name. The higher his position, the more he's shunned. For if a prince be a habitual gambler his reputation for the management of affairs and public business is lowered in the general opinion.

"When Stilbon, that wise ambassador who was sent in great pomp from Sparta to make alliance with Corinth, arrived there, he happened to find all the leading men of the country playing at dice. So he slipped away home to his own country as soon as he could, saying, 'I'm not going to lose my good name there or take upon myself the reproach of allying you to a set of gamblers. Send some other ambassador, for upon my honour I prefer to die rather than ally you with dice-players. I do not choose to be the agent of a treaty between gamblers and a nation as glorious in honour as yours.' That's what this wise philosopher said.

"And look at King Demetrius also: history tells us that the King of Pathia sent him a pair of golden dice in scorn because he was a confirmed gambler; on which account he held Demetrius' glory and renown null and void. Princes should find other and better ways of killing time.

"Now I'll say a word or two on the subject of swearing and perjury, as treated by the ancient authorities. Blasphemy is an abomination, and perjury even more reprehensible. Almighty God forbade us to swear at all: witness St Matthew, and especially what the holy prophet Jeremiah says of swearing: *'Thou shalt swear*

... in truth, in judgement, and in righteousness.' But idle swear-
ing is a sin. Behold and see, in the first part of the Tables of the
Law, the second* of the holy commandments of Almighty God is
this: *'Thou shalt not take the Name of the Lord thy God in vain.'*
Notice that He forbids swearing of this kind before murder and
many other damnable sins. I say that's how it stands according to
the order of the commandments: anyone who knows them knows
it's God's second commandment. And moreover, I'll tell you
plainly that if a man's oaths are too outrageous, vengeance shall
not depart from his house. 'God's heart!' 'God's nails!' 'By the
blood of Christ at Hailes, my throw was a winning seven, yours
five and three!' 'God's arms! Cheat me and this dagger runs
through your heart!' Such is the harvest of the dice, those two
cursed bits of bone: perjury, anger, cheating, murder. Now for
the love of Christ who died for us, abandon all kinds of swearing!
But now, sirs, I must tell my tale.

"My tale is of three revellers. Long before any bell had rung for
six o'clock prayers they were sitting drinking in a tavern. And as
they sat they heard a handbell clinking in front of a corpse being
carried to its grave. One of them called the boy and said, 'Run
and find out whose corpse it is that's passing by. Look alive, and
see you get his name right.' 'Sir,' answered the boy, 'there's no
need to do that; it was told me two hours before you came here.
He was indeed an old friend of yours. Last night he was suddenly
slain as he sprawled blind drunk upon a bench. There came a
prowling thief—men call him Death—who is slaying everybody
in the country, and speared him right through the heart and made
off without a word. He's killed thousands in the plague that's
going on. And, sir, it seems to me you need to be careful before
you confront such an adversary. You must always be ready to meet
him—so my mother taught me. I can tell you no more.'

"The innkeeper broke in: 'By St Mary, what the child says is
true. This year he's slain every man, woman, child, farmhand,
and serving-lad in a big village a mile or more from here, where
I believe he lives. It's wisest to be prepared lest he does you some
injury.'

" 'Eh?' said the reveller. 'God's arms! Is he such a peril to meet?

---

* He means the third; but in Chaucer's day the first two commandments
were considered as one.

By the holy bones of God I vow I'll search him out in the streets and highways! Listen, fellows, we three are one—let's each hold up his hand and swear eternal brotherhood one to another, and then we'll kill this false traitor Death. By the splendour of God, that slayer shall be slain before night!'

"Together the three of them pledged themselves on their word of honour to live and die for one another as if they were indeed brothers of one blood. Then up they leapt, drunk with rage, and set out towards the village of which the innkeeper had spoken, all the while tearing Christ's blessed body to pieces with their frightful oaths—death to Death if only they could catch hold of him!

"They had not gone fully half a mile when a poor old man met them just as they were about to climb over a stile. This old man humbly greeted them with a 'God save and keep you, sirs!' But the most arrogant of the three revellers retorted: 'Be damned to you for a yokel! Why are you all muffled up to the eyes? And why live on into your dotage?'

"The old man looked him hard in the face and said, 'Because if I walked from here to India I could find no man in any town or hamlet who will exchange his youth for my age. And therefore I must endure my old age for as long as God wills—not even Death, alas, will take my life. So like a restless prisoner I walk, knocking with my staff night and day upon the earth, my mother's door, and saying, "Dear mother, let me in! See how my flesh, blood and skin wither away! Ah, when will my bones be at rest? Mother, I would exchange with you all the clothes I have in that wardrobe which has stood so long in my chamber, for one haircloth shroud to wrap me in!" But she still won't grant me that favour, which is why my face is so pale and wan.

" 'But, sirs, it is poor manners on your part to speak so rudely to an old man who has in no way offended you. As you can plainly read for yourselves in Holy Writ, *"Thou shalt rise up before the hoary head, and honour the face of the old man."* Therefore I give you this advice: don't harm an old man now, any more than you would wish to be harmed in your old age should you survive so long. And God be with you wherever you journey. I must go whither I have to go.'

" 'No, by God! Not so fast, old fellow,' returned the other gambler. 'By St John, you're not getting off so easily! Just now you

spoke about that traitor Death who slays all our friends the coun-
try round. On my oath you're his spy! Tell me where he is or
you'll pay dearly for it, by God and the holy sacrament! You and
he are in league to kill us young folk, and that's the truth, you
lying thief!'

"'Well, sirs', he replied, 'if you're so anxious to find Death, turn
up this winding road; for I swear I left him under a tree in that
grove, and there he'll wait, nor will your bluster make him hide.
Do you see that oak? Right there you'll find him. May the Lord
who redeemed mankind save and amend you!' Thus spoke the
old man; and each of the revellers set off running till he came to
the tree, where they found a heap of fine, new-minted golden
florins—very nearly eight bushels, it seemed to them. Then they
sought Death no longer but set themselves down beside the
precious hoard, overjoyed at the sight of the beautiful gleaming
florins. The worst of the three was first to speak.

"'Brothers,' said he, 'mark what I say; for though I joke and
play the fool I have my wits about me. Fortune has given us this
treasure that we may spend the rest of our lives in mirth and revel.
Easy come, easy go; that's how we'll spend it. What! Splendour of
God, who'd have thought we'd have had such luck today? Now if
only this gold could be got away from here and carried home to
my house—or yours, I mean—we'd be in the seventh heaven. For
it's perfectly plain all this gold is ours. But it certainly can't be
done in the daytime. People would say we were highwaymen and
have us strung up for stealing our own treasure. No, it must be
carried off at night with all possible prudence and caution. There-
fore I suggest we draw lots and see where the lot falls. Then the
one who draws the longest straw shall run rejoicing to the town
as fast as he can and bring us bread and wine on the quiet, while
the other two keep a sharp watch over the treasure. If he loses no
time, tonight we'll carry the treasure to whatever place we agree
is best.'

"He covered the straws in his fist and told the others to draw
and see where the luck would fall. It fell to the youngest of the
three, who at once set off towards the town.

"As soon as he had gone, the one said to the other: 'As you
know, you're my sworn brother; and now I'll tell you something
to your advantage. Our friend has gone as you can see; and here's

gold a-plenty to be divided between the three of us. But suppose I could work it so that it were shared between us two, wouldn't that be doing you a good turn?'

"'I don't see how it can be done,' replied the other. 'He knows the gold is here with us. What are we to do? What shall we say to him?'

"'Shall it be secret?' said the first rascal. 'Then I'll tell you in a couple of words what we'll do to bring it off.'

"'Agreed,' said the other. 'Never fear, I give you my word I shan't let you down.'

"'Well,' said the first, 'as you know we are two, and two are stronger than one. Wait till he's settled, then jump up as if you were going to scuffle with him in joke; and I'll thrust him through the side—and while you're pretending to wrestle, mind you do the same with your dagger. Then, my dear fellow, all this gold can be shared between me and you, and we'll be able to dice to our hearts' content and do whatever we please.' And so these two scoundrels agreed to kill the third as I have said.

"Now, the youngest, the one that went to the town, kept turning over and over in his heart the beauty of those shining new florins. 'O Lord,' said he, 'if I could only have all that treasure for myself alone, what man alive under God's heaven would live so happily as I!' And in the end the Devil, our common foe, put it into his head to buy poison with which to kill his two friends. You see, the Devil found him living such a bad life that he was given leave to bring him to perdition: for the young man fully intended to kill both of them without the least remorse. And without wasting any more time, off he went to an apothecary in the town and begged him to sell him some poison to put down his rats—and there was also, he said, a polecat in his yard that had been killing his chickens; so he was anxious to settle accounts with the vermin that nightly plagued him.

"The apothecary answered, 'I'll give you something. As I hope for heaven, this poison is so strong and violent there's no living creature in the wide world but must lose its life at once, yes, drop dead in less time than it takes to stroll a mile, should it eat or drink as little of this mixture as would cover a grain of wheat.'

"The villain took the box of poison in his hand, then ran to the next street where he found a man from whom he borrowed three large bottles. He poured the poison into two of them, keeping the third clean for his own use; for he expected to work all night carrying off the gold. And when that wastrel—Devil take him!—had filled his three big bottles with wine he returned to his friends.

"Is there need to elaborate? For they slew him on the spot, just as they had planned earlier; and when it was done, one of them said, 'Now let's sit down and drink and be merry; and afterwards we'll bury his body.' And saying this he happened to take up the bottle with the poison in it and drank, giving it to his friend to drink as well; whereupon they both perished on the spot.

"And truly, I don't suppose that the physician Avicenna can have set down in any section of his *Book of the Canon in Medicine* more horrible symptoms of poisoning than those two wretches exhibited before they died. Thus the two murderers as well as the treacherous poisoner met their end.

"O iniquity of iniquities! Murderous traitors! O wickedness! O Greed, Lust, and Gambling! You blasphemer against Christ with your great villainous oaths born of habit and pride! O mankind, how is it that you are so false and unkind towards your Creator, who made you and redeemed you with His precious heart's blood?

"Now, dear brethren, God forgive you your trespasses and keep you from the sin of avarice! My holy pardon can cure you all if you make an offering of silver pence—or gold nobles, silver brooches, spoons, or rings. Bow down your heads under this holy bull! Come along, ladies, make an offering of your wool! I'll enter your names now in my roll, and you shall go to the bliss of heaven! By my holy power I absolve you as clean and clear as the day you were born—all those who make offerings!"

'—There! That, sirs, is how I preach. And may Jesus Christ, true healer of our souls, grant that you receive His pardon, for that is best, I'll not deceive you.

'But, sirs, there's one thing I forgot to say in my discourse. In my bag I've got relics and pardons as good as any in Britain, given me by the Pope's hands! If any of you be willing to make a devout offering and have my absolution, come forward now and kneel down here and humbly receive my pardon. Or you can take my pardon as we go along, brand new at every milestone, so long as you renew your offerings in good sound coin, silver or gold! What an honour for all of you here to have a capable pardoner to absolve you in case anything should happen as you ride through the land! Who knows, one or two of you may fall from his horse and break his neck. Think what a protection it is for you all that I, who may absolve high and low when the soul leaves the body, should have fallen in with your company! My advice is that our Host here should make a start, for he's the one most wrapped in sin. Come forward, Master Host! Make your offering first, and you shall kiss every one of these relics—all for sixpence! Come on, unbutton your purse!'

'No! No!' cried our Host, 'Christ damn me! Lay off, I'm a Dutchman if I do! You'd make me kiss your old breeches and swear they were a saint's relic, though smeared with your behind! By the True Cross Saint Helena found, I'd rather have your ballocks in my hand than your relics and holy souvenirs! Have them cut off and I'll help you carry them—we'll have them set in a pig's turd!'

The Pardoner answered not a syllable; he was too furious to speak.

'Well, I'm not going to joke with you any more, or with anybody who can't keep his temper,' said our Host. But at this, seeing that all the others were laughing, the good Knight cut in: 'No more of this, that's quite enough! Cheer up, Master Pardoner, and give us a smile; and as for you, Master Host, my dear fellow, I ask you to kiss the Pardoner. Come over here, Pardoner, I beg you, and let's laugh and enjoy ourselves as before.' Then they kissed and rode on their way.

'Were there no books at all on the subject, my own experience gives me a perfect right to talk of the sorrows of marriage; for, ladies and gentlemen, since I was twelve years old—the living God be thanked!—I've married five husbands in church (if it be allowable for me to wed so often), each of them a man of standing in his own sphere. To be sure, not long ago I was told that as Christ went but once to a wedding—at Cana in Galilee—He showed me by that same precedent I was not to be married more than once. Also I was to bear in mind the sharp words that Jesus, God and Man, spoke beside a well when He reproved the woman of Samaria: "Thou hast had five husbands and he whom now thou hast is not thy husband"—that's what He said, to be sure. But what He meant by it I cannot tell; all I ask is, why wasn't the fifth man the Samaritan's husband? How many could she have in marriage? In all my life I've never heard a definition of the number. People can surmise and interpret right and left; all I know for certain is, God expressly commanded us to increase and multiply: an excellent text which I can understand well enough. And I know very well that He said my husband should leave father and mother and cleave to me. But He made no mention of number, of bigamy or octogamy—so why should people talk as if it were a disgrace?

'Take that wise king, King Solomon; I bet he had more wives than one. I wish to God it were lawful for me to be solaced half as often! What a heavenly gift he must have had for all his wives! No man alive has anything like it! So far as I can make out, Lord knows this noble king had many a merry bout with each on the first night, so full of life was he! Blessed be God that I have married five! I rummaged out the best they had from the bottoms of their purses and strongboxes: just as different schools makes the scholar perfect, and different jobs are bound to make perfect the workman, I've been trained by five husbands.* And welcome be

* The six lines which I have translated by this sentence do not appear in most MSS, but are certainly genuine, though Chaucer may have meant to cancel them.

the sixth whenever he comes! The truth is, I don't want to keep chaste for ever. As soon as my husband departs this world some other Christian shall marry me, for then, says the Apostle, I am free to wed in God's name where I please. He says it's no sin to be married: better to marry than to burn. What do I care if people rail at that villainous Lamech and his bigamy? All I know is that Abraham was a holy man, and Jacob too so far as I can tell; and both of them (like many another holy man) had more than two wives. Can you tell me where Almighty God has at any time expressly prohibited marriage? Kindly answer me that. Or where has He commanded virginity? No question, you know as well as I do that when the Apostle Paul spoke of virginity he said he had no precept for it. A woman may be advised to stay single, but advice is not a command. He left it to our own judgement: for had God commanded virginity, by doing so He would have condemned marriage. And surely, if seed were never sown, where would virginity come from? At any rate Paul dared not command a thing for which his Master gave no behest. There's a prize going for virginity—let him win it who can, we'll see who'll make the running!

'*But this call is not for everyone, only where God, of His power, chooses to bestow it. All I know is, the Apostle was a virgin; and though he said he wished all men were even as himself, all that's only exhortation to virginity. And he allowed me to become a wife by way of concession, so if my husband should die it's no sin to marry me, not even bigamy. Yet "it were good for a man not to touch a woman"—the Saint meant in his bed or couch, for it's risky to bring fire and tow together; you'll understand the metaphor! Well, by and large he held that virginity was better than marriage because flesh is frail—frail I call it, unless the two mean to live in continence all their married life.*

'*I grant all this; I don't begrudge that virginity should be preferred to bigamy. It pleases some to keep themselves pure in body and soul; of my own case I won't boast. As you know, the master of a household doesn't have all his utensils made of gold; some are of wood yet do him good service. God calls folk to him in different ways, and each has his own peculiar gift from God—some one thing, some another, just as it pleases Him to assign them. Virginity is a great perfection, and so is devout married chastity;*

but Christ, the wellspring of perfection, didn't tell everybody he ought to go and sell all that he had and give it to the poor, and so follow in His footsteps. He spoke to those who wish to live a life of perfection; and if you don't mind, ladies and gentlemen, I'm not one of them. I mean to bestow the best years of my life on the acts and rewards of marriage.

'And tell me, to what end were organs of generation made, and what was a man made for? You can be sure they weren't made for nothing. Twist it as you like, argue back and forth to prove they were made for the discharge of urine, that our little differences are there to tell male from female and for no other reason—did somebody say no? Experience teaches us the contrary. And so as not to vex the scholars I'll say this: They were made for both purposes, that's to say both for use and pleasure of generation, wherein we do not displease God. Why else should it have been laid down in books that a man must pay his wife her due? And what would he make his payment with if he didn't use his wretched instrument? It follows they were given to all creatures for procreation as much as for the discharge of urine.

'But I'm not saying that everyone with the sort of equipment I spoke of is meant to go and use it in the act of generation. In that case no one would bother about chastity. Christ, like many a saint since the beginning of the world, was a virgin and formed like a man; yet they always lived in perfect chastity. I've nothing against virginity. Let virgins be loaves of the finest wheat-flour, and call us wives barley-bread; and yet as St Mark can tell you it was with barley-bread that Our Lord Jesus refreshed thousands. I'll persevere in the state to which God has called me; I'm not particular. As a wife I'll use my instrument as generously as my Maker gave it. If I be grudging, the Lord punish me! My husband shall have it night and morning whenever he wants to come and pay his dues. I shan't stop him! A husband I must have, one that is both my debtor and my slave; and so long as I'm his wife he'll have his "tribulation of the flesh". While I'm alive I'm given "the power of his own body" and not he. That's what the Apostle Paul told me; and he bade our husbands love us well. I entirely approve of this view—'

Up leapt the Pardoner: 'Well, madam,' said he, 'by God and St John, you make a splendid preacher on this topic. Alas! I was just about to wed a wife; but why should my body pay such a price? I'd rather never marry anyone at all.'

'Just you wait!' she retorted. 'My tale hasn't begun. No, you'll drink from a different barrel before I've done, and it won't taste as good as ale. And when I've finished telling you about the tribulations of matrimony—in which I'm a life-long expert, that's to say I've been a scourge myself—then you can decide whether you want to taste of the barrel I'm going to broach. Be very careful before you come too near it; for I'll tell you a dozen cautionary tales. "Those who won't be warned by others become a warning to others"—those are Ptolemy's very words, as you'll find if you read his Almagest.'

'Madam,' said the Pardoner, 'let me entreat you to be good enough to go on as you've begun—tell your story and spare no man! Teach us young fellows your technique.'

'Very well then, since it seems to please you,' said she; 'but I only hope that no one in this company will take offence if I say what comes into my head, for I only mean to amuse. Now, sirs, I'll get on with my story.

'May I never drink another drop of wine or ale if I lie, but three of those husbands of mine were good, and two bad: the good three were rich and old, and could barely keep the contract that bound us—you know what I mean by that! So help me God it makes me laugh whenever I think how unmercifully I made them work of nights! And I thought nothing of it, that I swear! They'd given me their land and treasure, so I didn't need to trouble myself further to win their love or show them respect. Heavens above, they loved me so much I set no value on it. A sensible woman only busies herself to win love where there's none. But as I had them in the hollow of my hand and they'd given me all their lands already, why bother to please them except for my own profit and amusement? My word, I worked them hard—many's the night I made them bawl! I don't suppose they'd have won the Dunmow Flitch like some! Yet I ruled them so well in my own way that each was perfectly happy; they were always ready to bring me pretty things from the fair. How glad they were when I spoke to them nicely, for God knows how viciously I scolded.

'Now listen, you wise wives who know what I'm talking about, and I'll tell you how well I managed.

'This is the way to talk to them and put them in the wrong. For there's no man who can lie and perjure half so boldly as a woman. I'm not speaking of clever wives but of when they make mistakes. A really clever wife who knows her business can make her husband believe that black is white and bring in her own maid as witness in support. But listen to the way I used to go on:

'"Is this the best you can do, you old dotard? Why is my neighbour's wife so smart and gay? She's respected wherever she goes while I've got to sit at home; I've no clothes fit to wear! What are you doing in her house? Is she that pretty? Are you so amorous? What were you whispering to the maid? You old lecher, give it a rest! And whenever I have a harmless chat with a friend or walk over to his house for a bit of fun you rage at me like a fiend! Home you come, drunk as an owl, and sit on your bench lecturing and making monstrous accusations! You say it's a great misfortune to marry a poor woman because of the expense; but if she's rich and well-connected then you say it's torture to have to put up with her pride and disconsolate airs. O you rascal, if she's beautiful you say all the lechers will be after her, that her chastity won't last a moment because she's assailed on every side!

'"You tell me that some want us for our riches, some for our figures, some for our beauty; while some desire a woman because she can dance or sing; or for her breeding and conversation; or for her slender arms and hands—and so, by your account, the devil takes the lot! A fortress besieged at all points can't hold out for long—so you say.

'"And if she's ugly, then you say she wants every man she sets eyes on, and fawns on them like a spaniel until she finds some man to do business with her! There's no goose on the lake so grey it won't find its gander, says you. And then you say it's hard to control a girl no man would willingly keep! Miserable wretch, that's how you go on when you go to bed, muttering that no sane man need marry, nor any man who hopes for heaven! Thunder and lightning break your shrivelled neck!

'"Says you, a leaky roof, a smoking chimney and a scolding wife drive a man out of his own home. Oh! Bless us all, what ails the old man that he grumbles so?

'"Then you say we women are ready to hide our faults until the knot's safely tied, and then we show them. A blackguard's proverb if ever there was one!

' "You tell me that oxen, asses, horses, and hounds can be tried out at leisure before you buy them, and so can basins, washing-bowls, spoons, stools, and household goods like that, besides pots and clothes and dresses; but no one tries out a wife until they're married—wretched old dotard! And then, says you, we reveal our faults.

' "You also say it vexes me if you aren't forever saying how pretty I am, gazing on my face and paying me compliments wherever we go; or if you forget to make a fuss of me on my birthday; or if you aren't polite to my nurse, my chambermaid, and my father's family and friends—that's what you say, you old barrelful of lies!

' "You've even got hold of a false suspicion of our apprentice Jankin because of his curly golden hair, and the way he squires me wherever I go. I wouldn't have him if you died tomorrow! But tell me this, you wretch: why do you hide away the keys of the strong-box from me? It's my property as well as yours, for goodness' sake! What, do you want to make the mistress of the house look a fool? Now, by St James, you can rave as you please but you shan't have both my body and my goods; no matter what you do, one or the other you must forgo! And what's the use of all your snooping and spying? I sometimes think you want to keep me locked up in your strongbox! What you ought to say is, 'Dear wife, go where you like and have your fun; I won't listen to any tittle-tattle. Dame Alice, I know you're a true and faithful wife.' We cannot love a man who keeps a check on our comings and goings; we must be free.

' "Blessed above all others be the wise philosopher Master Ptolemy, for he has this proverb in his Almagest: 'Wisest of all is he who cares no whit who is richer than himself.' From this proverb you should understand there's no call to fret how well off other people are when you've got enough for yourself. For, you old dotard, don't worry, you'll have cunt enough tonight if you want it! Was there ever anyone so miserly as to refuse another man a light for his candle from his lantern—it won't make it any dimmer, for goodness' sake! Why grumble if you've enough?

' "Then you say our chastity's in danger if we make ourselves gay with clothes and jewellery; and then, you brute, you've got to back yourself up with this text from St Paul: 'Let women adorn themselves with modest apparel, with shamefastness and sobriety,' *says he,'and not with broidered hair, and fine jewellery or gold, or pearls, or costly array.' I'll take as much notice of your texts and rubrics as a flea!*

'"*And once you said I was like a cat, because when you singe its skin it stays at home, but when its coat is sleek and smart it won't stay half a day in the house, but goes off first thing in the morning to show off its coat and go caterwauling after the toms. Which means, Sir Brute, that if I'm looking smart it's because I want to run out and parade my miserable rags!*

'"*Sir Old Fool, what's the use of spying? Even if you begged Argus with his hundred eyes to guard me as best he can, I tell you he wouldn't be able to keep me unless I wanted—I'd put it across him if it killed me!*

'"*You also said there are three things that trouble the whole earth, and none can endure the fourth. O sweet Sir Brute, Jesus shorten your life! Still you preach away, saying an odious wife is reckoned one of these misfortunes. Aren't there any other comparisons to use in your parables without dragging in an innocent wife?*

'"*Then you liken a woman's love to Hell, to a barren waterless land, and to burning naphtha; the more it burns the more eager it is to consume whatever will burn. Just as worms destroy a tree, a woman destroys her husband—everyone who is chained to a wife knows this. That's what you say!*"

'As you can see, ladies and gentlemen, that's how I made my old husbands firmly believe they talked when they were drunk; it was all lies, but I got my niece as well as Jankin to bear me out. Lord! the trouble and grief I gave them! And they quite innocent, by God's sweet passion! Like a horse, I'd bite one moment and whinny to be petted the next. I'd scold even when I was in the wrong; or I'd have been done for, often as not. When you go to the mill to grind, it's first come, first served; I'd get in first with my reproaches and so put a stop to our strife. They were glad enough to find a quick excuse for things they'd never in their lives been guilty of.

'I'd accuse my husband of wenching, when he was so ill he could hardly stand; yet it tickled him to the heart, because he thought it showed how fond of him I was! When I walked abroad at night I'd swear it was to spy out the girls he slept with, and that *gave me cover for plenty of fun. Such mother-wit is granted us at our birth; God has given lies, tears, and spinning by nature to all women while they live. So I can boast of one thing: in the end I got the better of my husbands in every way, by force, cunning, or one means and another, such as keeping up an everlasting grumbling and natter. Especially in bed their luck was out; that's where I'd scold and do them out of their fun. When I felt my husband's arm come over my side I wouldn't stay another moment in the bed until he'd ransomed himself to me; and then I'd let him do his foolishness. As I always say, everything has its price. Who can lure home a hawk when he's empty-handed? To get what I wanted, I'd put up with all his lust and even pretend an appetite for it, though I never had much taste for old bacon; and that's really what turned me into a scold. For I wouldn't spare them, even at their own table, though the Pope himself sat next to them; I paid them out word for word I tell you! So help me God Almighty, were I to make my will and testament here and now there's never a word I owe them that isn't paid in full. I managed it so cleverly they found it best to give up; otherwise we'd never have had any rest. He could look like a raging lion but he wouldn't get his satisfaction. Then I'd say, "Darling, look at Wilkin, our sheep! How tame he is! Come to me, sweetheart, let me kiss your cheek! You should be meek and patient too, and have a gentle scrupulous conscience yourself, since you keep on preaching about Job's patience. Be patient always; practise what you preach, for if you don't we'll certainly teach you how much better it is to have peace in the house. No doubt one of us must knuckle under; and since a man is more rational than a woman is, you ought to be the one to give way. What makes you groan and moan so? Is it just that you want my cunt all for yourself? Why, take it all, have the lot! By St Peter, how you love it! Were I to sell my pretty puss I could go dressed as fresh as a rose, but I'll save it just for you. Heaven knows, you're to blame; I'm only telling you the truth."*

'That's how our arguments used to go. Now I'll speak of my fourth husband.

'My fourth husband was a rake, that's to say he kept a mistress; and I was young and turbulent, strong, stubborn, and gay as a lark. When I'd drunk a glass of sweet wine, O I'd dance to the *lute and sing like a nightingale! That filthy ruffian Metellius, the pig who beat his wife to death because she drank wine, wouldn't have deterred me from drinking if I'd been his wife! And after wine I'm driven to thinking about Venus, for as sure as cold engenders hail a lickerish tail goes with a lickerish mouth. Fill a woman with wine and her defences are down, as lechers know by experience!*

'But, Lord Christ! When it all comes back to me, and I recall my youth and gaiety, it tickles me to the roots of my heart. To this day it does my heart good that in my time I've had my fling. But age, alas! that cankers everything, has stripped me of my beauty and go. Goodbye, let them go, and the devil go with them! What's left to say? The flour's all gone, and now I must sell the bran as best I may. Even so I mean to rejoice! Now I will tell about my fourth husband.

'I was saying it rankled my heart that he took delight in any other woman. But, by God and St Joce, he was paid in full! I made him a cross from the same wood. Not sluttishly, and not with my body; but I certainly made eyes at other folk till I had him stewing in his own juice with rage and jealousy! By God! I was his purgatory on earth; may his soul be in paradise now! For the Lord knows he sat and bawled often enough when the shoe pinched. No one, only God and he, knew how sorely or in how many ways I tormented him. He died when I came back from Jerusalem and now lies buried in the chancel under the rood-beam; though his tomb is nothing like that elaborate sepulchre of Darius, so subtly carved by Apelles. It would have been a waste to give him a rich burial. Farewell to him, God rest his soul! He's in his grave now, in his coffin.

'Now I'll tell of my fifth husband. I pray God keep his soul from hell! And yet to me he was the worst of the lot, as I can feel on every one of my ribs and always shall till my dying day. But in bed he was so gay and spirited, and whenever he wanted my pretty puss, how well he knew how to coax! Though he'd beaten every bone in my body he could win back my love in a moment. I think I loved him best because he was sparing of his love to me. We women have, and I'll tell you no lie, a queer fancy in these things. Whatever is not easily to be had we'll cry and beg for all day long. Forbid us a thing and we want it; pursue us, and we'll run away.

We aren't eager to set out all we have to sell; a big crowd at the market makes goods the dearer; if they're priced too cheap people think them worthless—as every wise woman knows.

'My fifth husband—may God bless his soul!—whom I took for love and not for money, was at one time an Oxford scholar; and he had left college and taken board and lodging with my best friend, who lived in our town. God keep her soul! Her name was Alison. As I live, she knew my heart and secret thoughts far better than our parish priest. I confided everything to her. Did my husband piss against a wall, I told her. Had he done a thing that could have cost him his life, I'd have told her, and another good woman, and my niece also, whom I loved; I'd have told them every one of his secrets. I did, often enough, God knows, and as often it made his face burn red with downright shame while he blamed himself for telling me his most private secrets.

'And it so happened one Lent (I was always calling on my friend, for I loved to have fun and to walk abroad in March and April and May, going from house to house to hear the different gossip) that Jankin the scholar, my friend Dame Alison and myself went into the fields. My husband was in London all that Lent; I had the more leisure to amuse myself, for seeing and being seen by the gay crowd. How could I know where or in what place my luck would turn? So I went to evening festivals, and processions, and pilgrimages, and weddings, and these miracle plays, and listened to sermons, dressed in my gay scarlet gowns. Trust me, no moth, worm, or insect had the chance to devour them, and why? They were well used.

'Now I'll tell what happened to me. I was saying we were walking in the fields, this scholar and I, and indeed we got on so well that I began to look ahead and spoke to him: I told him that if I were a widow he should marry me. Indeed—I don't speak out of conceit—I was never without foresight in the matter of marriage, as well as in other things. I wouldn't give a leek for the mettle of a mouse that has only one bolthole: for if that fails, it's all over.

'I made him believe he'd bewitched me—my mother taught me that trick. Also I said I'd dreamed of him the whole night long, and in the dream he tried to kill me where I lay; the bed was drenched in blood! Yet I hoped he'd bring me luck, for blood signifies gold, or so I'd been taught. And it was all lies; I dreamed

*nothing of the kind. But in this as in most other matters I was as
usual following my mother's teaching.*

'*But now, sirs, let me see—what was I going to say? Aha! I have
it again—I'd lost the thread.*

'*All the same, when my fourth husband was laid upon his bier
I wept and looked mournful, as wives should, for it's the custom;
and I covered my face with my kerchief. But as I was already
provided with another mate I promise you I cried but little.*

'*The next day my husband was carried to the church, followed
by the neighbours who came to mourn him. One of them was
Jankin, the scholar. So help me God, when I saw him follow the
bier I thought, what a fine clean pair of legs and feet! And I lost
my whole heart to him. I should think he was about twenty years
old; and I was forty, to tell the truth. But I had the itch for it still.
I was gap-toothed, but it suited me; I carried Saint Venus' birth-
mark. So help me God, I was a gay one; pretty and rich, and
young, and joyous; and truly, as my husbands told me, I had the
best whatnot that might be. Certainly Venus influences all my
feelings, Mars my courage; Venus gave me my desire and lecher-
ousness, Mars my sturdy boldness. Taurus was in the ascendant,
and Mars in it, when I was born. Alas, alas, that ever love was sin!
I followed my inclination always, guided by my stars; which made
me so that I never could deny my chamber of Venus to any likely
lad. Yet on my face I have the mark of Mars, and also in another
private place. As sure as God's my salvation I never used discretion
in love but followed my appetite always, let the man be dark or
fair or tall or short. So long as he pleased me I took no heed how
poor he was or what his rank might be.*

'*What else is there to say? Well, at the end of the month, this
handsome scholar, the debonair Jankin, had married me with all
due ceremony; and I gave him all the lands and rents that had
been given me beforetime. But I repented bitterly of it afterwards;
he would let me do nothing I wanted. By God! He once gave me
such a box on the ear for tearing a page out of his book that I went
deaf from the blow. I was stubborn as a lioness, with a real quar-
relsome tongue; and walk I would, as I did before, from house to
house, though he swore I shouldn't. And because of this he'd keep
lecturing and telling me old stories from Roman history, of how
one Simplicius Gallus left his wife and forsook her for ever, only*

because he saw her look out of the door one day without a hat on.
He told me about Whatsisname, another Roman, who also de-
serted his wife because she went to the midsummer games without
his knowing. And then he'd take his Bible and look up that
proverb of Ecclesiasticus which absolutely forbids a man to allow
his wife to gad about. Then, never fear, out he'd come with

> Whoever builds a house out of willows
> Or rides a blind horse over the fallows
> Or lets his wife run after saints' haloes
> Really deserves to be hung on a gallows.

But it was all for nothing; I didn't give a bean for his proverbs or
for his old saw; I wouldn't be reformed by him either. I can't bear
a man who tells me my faults; nor, Lord knows, can others be-
sides myself. It made him absolutely mad with rage at me; I
wouldn't give way at any point.

'And now, by St Thomas, I'll tell you the true story of why I
ripped a page out of his book, and made him hit me so hard that
I went deaf.

'He had a book he loved to read, and was always reading it from
morning to night: he called it Valerius and Theophrastus, *and*
was always chuckling over this book. There was also a book
written against Jovinian by a learned man who lived in Rome, a
cardinal called St Jerome; and books by Tertullian, Chrysippus,
Trotula, and Heloise, who was an abbess not far from Paris; also
the Parables of Solomon, *and Ovid's* Art of Love; *these and many*
another were all bound together in one volume. And night and
day it was his custom, whenever he had leisure or the time to
spare from other work, to read about wicked women in this book,
till he knew more legends and biographies of them than there are
good women in the Bible. For, make no mistake, it's an impossi-
bility that any scholar should speak good of women, except in the
case of the lives of female saints; certainly not any other sort of
woman! As the lion asked the fellow who showed him a picture
of a man killing a lion, "Who was the painter?" Tell me who!
By God, if women had written as many histories as these cloistered
scholars, they'd have recorded more wickedness on the part of men
than all the sons of Adam could ever put right. Scholars are chil-
dren of Mercury, women of Venus; and the two are at cross

purposes in all that they do. For Mercury loves wisdom and knowledge; Venus, revelry and extravagance. In astrology, the exaltation of one is the dejection of the other, owing to their different natures. Thus, when in the sign of Pisces, Mercury, Lord knows, is in dejection and Venus in exaltation; but Venus falls where Mercury is raised. Therefore a woman is never praised by a scholar. For when he's senile, and about as much use as an old boot at making love, then your scholar sits down and writes drivel about women being unable to keep their marriage vows.

'But to get back to the point, I was telling you how I was given a beating because of a book. One night Jankin, my husband, sat reading his book by the fire. First he read about Eve, whose wickedness brought all mankind to misery, so that Jesus Christ Himself, who redeemed us with His heart's blood, was slain. Here's a text that expressly says woman was the perdition of all mankind.

'Then he read to me how Samson lost his hair; his sweetheart cut it off with the shears while he slept, and through that betrayal he lost both his eyes.

'And then, forsooth, he read to me about Hercules and Dejanira, who was the cause of his setting himself on fire.

'He forgot none of the grief and trouble Socrates had with his two wives; how Xantippe threw piss over his head. The poor man sat there like a corpse, and wiped his head without daring to say more than this: "Before the thunder stops, down comes the rain!"

'And he savoured the wickedness of the story of Pasiphae, who was Queen of Crete—for shame, it's too gruesome; not another word about her horrible delights and desires!

'And it was with the greatest relish he read of Clytemnestra, who treacherously put her husband to death that she might satisfy her lust.

'As he related to me how Amphiarus came to lose his life at Thebes. My husband had a tale about his wife Eriphyle, who for the sake of a golden buckle secretly revealed to the Greeks the place where her husband had hidden himself; he got a short shrift at Thebes.

'He told me of Livia and Lucilia, both of whom put their husbands to death, the one for love and the other for hate. Livia poisoned her husband late one evening, because she hated him; while the concupiscent Lucilia loved her husband so much that,

in order he should think only of her, she gave him so strong an aphrodisiac he was dead before morning. Thus, one way or another, husbands have the worst of it.

'Next he told me how one Latimius grumbled to his friend Arrius about a tree that grew in his garden, on which, said he, his three wives had hanged themselves out of dudgeon. "My dear friend," answered Arrius, "give me a cutting from that wonderful tree, and I'll plant it in my own garden!"

'Of wives of later days he read how some murdered their own husbands in their beds and let their lovers have them while the corpse lay stretched all night upon the floor; how some drove nails through their husbands' brains while they slept, and so killed them; while others put poison in their drink. The heart cannot conceive the evil he spoke; and besides he knew more proverbs than the world has weeds and grass. "Better to live with a lion or a hideous dragon than with a woman given to scolding," said he. "Better to dwell in the corner of a housetop than with a brawling woman in a house; they are so wicked and contrary, they always hate what their husbands love," said he. "A woman casts off shame when she casts off her smock," said he, and furthermore, "A fair woman, unless she be chaste also, is like a gold ring in a sow's nose." Who could guess or imagine the pain that was in my heart, or the torment?

'And when I saw he'd never finish reading that accursed book but go on all night, suddenly I tore three pages out of it even as he read, and at the same time caught him such a blow on the cheek with my fist that it tumbled him over backwards into the fire. Then up he jumped like a wild beast and gave me such a punch on the head I lay for dead on the floor. And when he saw how still I lay he took fright and would have run off, if I hadn't come to at last. "O, have you killed me, you dirty thief?" I said. "Have you murdered me for my land? Yet before I die I'll kiss you." Then he came close and kneeled down gently beside me, saying, "Alison, my dearest love, so help me God I'll never strike you again. You've only yourself to blame for what I did. Forgive it me for mercy's sake!" But once again I hit him on the cheek and said, "You robber, that's on account! I can't speak any more, I'm dying!" But at last, after no end of grief and trouble, we made it up between us. He gave over to me the reins; I *had the governing of our house and land, and of his tongue and fist as well; and I made him burn his book on the spot. And from that moment when by winning mastery over him I'd got the upper hand, and he'd said, "My own true wife, do as you please as long as you live; look after your honour and my goods" —from that day we never had a quarrel. So help me God, there's not a woman from Denmark to the Indies who could have been kinder to him than I, or more true—and so was he to me. I pray to God who reigns in glory in His dear mercy to bless his soul. And now, if you'll listen, I'll tell my tale.'*

*When he had heard all this, the Friar laughed. 'Now, madam,'
said he, 'as I hope for bliss, that was a long preamble to a tale!'
But the Summoner cut in when he heard the Friar sing out. 'See
here!' cried the Summoner. 'God's arms! A friar's always butting
in. Look, fellows, these friars are just like flies, always falling
into other people's food and getting mixed up with all their
concerns. What do you mean, "perambulation"? What! Amble,
trot, or shut up and sit down! You're spoiling our fun like this.'*

*'So that's what you think, Master Summoner?' retorted the
Friar. 'Well, before I go, I give you my word I'll tell a tale or two
about a summoner that will set everyone here laughing.'*

*'Try it and see, Friar, and damn your eyes,' said the Summoner.
'And before I come to Sittingbourne I'm damned if I don't tell
two or three tales about friars that will leave you lamenting, for
I can see you're losing your temper.'*

*Our Host bellowed, 'Quiet! Shut up at once!' Then he said,
'Let the lady tell her story. You're behaving as if you'd had too
much ale to drink. Go on, madam, tell your tale; that would be
best.'*

*'I'm quite ready, sir,' said she, 'whenever you please; that is,
if I have permission from this good Friar.'*

'By all means, madam,' said he. 'Tell away, and I'll listen.'

THE
WIFE OF BATH'S
TALE

In the old days of King Arthur, whose renown is celebrated among the Britons, the whole land was filled with troops of fairies. The Elf-Queen and her joyous company danced many a time on many a green field. That was the old belief, I've read; I speak of many hundred years ago. But no one sees the fairies any more, for nowadays the prayers and overflowing Christian charity of limiters and other saintly friars, who go about every nook and corner of the country thick as motes in a sunbeam, blessing halls, chambers, kitchens, and bedrooms; cities, boroughs, castles, towers, and villages; barns, dairies, and cowsheds; have seen to it there are no fairies. Where elves used to go, there now walks the limiter himself morning and afternoon, saying his matins and holy offices as he goes about his district. And nowadays women can wander safely under every bush and tree; the only satyr they'll meet is a limiter, and all he'll do is take their honour.

Well, it so happened that in King Arthur's court there was a gay young knight; and one day he was riding home from hawking by the river when he chanced to see a maiden walking all by herself; and in spite of all she could do he took her maidenhood from her by main force. This outrage made a great stir. There was much petitioning of King Arthur, till by due course of law the knight was condemned to death. He would have had his head struck off (such, apparently, was the law in those days) had not the queen and many other ladies kept importuning the king for mercy, till at last he granted him his life and handed him over to the queen that she might decide whether to slay or spare him, just as she pleased.

The queen gave the king her heartfelt thanks, and a day or two later found opportunity to speak to the knight: 'You are still in a very serious position,' said she, 'for your life is not yet safe. But I will grant you your life if you can tell me what it is that women most desire. Take care! Take care! Keep your neckbone from the steel! Still, if you cannot give the answer at once,

I shall grant you leave to go away for a twelvemonth and a day and find a satisfactory answer to this question. And before you go I must have assurance that you will yield yourself up in this court.'

Sad was the knight, and sorrowfully he sighed; however, he had no other choice. At last he decided to go away and return at the end of the year with whatever answer God might provide him. So he took his leave and set off.

He visited every house and all places where he thought he might have the luck to learn what it is that women love most; but in no country could he find two people who agreed with one another on the subject.

Some said women love riches best; some said honour; some said merry-making; some said rich attire; some, that it was the pleasures of the bed, and being often widowed and remarried. Some said our hearts are most content when we are indulged and flattered, which I must admit is very near the truth. A man can win us best by flattery; by attentiveness and being made a fuss of we are all of us ensnared.

And some said we love best to be free to do just as we please, and have no one to criticize our faults but tell us instead we're sensible and not in the least silly; for in all conscience there's not one of us who won't kick when scratched on a sore spot by somebody telling the truth. Try it and see; no matter how wicked we may be inside, we always wish to be thought virtuous and wise.

Yet others say we take great delight in being thought discreet, dependable and firm of purpose, incapable of betraying anything we are told. But that idea isn't worth a rake-handle. For heaven's sake, we women can keep nothing hidden. Witness Midas—would you like to hear the story?

Ovid, among other little matters, says that Midas had two asses' ears growing on his head under his long hair, a blemish which he carefully hid from view as best as he could; only his wife knew about it. He loved her above all things, and trusted her too; and he begged her to tell no living creature about his disfigurement. Oh no, she swore, not for the whole world would she do such wrong and injury as sully her husband's name; if only for her own shame's sake she wouldn't tell. But nonetheless she thought she'd die if she kept a secret for so long; it seemed to swell so painfully against her heart she felt she must speak or burst. And since she didn't dare tell it to anyone she ran to a marsh near by—her heart on fire till she got there—and laid her mouth against the water like a bittern booming in the mud: 'Water, don't betray me with your noise,' said she, 'I'm telling it to you and no one else—my husband has two long asses' ears! Now it's out I feel ever so much better. I couldn't have held it in much longer, that's certain.' This shows you we cannot keep anything secret; we can hold on for a while, but it must out. If you want to hear the rest of the tale, read Ovid; you'll find it all there.

But to get back to the knight in my story. When he saw that he couldn't discover it—what women love most, I mean—his heart was heavy in his breast. But he set off home, for he might not stay; the day had come when he must turn homeward. And as he went gloomily upon his way he happened to ride by the edge of a forest, where he saw four-and-twenty ladies and more dancing in a ring. Eagerly he drew nearer, hoping to learn some wisdom. But—presto! before he had quite reached them the dancers vanished he knew not where. Save for an old woman sitting upon the green he could see no living creature; and she was the ugliest person you could imagine. This old woman got up at the knight's approach and said, 'Sir Knight, there's no road on from here. Tell me what it is you seek; that may be best, perhaps; we old folk know a great many things,' said she.

'Good mother,' the knight replied, 'the truth is I am as good as dead unless I can say what it is that women most desire. If you could tell me that, I'd reward you well.'

'Put your hand in mine and pledge me your word that you will do the first thing I ask of you if it lies in your power,' said she, 'and before night I shall tell you what it is.'

'Agreed,' said the knight, 'I pledge you my word.'

'Then,' said she, 'I dare aver your life is safe; for I'll stake my own that the queen will say as I do. Show me the proudest of them all wearing her coverchief or jewelled cap and see if she dares deny what I shall tell you. Now let us set off without more talk.' Then she whispered her message in his ear, telling him to cheer up and be no more afraid.

When they arrived at the court the knight announced that according to his promise he had kept his day, and was ready with his answer. Many a noble matron, many a maid, and many a widow also (for they have so much wisdom) were there assembled to hear his answer, with the queen herself sitting in the chair of justice. Then the knight was bidden to appear.

All were commanded to be silent while the knight told the court what it is that earthly women love the best. The knight, far from standing dumb as an ox, gave his answer at once. He spoke in ringing tones so that the whole court heard it.

'My liege lady,' he began, 'in general women wish to have sovereignty over their husbands as well as their lovers and to be in authority over them. Though I should answer for it with my life, this, I say, is your greatest desire. Do as you please: I am here at your mercy.' Not a matron, maid, or widow in the whole court contradicted what he had said: all declared he deserved to keep his life. And at that the old woman the knight had seen sitting on the green jumped up. 'Mercy, sovereign lady!' she cried. 'See that justice is done to me before your court disperses. I taught the knight that answer, for which he pledged me his word to perform the first thing I asked of him if it lay in his power. And so, Sir Knight, I pray you before all the court,' she said, 'to take me for your wife; for well you know I have saved you from death. If what I say is false, deny it upon oath.'

'Alas! Alas!' replied the knight. 'I know only too well that I made that promise. For the love of God, make some other request—take all my goods but leave me my body.'

'No indeed,' said she. 'A curse on us both if I do! Old, poor, and ugly as I am, for all the gold and ore that's buried under the earth or lies above it, I wouldn't be anything but your wife and your lover too.'

'My lover!' cried he, 'you mean my damnation! Alas that ever one of my family should be so vilely misallied!'

But nothing would avail. In the end he was compelled to agree to marry her and take the old woman to his bed.

Now perhaps some of you will say that I don't bother to describe all the preparations and rejoicing that went on at the wedding out of laziness; but to that I'll give a short answer: there was no rejoicing and no wedding-feast whatsoever, nothing but grief and gloom. For he married her secretly the next morning, and hid himself like an owl for the rest of the day; he was so miserable at the ugliness of his wife.

The knight suffered much anguish of mind when he was brought to bed with his wife. He tossed and twisted back and forth; and all the while his aged wife lay there smiling. Then she said, 'Bless us, dear husband! Does every knight behave like this with his wife? Is this the custom of King Arthur's court? Are all his knights so standoffish? I'm your wife as well as your sweetheart; she who saved your life. Truly, up to now I haven't done you a wrong. So why behave to me like this on our first night? You're like a man out of his wits. What have I done wrong? For God's love, tell me, and I'll put it right if I can.'

'Put it right!' exclaimed the knight. 'Alas! It can never, never be put right. You're hideous, and old, and low-born besides. It's little wonder if I twist and turn. I wish to God my heart would burst.'

Said she, 'Is that the reason for your distress?'

'Indeed it is and no wonder,' he replied.

'Now, sir,' she retorted, 'I could set all this right in less than three days if I wanted to, so you might as well behave nicely to me.

'But since you speak of the kind of nobility that's derived from ancient possessions, and think people should be noblemen on that account—that kind of pride's not worth a rap. The man who's always virtuous, in public and private, and ever strives to perform as many noble acts as he can—take him for the greatest nobleman. Christ wishes us to claim our nobility for Him, not from our fathers on account of their ancestral wealth; for though they may give us all their heritage—for which we claim to be high-born—they can by no manner of means bequeath to us their virtuous way of life, that alone entitles them to be called noblemen, and bids us follow their example.

'On this subject Dante, the wise Florentine poet, is particularly eloquent. Dante's verses go like this:

> *It's rarely man's excellence rises by*
> *The branches, because God in His goodness*
> *Desires us to claim from Him nobility.*

For we can claim nothing from our ancestors except temporal things, which may be hurtful and injurious. And everyone knows as well as I do that if nobility were implanted by nature in any particular family, so that the whole line inherited it, then they would never cease to perform noble deeds in private and in public; they would be incapable of evil-doing and vice.

'Take fire, carry it to the darkest house between here and Mount Caucasus, then shut the doors and leave it; yet the fire will burn and blaze as brightly as if twenty thousand people were there to watch: that fire, I'll stake my life, will continue to perform its natural function until it dies.

'From this it may be easily seen that nobility is not dependent on possessions, since people do not always conform to pattern, while fire is always fire. For God knows one often enough sees a lord's son behave viciously and shamefully. Whoever wants to be honoured for his nobility because he was born of a noble family with noble and virtuous ancestors is not noble, though he be a duke or earl, if he does not himself perform noble deeds or follow the noble example of his dead ancestors; for it's a scoundrel's wrong and vicious actions that make the churl. Nobility is no more than the renown of your ancestors; they won it for their great goodness—which has nothing to do with you; your nobility comes from God alone. Thus our true nobility comes by grace; it is by no means assigned to us along with our worldly position.

'Think how noble (as Valerius says) was that Tullius Hostilius who rose from poverty to the highest rank. Read Seneca, and Boethius as well; there you will find it explicitly stated that a nobleman is undoubtedly a man who does noble deeds. And therefore, my dear husband, I conclude that although my ancestors might have been of humble birth, yet Almighty God may grant me the grace to live in virtue, as I hope He will. Only when I begin to eschew evil and live in virtue am I noble.

'As for the poverty you reproach me with, the Lord on high (in Whom we believe) chose to live a life of voluntary poverty. Surely it's plain to every man, woman and child that Jesus, the King of Heaven, would never have chosen to lead a wicked kind of life. Poverty is honourable when it's cheerfully accepted, as Seneca and other learned men will tell you. Whoever is contented in his poverty I hold to be rich though he have no shirt to his back. He who covets is a poor man, because he wants what he cannot get; but he who has nothing and covets nothing is rich, though you may think him no more than a peasant. Juvenal has a happy saying about poverty: "When a poor man makes a journey he can laugh at thieves." I'd say poverty is a hateful good; it's a great incentive to busy endeavour, and a great promoter of wisdom in those who accept it with patience. Though it may seem hard to bear, poverty is a kind of riches, one which no one will try to take away from you. If a man be humble, poverty generally brings him to a knowledge of God and of himself. Poverty is a spyglass, it seems to me, through which one can see one's true friends. And therefore, sir, since I do not offend you in this, you can no longer reproach me for my poverty.

'Next, sir, you reproach me for being old. But indeed, sir, even if there were no authority for it in books, honourable gentlemen like yourself say that people should respect an old man, and call him 'Sir' out of good manners; I could find authorities for this, I imagine.

'Then you say I am old and ugly; but on the other hand you've no fear of being made a cuckold; for, as I live, dirt and age are the best guardians of chastity. But I know what delights you and I'll satisfy your grosser appetites.

'Now choose,' said she. 'Choose one of two things: either to have me old and ugly for the rest of my life, but a faithful, obedient wife; or else to have me young and fair, and take your chance with all the men who will resort because of me to your house—or to some other place perhaps! The choice is yours, whichever you please.'

The knight thought it over, sighing heavily the while; and at last he made this reply:

'My lady and my love, and my dearest wife, I trust myself to your wise guidance; do you yourself choose whichever may be the most pleasing and honourable for both of us. I care not which of the two you choose, for whatever pleases you will satisfy me.'

'Then have I gained the mastery over you,' cried she, 'since I may choose and rule as I wish?'

'Indeed, yes,' said he, 'it's best, I think.'

'Kiss me,' she said, 'we'll not quarrel any more; for upon my honour, to you I shall be both—I mean I shall be beautiful as well as good. I pray God to send me madness and death if I am not as good and true a wife to you as ever there was since the world began. And tomorrow morning, if I be not as fair to see as any lady, queen, or empress from east to west, then dispose of my life as you please. Lift up the curtain and look.'

And when the knight saw that it was really so, that she was as young as she was lovely, he caught her up in his arms for joy; his heart was bathed in a bath of bliss. He kissed her a thousand times in a row, and she obeyed him in everything that could delight or give him pleasure.

And thus they lived in perfect joy for the rest of their lives. And may Jesus Christ send us husbands who are submissive, and young, and spirited in bed; and may He send us grace to outlive those we marry; and also I pray Jesus to shorten the days of those who'll not be governed by their wives; and as for old, bad-tempered, pennypinching skinflints, God's plague upon them!

That worthy Limiter, the good Friar, kept casting black looks in the direction of the Summoner. For decency's sake he had so far refrained from abuse, but at length he said to the Wife of Bath: 'God bless you, Madam! Believe me, you have here touched upon a very difficult subject of debate in the Schools. I must say you've made a number of excellent points; but, Madam, there's no need to discuss other than the very lightest topics as we ride on our way. For heaven's sake let's leave books and authorities to the preachers and schools of divinity. But if it would please the company, I'll tell you a good story about a summoner—Lord knows you have only to hear the name to know no good may be said of them—I pray that none of you take offence! A summoner is a fellow who runs around with summonses for fornication and gets beaten up at every town's end.'

Here our Host cut in: 'Ah, sir, a man of your position ought to be a little more civil and polite. We'll have no quarrelling in company! Tell your story, and leave the Summoner alone.'

'No matter,' said the Summoner; 'let him say to me whatever he likes; when my turn comes, by God! I'll pay him out every farthing—I'll show him what an honourable thing it is to be a wheedling Limiter: I'll tell him what kind of a job he has, no fear.'

'Be quiet!' answered our Host, 'enough of this!' Then he turned to the Friar, saying, 'My dear sir, begin your tale.'

THE FRIAR'S TALE

In my part of the world there once lived an archdeacon, a man of high position and a stern meter-out of penalties for witchcraft, fornication, slander, adultery, robbing churches, breaches of wills and contracts, neglect of the sacraments, simony and usury, as well as many other kinds of offence we need not now go into. To be sure, he came down heaviest upon whoremongers—if they were caught he made them squeal; and those who hadn't paid up their tithes he'd haul over the coals as soon as any person complained of them; he never missed the chance of a fine. If tithes and offerings were too small he'd make the people sing out, for before the bishop hooked them they were put in the archdeacon's book, when, being under his jurisdiction, he had power to visit them with punishment. He had a summoner ready to his hand —there was no slyer lad in the country, for he'd set up a cunning network of spies who kept him well informed of anything he might turn to advantage. He'd excuse a whoremonger or two if they'd lead him to a couple of dozen more. No matter if it drives the Summoner here madder than a March hare, I'll not skimp my account of his knavery—we friars are out of their power, they've no jurisdiction over us and never will have as long as they live—

'St Peter! So are the women of the stews out of our charge!' cried the Summoner.

'Shut up and be damned to you!' shouted our Host. 'Let him get on with his story. Go on, my dear sir, leave nothing out; never mind the Summoner's railing.'

This lying thief, this summoner (the Friar continued), had whores always at his beck and call, like lures for a hawk, who told him all the secrets they came across, for theirs was no new friendship. They were his private spies, and he made a good profit for himself thereby; his master did not always know how much he got. He could summon without warrant some illiterate yokel on pain of excommunication, who'd be only too glad to fill his pockets or stand him big dinners at the ale-house. Judas was a thief and had the bag: just such a thief was he, for his master got less than half his dues. Let me do him justice: he was a thief, a pimp, a summoner! And he had whores in his pay, so whether it was the Reverend Robert or the Reverend Hugh that lay with them, or Jack, or Ralph or whoever, they brought it to his ears. He had an understanding with the girl—he'd fetch a forged warrant and summon both before the chapter, when he'd fleece the man and let the girl go. Then he'd say, 'Friend, for your sake I'll strike her name off our black list; you needn't trouble yourself further about this affair. I'm your friend; I'll do what I can for you.' Indeed he knew more swindles than it's possible to tell, even if I took two years. No hunting dog is better at picking out a wounded deer than this summoner at winding some sly whoremonger, some adulterer or fancy woman. And as this accounted for the best part of his income he gave his whole mind to it.

Well, one day it so fell out that this summoner, on the prowl as usual, rode out to summons some old bag, a widow, with the idea of robbing her on some pretence or other; when he happened to see, riding ahead of him by the edge of a forest, a gaily-dressed yeoman carrying a bow with sharp bright arrows. He wore a short green coat and on his head a hat with a black border.

'Greetings,' said the summoner, 'well met, sir!'

'Welcome to you and all good men,' replied the other. 'Where are you going in the greenwoods? Do you ride far today?'

'No,' answered the summoner, 'I'm only going to ride to a place near by to collect a rent owning to my master.'

'Then you're a bailiff?'

'Yes,' said he, for he didn't dare admit he was a summoner because of the very shame and stink of the name.

'Lord bless you!' said the yeoman. 'My dear fellow, I'm a bailiff myself. I'd like to make your acquaintance as I'm a stranger in these parts; your friendship too, if you will. I've gold and silver laid away; if ever you happen to visit our shire I'll put it at your disposal, just as much of it as you please.'

'A thousand thanks, upon my word!' cried the summoner. They both shook hands and pledged themselves to be sworn brothers for life. Then they rode on talking gaily.

This summoner was as full of chatter as a butcher-bird of spite; he was always asking questions. 'Where is it that you live, brother,' he asked, 'in case I should look you up one day?' And the yeoman mildly replied, 'Far in the north country, my friend, where I hope I'll see you some time. I'll give you such careful directions before we part that you'll never miss the house.'

'Well, brother,' said the summoner, 'while we ride along I'd like to ask you to teach me some of your dodges, and tell me frankly how to make the most I can out of my job, since you're a bailiff like myself. Don't let any scruples of conscience hold you back—as one friend to another, tell me how you make out.'

'Well, upon my word, my dear fellow,' he replied, 'if I am to give you a faithful account, my wages are small and scanty enough; my master's a tight man and a hard, and my job's pretty onerous; so I make my living by extortions. In fact I take anything I'm given—at any rate, by hook or crook, I manage to cover expenses from one year to the next. And frankly, that's the best I can say.'

'Well, it's just the same with me, really,' said the summoner. 'God knows I'm ready to take what I can, unless it's too hot or too heavy! I've no scruples at all about what I can get from a private deal on the side. If it weren't for my extortions I wouldn't be able to live. I don't mention such harmless dodges at confession. I've no conscience whatever, nor bowels of compassion —devil take the whole pack of father-confessors! By God and St James, we are well met! But now, dear brother, tell me your name,' said the summoner. As he spoke the yeoman began to smile a little.

'My friend,' said he, 'do you really want me to tell you? I am a fiend; my dwelling is in Hell, and I'm riding here on business, to see whether people will give me anything. My pickings are my whole revenue. It seems you're riding on the same errand

—to make a profit, never mind how; it's the same with me, for at this very moment I'd ride to the end of the world to catch my prey.'

'Ah! said the summoner. 'Bless us, what are you saying? I really thought you were a yeoman. You're formed like a man, as I am; have you then a fixed shape of your own in Hell, where you're in your natural state?'

'No indeed, we have none there,' replied the other, 'but we can adopt one when we like, or else make you think we have forms, sometimes like men, sometimes like apes; I can even go about like an angel. There's nothing wonderful in it; any wretched conjurer can deceive you. And, excuse me, I know a bit more about the technique than they do.'

'Why do you go around in different shapes instead of the same one all the time?' asked the summoner.

'Because we want to take such forms as best enable us to catch our prey,' replied the other.

'What makes you go to all this trouble?'

'Very many reasons indeed, good Master Summoner,' said the fiend, 'but there's a time for everything: the day is short, it's past nine already, and as yet I've taken nothing today. If you don't mind I'll concentrate on business instead of discussing our talents. Anyway, dear brother, your wits are too scant to understand, even if I explained them to you. But since you ask why we take all this trouble, it's because we are sometimes God's instruments and, when it pleases Him, a means of carrying out His commands upon His creatures in various modes and forms. It's true we have no power without Him, should He wish to oppose us. Sometimes, at our asking, we are given leave to vex the body but not the soul—for example Job, whom we tormented; and sometimes we have power over both, that's to say over the soul as well as the body. At other times we're allowed to seek out a man to vex his soul, though not his body. All's for the best—if he withstands our temptation that's one cause of his salvation, even if it's our aim to catch him, not that he should be saved. Sometimes we are people's servants, as in the case of the archbishop of St Dunstan—I myself was a servant to the Apostles.'

'Now tell me truly,' asked the summoner, 'do you always

make new bodies for yourselves out of the elements like this?'

'No,' replied the fiend, 'we often simulate them; sometimes we take on the bodies of the dead in many various ways and speak as fluently and reasonably as Samuel to the Witch of Endor—though some people say it wasn't Samuel; but I've no time for your theology. But joking apart, I warn you of one thing—at all events you'll find out what our real shape is. Hereafter, my dear fellow, you'll come to a place where you'll have no need to learn from me. Your own experience will enable you to lecture on the subject like a professor, better than Virgil when he was alive, or Dante either. Now let's ride on quickly, for I'd like to keep company with you till such time as you forsake me.'

'That shall never happen!' cried the summoner. 'I'm a yeoman, and pretty widely known; I always keep my word, as in this case—were you Satan himself I'd keep faith with my sworn brother, since in this matter each of us has sworn to be true brothers and go about our business in partnership. Take your share of whatever people give you and I'll take mine; in this way we'll both make a living. And if either of us earns more than the other, let him be honest and share it with his friend.'

'Agreed,' said the devil. 'There's my word on it.' And with that they rode on their way. But just at the entrance of the village where the summoner meant to go they saw a carter driving a cartload of hay. The road being deep in mud, the cart was stuck; the carter was laying about him and yelling like mad: 'Hup, Brock! Hup, Scot! Never mind the stones! The fiend fetch you, hide and all as you were born! You've given me enough trouble—devil take the lot, horse, cart and hay!'

Said the summoner, 'We're going to have some fun here.' And he covertly drew near the fiend as if he had noticed nothing, whispering in his ear: 'Hear that, brother, just listen to that! Didn't you hear what the carter said? Take it now, he's given it to you—hay and cart and his three nags thrown in.'

'Lord, no, not a bit of it,' said the devil. 'Trust me, that's not what he means. Ask him yourself if you don't believe me—or wait a minute, and you'll see.'

The carter gave the horses' cruppers a thwack and they began to strain and heave. 'Hup now! Jesus bless you and all His handiwork, great and small! Well tugged, old grey! That's my boy!

God and St Loy save and keep you! Thank God my cart's out of the mud.'

'There, brother,' said the fiend, 'what did I tell you? My dear fellow, that just shows you: the yokel said one thing but meant another. Let's get on with our journey—there's no rake-off here for me.'

When they were a little way out of the town the summoner whispered to his friend, 'Brother, there's an old bag who lives here who'd almost as soon cut her throat as give up a penny of her goods. I mean to get twelve pence out of her even if it should drive her out of her wits—else I'll summons her to our court, though God knows she hasn't any vices so far as I'm aware. But as it looks as though you can't earn your keep in these parts, watch me and I'll show you.'

The summoner knocked upon the widow's door. 'Come out, you old harridan!' he shouted, 'I bet you've got some priest or friar in there with you!'

'Who's knocking?' exclaimed the woman. 'Benedicite! God save you, sir! What might your honour be wanting?'

Said the summoner, 'Here's a writ of summons: on pain of excommunication see that you present yourself before the arch-deacon tomorrow to answer for certain matters to the court.'

'Lord, O Lord,' cried she, 'may Christ Jesus, King of Kings help me, for I can't! I've been sick this many a day; I just can't go so far! It would be the death of me—my side pricks me so! May I not have a copy of the writ, good Master Summoner, and let my attorney answer whatever I'm accused of?'

'Very well,' replied the summoner, 'pay up then—let's see—twelve pence will do—and I'll acquit you. I'm not making much out of this—my master takes the profit, not me. Get on with it, I'm in a hurry to be off—give me twelve pence! I can't stay here all day.'

'Twelve pence!' she cried. 'May Our Lady Saint Mary deliver me from trouble and sin! Were you to give me the whole wide world, I haven't got twelve pence in my pocket. Can't you see I'm old and poor? Show charity to a poor wretch like me!'

'Never!' said the summoner, 'though it should ruin you. The foul fiend fetch me if I let you off!'

'Alas!' she cried, 'God knows I've done no wrong.'

'Pay up, or by the sweet Saint Anne I'll carry off your new frying-pan to pay that old debt you owe me! I paid your fine to the court that time you made a cuckold of your husband.'

'You lie!' cried she, 'by my salvation, up till now I've never been summoned to your court in all my life—neither as wife nor widow! Nor has my body ever been anything but faithful! To the black hulking devil I give you—you and my frying-pan!'

When the devil heard her cursing on her knees like this he said, 'Come now, good Mother Mabel, do you really mean what you say?'

'The devil fetch him before he dies, pan and all, if he doesn't think better of it,' said she.

'Not likely, you old cow,' cried the summoner, 'I've no mind to repent for anything I've had of you—I'd sooner take your smock and every last stitch from your back!'

'Now take it easy, brother,' said the devil. 'Your body and this frying-pan are mine by right; and tonight you're coming along with me to Hell, where you'll learn more about our secrets than any doctor of divinity.' And with that the foul fiend grabbed hold of him; body and soul, off he went with the devil to take the place assigned to summoners. And may God, who made mankind after His image, guide and protect us one and all and grant that summoners become good men!

And, ladies and gentlemen (continued the Friar) if this summoner here would give me time I could have told you, on the authority of Christ, St Paul, St John and many others of our teachers, of such frightful agonies as would strike terror to your hearts—though no tongue may describe them even if I took a thousand years telling you of the torments of that cursed house of Hell. But, to save us from that cursed place, watch and pray Jesus of His mercy to guard you from the tempter Satan. Listen to this proverb, and reflect: 'The lion lies ever in wait to slay the innocent if he can.' Always keep your hearts prepared to withstand the fiend who means to make you his thrall and bond-slave. He is not permitted to try you beyond your strength, for Christ will be your champion and your knight. And pray that these summoners repent of their misdeeds before the Devil gets hold of them.

The Summoner stood up in his stirrups, wild with rage at the Friar, and shaking like an aspen leaf in his anger.

'Gentlemen,' said he, 'I ask only one favour: now that you've heard the lies of this two-faced Friar I beg you to be good enough to allow me to tell a tale of my own. The Friar boasts he knows all about Hell—and God knows it's not to be wondered at, for there's little to choose between friars and fiends. Lord bless us, you must often enough have heard the story about the friar who had a vision in which his soul was snatched off to Hell; and when an angel took him round to show him all the torments he didn't see a single friar in the whole place, though he saw plenty of other folk in trouble. So the friar said to the angel: "Tell me, sir, have friars so much grace that none of them ever come here?" "Far from it," said the angel, "there are millions of them!" And he took him down to see Satan. "As you see, Satan has a tail bigger than the mainsail of a carrack," said he. "You there, Satan! Hold up your tail and show us your arse: let the friar see where friars nest in Hell!" The next moment, like a swarm of bees from a hive, a troop of twenty thousand friars came scurrying out of the devil's arse and swarmed all over Hell before returning as fast as they could, every single one of them creeping back into the devil's arsehole; when he clapped his tail upon them and lay still. When the friar had seen enough of the torments of this dreadful place, God in His mercy restored his soul to his body, and he awoke. Yet even then he quaked with terror, for he couldn't get out of his mind that natural home of all his tribe, the devil's bum. God save you all except this damned Friar! And so I'll end my prologue.'

THE
SUMMONER'S
TALE

Ladies and gentlemen, I believe there is in Yorkshire a marshy region called Holderness, where there was a Limiter who went round preaching—and begging too, no doubt. Now one day it happened that this friar had preached in a church in his usual style. In his sermon he particularly exhorted the people above all to buy masses for the dead, and for the glory of God to give the wherewithal to build churches where divine service is honoured; not where it's swallowed up and wasted, nor where there's no need to give—the beneficed clergy for example, who (thanks be to God!) are able to live in ease and plenty. 'Masses for the dead rescue the souls of your friends, both young and old, from Purgatory—indeed they do, even when hastily run through; not that a priest is to be thought frivolous and pleasure-loving because he only sings one Mass a day. O deliver those poor souls apace! How terrible to bake and burn, clawed with flesh-hooks, spitted upon an awl! Make haste, make haste, for Jesus' sake!' And when he'd made all his points, the friar gave the benediction and went his way.

When the folk in church had given him what they thought proper he set off without waiting another minute. He went poking and prying round the houses, with his bag and tipped staff held high, begging for flour, cheese, or a little corn. His companion had a staff with a horn tip, a pair of ivory writing-tablets and an elegantly-polished stylus, and stood there writing down the names of everyone who gave anything, as if to guarantee he'd pray for them. 'Give us a bushel of wheat, or malt, or rye, or just a bun or a bit of cheese, or whatever you like—it's not for us to choose; a halfpenny, or a penny for Mass; or give us a bit of your brawn if you've got some; a piece of your blanket, sweet madam, dearest sister—look! I'm writing down your name—bacon, or beef, whatever you can find.'

A sturdy serving-lad who looked after the guests at their hostel always followed behind, carrying a bag; and whatever they were given, he slung it on his back. Once outside the door he'd scrape out every one of the names he'd just written on the tablets; he served them up nothing but fables and claptrap—

'There you lie, you Summoner!' cried the Friar. 'Sweet Mother of Christ, be quiet!' shouted our Host. 'Get on with your story and leave out nothing.' 'Trust me, I won't,' said the Summoner.

So he went along from house to house, till he reached one where he used to be better entertained than in any of the others. The master of the house, the owner of the place, lay sick and bedridden upon a low couch. *Deus hic!* Good day, friend Thomas,' said the friar in a polite, gentle voice. 'God reward you, Thomas! How many happy times I've had on this bench; many's the splendid meal I've eaten here.' He shooed the cat from the bench and put down his stick, hat and bag, and settled down comfortably. (His companion had gone off into town with his serving-lad, to the hostelry where he meant to spend the night.)

'Dear master,' said the sick man, 'how have you been since the beginning of March? I've not seen you for a fortnight or more.'

'God knows I've been working cruelly hard,' replied he. 'I've been offering up many precious prayers specially for your salvation, and for our other friends, God bless them! I've been to Mass at your church today, and preached a sermon to the best of my modest powers; it didn't altogether follow the text of Holy Writ, which I imagine you'd find too hard: that's why I have to interpret it all for you. Interpretation is a splendid thing to be sure. "The letter killeth," as we scholars say. I was teaching them to be charitable and spend their money judiciously. And I saw your good lady there—now, where is she?'

'I expect she's outside in the garden,' said the man. 'She'll come in presently.'

'Ah, master, welcome to you, by St John!' cried his wife. 'I hope you're keeping well?'

The friar rose gallantly to his feet and gave her a hug; sweetly he kissed her, chirruping like a sparrow with his lips. 'Never better, madam! Your servant in all things—God be thanked, who gave you soul and life! God bless me, I saw no prettier woman in church today!'

'Well, may God mend my blemishes,' said she. 'In any case you're most welcome, that's a fact!'

'A thousand thanks, madam; it's what I've always found. But if you'd be good enough to excuse me—don't put yourself out, I beg—I'd like to have a little talk with Thomas. These curates are so negligent and slow when it comes to delicate examination of the conscience in confessional—but preaching is my forte, as well as the study of the words of St Peter and St Paul. I go about fishing for Christian souls to render Christ Jesus his proper dues; my whole aim is to spread His gospel.'

'Then, if you don't mind, dear sir,' said she, 'give him a real scolding; for by the Holy Trinity he's as cross as a bear, though he has everything he can possibly want. Even though I cover him up at night and keep him warm, and put my arm or leg over him, he only grunts like the pig in our sty. That's all the fun I get out of him; there's no pleasing him at all.'

'O Thomas, *je vous dis,* Thomas! Thomas! That's the devil at work; this must be put right! Anger is one thing that Almighty God forbade; I shall have to say a word or two about it.'

'Well, sir,' said the woman, 'before I leave, what would you like for dinner? I'm just about to see to it.'

'Well, madam,' said he, *'je vous dis sans doute* a simple meal with you would be enough—if I could have a little chicken-liver, and just the thinnest slice of your soft bread, and after that—only you won't kill any animal on my account, I hope—a roast pig's head. I need but little sustenance—my spirit draws its nourishment from the Bible. This poor body is so inured to waking and watching that my stomach is destroyed—dear madam, I beg you not to take it amiss if I confide in you so frankly—by the Lord, I assure you there aren't many people I'd tell these things.'

'O sir,' said she, 'just one word with you before I go. In these last two weeks, soon after you left town, my child died.'

'I saw his death in a revelation while I was in our dormitory at home,' replied the friar. 'As God is my judge, I'll go so far as to say that in my vision I saw him born into bliss less than half an hour after his death. So did our sacristan and infirmarian, who have been true friars these fifty years—they've just celebrated their jubilee (God be thanked for His gifts!) and may now walk unaccompanied when they go outside the friary. And I arose, and so did the rest of the convent, without any noise or clatter of bells; the tears were trickling down my cheek, and we sang the *Te Deum* only—save that I offered up a prayer to Christ to thank Him for His revelation. Believe me, dear sir, dear madam, our prayers are more effectual than those of the laity—even kings—and we see more of Christ's secrets. We live in poverty and abstinence while ordinary folk live well and spend extravagant sums on food, drink and unclean delights. We disdain all the pleasures of this world. Dives and Lazarus led different lives, and as a result won different rewards. Whoever would pray must fast and keep himself pure: fatten the soul but keep the body lean. We do as the Apostle says—mere food and clothing is enough for us, be they never so poor. The fasting and purity of us friars makes Christ accept our orisons.

'Remember, Moses fasted forty days and nights before Almighty God spoke with him on the mountain in Sinai. It was with an empty belly, having fasted for many a day, he received the Law written with God's finger. As you well know, Elijah fasted and meditated upon Mount Horeb long before he had speech with God, the healer of our souls.

'Aaron, who was in charge of the Temple and all the other priests, would never on any account drink anything intoxicating when they had to go into the temple to hold their services and pray for the people. Instead they watched and prayed there in abstinence lest they should perish. Take heed what I say! Unless those who pray for the people, mark my words, are sober—but no more of this; that will do. The Bible tells us that Our Lord Jesus Christ set us the example of fasting and prayer. Therefore we mendicants, we simple friars, are wedded to poverty, continence, charity, humility, frugality; to persecution for righteousness' sake; to tears, pity and purity. And so, what with your feasting at table, you can see that our prayers—I speak of us mendicants—are more acceptable than yours to the Almighty. If I'm not mistaken, for his greediness Man was first chased out of Paradise; in Paradise it's certain he was chaste!

'Now listen, Thomas, to what I'm going to say. I can't claim to have a text for it, but it's clear from the commentaries that Our dear Lord Jesus Christ was referring particularly to friars when He said "Blessed are the poor in spirit". Go through the whole Gospel and see whether it is nearer to our vows or to those of the bene-ficed clergy who wallow in their possessions—shame on their greed and pomp! And I despise them for their ignorance.

'It seems to me they're like Jovinian, fat as a whale and waddling like a swan, as full of wine as bottles in a buttery! Oh, they're very reverent when they pray—when they pray for the souls of the dead and say the psalm of David, they go "Burp! *Cor meum eructavit!** Burp!" Who follows Christ's footsteps and His gospel if not we who are humble, chaste, and poor—doers not hearers of God's word? And just as a hawk vaults high into the air in its upward swoop, so do the prayers of charitable, chaste, busy friars make their upward swoop into the two ears of God. Thomas, Thomas, as I live and breathe, were you not our brother you'd never prosper —no, by St Ive! We pray to Christ night and day in our chapter to send you health, strength, and the use of your limbs.'

'God knows I don't feel any difference,' said the sick man; 'so help me Christ, these last few years I've spent pounds and pounds on all kinds of friars and I'm none the better for it. I've used up almost the whole of my resources and that's a fact. I can kiss my gold goodbye—it's all gone.'

'O Thomas!' said the friar, 'is that what you've been doing? What need is there for you to seek out "all kinds of friars"? When a man's got the best doctor in town, what need for him to look round for others? Your inconstancy is your downfall. So you don't think it enough I should pray for you—or my convent either? Thomas, this is past a joke! If you are ill it is because we've been given too little! "Hey! Give this convent half a quarter of oats!" "Hey! Give four-and-twenty groats to that one!" "Hey! Give this friar a penny and let him go!" No, no, Thomas, it's no good! Split a farthing into twelve, and what's it worth? Look, anything that's complete in itself is stronger than when it's split up. Thomas, you'll get no flattery from me: you want our work all for nothing! The Lord God Who made the whole world says that a labourer is worthy of his hire. Now, Thomas, so far as I'm concerned I

* 'My heart is inditing a good matter'—Psalm XLV.

don't want a penny of your wealth; it's only that the whole convent prays so diligently for you, and is so diligent to build Christ's church also. Thomas, if you would learn to do good works, you may discover from the life of St Thomas of India whether the building of churches is a good thing. Here you lie, full of the wrath and anger with which the devil sets your heart on fire, scolding this simple innocent here—your meek, patient wife! And so, Thomas (please believe me, it's for your own good), don't wrangle with your wife! And I charge you to bear this proverb in mind—it's what the wise say touching the matter—"Be not as a lion in thy house, nor oppressive to thy servants, nor make thine acquaintance flee from thee." And, Thomas, once again I charge you: beware of her who sleeps in your bosom, beware of the snake with subtle sting that creeps stealthily under the grass: beware, my son, hear me patiently, and remember twenty thousand men have been destroyed through contending with their wives and sweethearts. In any case, Thomas, since you've got such a meek, saintly wife, what need have you to wrangle? Indeed, were you to step on the tail of a snake it would not be so cruel nor half so fell as a woman in wrath—vengeance is then their sole desire. Wrath is a sin, one of the seven deadly sins, abominable to the God of Heaven; and it is the destruction of the sinner. Any illiterate curate or parson can tell you homicide is bred of wrath; truly, it is the active agent of pride. Were I to speak of all the sorrow wrath brings, my homily would last till dawn. And so I pray God night and day that He grant no power to a wrathful man. It's a great pity, and a great evil, to set a wrathful man in a position of power.

'As Seneca tells us, there was once a choleric magistrate. One day during his term of office two knights rode out together. As fortune willed it, one returned home, but not the other. In due course the knight was brought before the judge, who said, "You have killed your companion; and for this I condemn you to death." To another knight he commanded: "Go, lead him out to die; these are my orders." Now as they went along the road to the place where he was to die, the knight who was supposed to be dead happened to turn up; so they thought the best plan was to bring the two of them once more before the judge. But when they said, "My lord, the knight did not kill his companion; here he stands, alive and well," the judge replied, "You must die, so help

me God! And by that I mean not one, or two, but all three of
you!" To the first knight he said, "I condemned you; you must
in any case die. As for you, you also must lose your head, since
you are the cause of your friend's death." And to the third knight
he said, "You failed to carry out my orders." And so he had all
three of them slain.

'Cambyses, besides being a man of wrath, was also a drunkard
and always took the greatest delight in behaving like a scoundrel.
One day a nobleman of his household who loved virtue and
morality happened to speak privately to him, saying, "If a lord
be a vicious man, he's lost; and drunkenness is a foul blot on any-
body's reputation, especially a lord's. There are plenty of eyes and
ears keeping watch on a lord, and he cannot tell where they may
be. For the love of God be more temperate when you drink! How
miserably wine makes a man lose control of mind and body!"

' "You'll soon see it's just the other way about," retorted Cam-
byses, "your own experience shall prove to you that wine does
people no such harm—I'd like to see the wine that could rob me
of steadiness of hand or eye." Out of malice he began to drink a
hundred times as much as before; and straightaway this vile,
wrath-filled scoundrel ordered the knight's son to be brought into
his presence, when he commanded him to stand in front of him.
Suddenly he snatched up his bow and drew the string to his ear,
letting fly an arrow which slew the child on the spot. "Now is my
hand steady or isn't it?" said he. "Have I altogether lost my
strength and judgement? Or has wine robbed me of eyesight?"
Why give the knight's reply? His son was slain; there's no more to
be said. So take care when you have dealings with the great. Let
"Placebo" be your cry, or "I will if I can", unless it's a poor man
you're dealing with—people ought to tell a poor man his faults,
but never a lord, though he should go to Hell.

'And look at Cyrus, that ireful Persian who destroyed the River
Gyndes because one of his horses was drowned in it when he set
out to conquer Babylon. He diminished that river till women
could wade over it. And what did Solomon say, the great teacher?
"Make no friendship with an angry man; and with a furious man
thou shalt not go, lest it repent thee." I'll say no more!

'Now, Thomas, my dear brother, forgo your wrath—you'll find
I'm dealing squarely with you. Don't keep holding the devil's

knife to your heart—anger makes you smart all too sorely—but make me a full confession instead.'

'No, by St Simon!' exclaimed the sick man. 'I've been shriven once today by my curate, I've told him everything; there's no need for me to confess again unless I choose, or out of humility.'

'Then give me some of your money to build our cloister,' said the friar, 'for to raise it, mussels and oysters have been our food while others have lived in ease and comfort. Even now, God knows, the foundations have hardly been completed, while not a tile of pavement has been laid in our buildings. By God, we owe forty-four pounds for stones!

'Now help us, Thomas, for the sake of Him who harrowed Hell! For otherwise we must sell our books. And if you lack our teaching the whole world must go to destruction! For, excuse me, Thomas, whoever deprives the world of us also deprives the world of its sun, so help me God! For who can teach and work as we can? And this for no short while,' said he, 'for I find it recorded that friars—the Lord be thanked!—have led their charitable lives since the time of Elijah or Elisha. Now, Thomas, help us for charity's sake!' And he fell upon his knees there and then.

The sick man was almost out of his wits with rage; he would have liked to see the limiter with his hypocritic lies in flames. 'I can only give you what I have in my keeping, and nothing else,' said he. 'You were saying just now that I am your brother?'

'Yes, certainly,' replied the friar. 'You may be sure of that. I brought your good lady your letter of fraternity with our seal.'*

'Well, then,' said he, 'I'll give something to your holy convent while I'm alive, and you shall have it in your hand in a moment —but on this condition, and this alone, which is, dear brother, that you divide it so that each friar has an equal share. You must swear this without fraud or cavil on the vows of your profession.'

'On my faith I swear it,' said the friar, and with that he laid his hand in the other's. 'Here's my promise; I shan't let you down.'

'Now put your hand down my back,' said the sick man, 'and probe carefully behind it. There, under my buttocks, you'll find something I hid in secret.'

---

* Letters of fraternity were granted under the conventual seal to laymen who had given benefactions to convents; in return they participated in the spiritual benefits the friars would confer.

'Ah!' thought the friar, 'I'll have that for myself!' And he thrust his hand down to the cleft of the man's buttocks, hoping to find a donation there. When the sick man felt the friar probing here and there about his arsehold he let out a fart—and no carthorse ever let off a fart so thunderous—right in the middle of the friar's hand.

Up sprang the friar like a wild beast. 'Ah, you treacherous yokel,' cried he. 'God's bones! You did it for spite, on purpose! You'll pay for this fart, I'll see to that!"

Hearing the row, the sick man's servants rushed in and chased out the friar. Purple with rage, he set off to find his companion and his belongings, grinding his teeth in fury till you'd have thought him a wild boar. He marched off at a smart pace to the manor-house, where dwelt a very important man whose confessor he had been from the beginning. This worthy was lord of the manor. He was eating at table when in came the friar in a terrible rage, almost incapable of saying a word.* But at last he brought out a 'God bless you!'

The lord of the manor stared at him, then said: 'Benedicite! What on earth's the matter, Friar John? It's easy to see there's something amiss—you look as if the wood were full of thieves! Now sit down and tell me what the trouble is; I'll put it right if I can.'

'It's an outrage!' cried he. 'Today, down in your village—God reward you, the meanest potboy alive would have been disgusted at the way I've been treated in your town. But nothing hurts me more than that hoary-headed old yokel blaspheming our holy convent as well!'

'Now, master,' said the lord of the manor, 'I beg you—'

'Not master, sir, but servant,' said the friar, 'though the Schools have done me that honour. God does not like us to be called "Rabbi", whether in the market-place or in your great hall.'

'Never mind all that,' said he, 'but tell me all your troubles.'

'Sir,' said the friar, 'today an odious wrong was done to my order and to myself, and therefore, *per consequens,* to the entire hierarchy of Holy Church—God amend it quickly!'

'You know best what ought to be done, sir,' said the lord of the

---

* Note Chaucer's irony: the friar had just been preaching a homily against wrath.

manor. 'Don't upset yourself—you're my confessor, the salt of the earth and the savour thereof! For the love of God calm down and tell me your trouble.' Then he told him what you've already heard —and you know well enough what that was.

The lady of the house kept perfectly quiet until she had heard the friar out.

'Eh! Mother of God!' said she. 'Blessed virgin! Is there anything else? Tell me truly.'

'What do you make of it, madam?' asked the friar.

'What do I make of it?' she exclaimed. 'Lord save me! I'd say it was the vulgar act of a vulgar fellow. What should I say? Lord send him misfortune! His sick head's filled with foolishness; I suppose he had some kind of a fit.'

'By God, madam,' said he, 'if I'm not mistaken I can be avenged in another fashion; I'll traduce him wherever I preach—that lying blasphemer who bade me divide in equal parts what cannot be divided—the devil fetch him!'

But the lord of the manor sat quietly there, like a man in a trance, turning everything over in his heart. 'How did the fellow have the imagination to set the friar a problem like that? I never heard of such a thing before. I swear the devil put it in his head! There wasn't such a conundrum to be found in the whole science of arithmetic till now. How could anyone prove each had an even share of the sound and smell of a fart? A vain, foolish fellow— damn his eyes! See here, gentlemen,' cried the lord, 'curse it all, whoever heard of such a thing before? An even share to each—tell me how? It's an impossibility; it can't be done! Ah, a foolish fellow—Lord send him misfortune! Like all other sounds, the rumbling of a fart is no more than a reverberation of air that dies away little by little. Upon my word, no man could judge whether it were equally divided. What, one of my villagers at that! Yet how scandalously he spoke to my confessor today! In my opinion he's a rank lunatic. Now eat your food and let the fellow alone— let him go hang himself, devil take him!'

But the lord's squire who carved the meat was standing by the table and heard every word of all these matters I've related. 'Pardon me, my lord,' said he, 'but for a bit of cloth to make me a gown I could tell you if I liked, Master Friar, so long as you don't get angry, how such a fart might be equally shared among your convent.'

'Tell, and you'll have your gown-cloth in a trice, by God and St John!' said the lord of the manor.

'My lord,' began the squire, 'so soon as the weather's fine, with no wind or disturbance of air, let a cartwheel be brought here into this hall—but see that it has all its spokes—twelve spokes is the usual number in a cartwheel. Then bring me twelve friars—and why? I believe thirteen friars make a convent; and your confessor here is worthy to complete the number. Then let them all kneel down together, every friar placing his nose firmly to the end of each spoke, like this. Your noble confessor—God save him!—must stick his nose right up under the hub. Next, have that fellow brought in here with his belly as stiff and taut as a drum; set him exactly on the axle of the cartwheel, and make him let out a fart. Then, I'll stake my life, you'll see demonstrable proof that the sound and stink travels equally to the ends of the spokes—save that this worthy confessor of yours shall have the first-fruits, as is only right and proper, seeing he's a man of particular eminence. The friars still have the excellent custom of serving important people first; and in his case it's certainly well-deserved. Today he instructed us so well as he stood preaching in his pulpit that as far as I'm concerned I award him first smell of three farts, and so will the rest of his convent, I'm sure, for he behaves himself in such a fine saintly fashion!'

The lord of the manor and his lady, and everyone except the friar, agreed that Jankin had debated the matter with the skill of a Euclid or Ptolemy. As for the old fellow, they agreed that only shrewdness and great intelligence could have made him speak as he did; he was certainly no fool or madman! And Jankin won his new tunic. That's the end of my story; we've almost reached the town.

'Sir Scholar of Oxford,' said our Host, 'you're riding along mum
and quiet as a new-married girl sitting at her dinner-table for the
first time; I haven't heard a word from your tongue all day. I take
it you're ruminating over some philosophical problem—but as
Solomon says, there's a time for everything. Come on, for mercy's
sake cheer up—this is no time to be meditating. Keep your
promise and tell us some pleasant tale: for all who have joined in
a game must obey the rules. Only don't sermonize us, don't try
and make us weep for our sins like some friar in Lent, and mind
your story doesn't send us off to sleep. Tell us a rattling tale of
adventure, and keep your flowers of rhetoric and your figures of
speech in storage till such time as you need the high-flown lan-
guage people use when they're writing to kings and such. Just for
now we beg you to speak simply so we may understand what you
say.'

Amiably the good Scholar replied, 'Host, I am under your rod;
you're in command for the time being, so I'm perfectly prepared
to bow to your ruling—within reason, that is. I shall tell you a
story I learned in Padua from an excellent scholar who was de-
servedly respected for all he did and said. He's dead and buried
now; I pray God rest his soul!

'This scholar was called Francis Petrarch, the poet laureate
whose sweet eloquence illumined all Italy with poetry, just as
Lignano did with philosophy, law, and other special branches of
learning. But death, which will not suffer us to live in this world
for the twinkling of an eye, has slain them both; all of us must die.

'But to go on with what I was saying about the distinguished
man who taught me this story. Let me explain that before writing
the main body of his tale he composed a prologue in the rhetorical
style in which he gave a description of Piedmont and the region
round Saluzzo. He also spoke of the Apennines, those tall hills
which form the boundary of western Lombardy, and in particular
Mount Viso where the Po has its source and beginning in a small
well, becoming ever larger as it flows eastward to Aemilia, Ferrara,

and Venice. All this would be far too long to give in detail, and indeed in my judgement seems irrelevant except to set the scene for his story. But here is his tale, which you may listen to if you wish.'

THE SCHOLAR'S TALE

n the western side of Italy, at the foot of bleak Mount Viso, there lies a rich abundant plain studded with cities and castles that were founded in the days of our forefathers. Many other goodly prospects are to be seen in this magnificent region, which is called Saluzzo. Of this country a marquis was once prince, as his great ancestors had been before him; every one of his subjects, rich and poor, was obedient to his beck and call. And thus through Fortune's favour he had lived for a long time in perfect happiness, loved and feared by both his lords and commoners. As for his ancestry, he was the noblest-born in Lombardy; in person handsome, strong, and youthful; moreover, he was most honourable and courteous, and prudent enough in ruling his country, except for one or two things wherein he was at fault. Walter was the name of this young prince.

But he was to be blamed in this: he gave no thought to what might happen in the future. His thoughts were wholly concentrated upon the pleasure of the moment, such as hunting and hawking the country round. Practically all other duties he let slide —worst of all, come what might, he would not marry a wife.

But his people felt so strongly on this point that one day they came flocking to him, and one of them—because he was the wisest and most experienced, or the man the prince was most likely to listen to, or perhaps because he was good at presenting a case like this—spoke thus to the marquis:

'O noble marquis, your humanity gives us confidence as well as the boldness to presume we may speak to you of what weighs on us whenever it may be necessary. Now deign of your graciousness, Sir, to allow us to make our sad complaint; let not your ears disdain to hear my voice.

'Though I am no more concerned in this matter than anyone else here present, yet forasmuch as you, my beloved prince, have always shown me your gracious favour, I am the more emboldened to ask you to give us a hearing for our petition; and may you, my lord, do as you think best. Indeed, sir, we cherish you and all your works and ever have; so much so that we cannot imagine how we could possibly live in greater felicity—except for one thing, Sir, if it please you: that you should choose to marry; then the hearts of your people would be quite set at rest. O bow your neck beneath that happy yoke men call marriage or wedlock: it is the yoke of dominion, not bondage! And consider, Sir, among your wiser thoughts, how our days slip by in one way or another; whether we sleep or wake, ride or roam, time is always flying and waits for no man. And though as yet you are in the first flower of youth, age is ever creeping nearer, quiet as a stone; while death menaces us at every age, striking down all sorts and conditions of men, and none escapes; for as surely as each one of us knows he must die, we are each one of us unsure of the day when death shall fall.

'Then believe the sincerity of our intentions, for we have never yet refused your behest. And, Sir, if you are willing to agree, as soon as possible we will choose you a wife born of the noblest and highest family in the whole country, so that—as far as we may judge—the choice shall appear honourable in Heaven's eyes. For the love of God on high, deliver us from this perpetual worry by taking a wife; for if it should ever happen (which God forbid!) that at your death your line should come to an end and some foreign successor take your inheritance—woe to us! woe! Therefore we entreat you to marry with all speed.'

This humble plea and their supplicating looks touched the marquis' heart with pity. 'My beloved people, you wish to force me to do something I never thought of doing,' he replied. 'I rejoiced in my freedom, a thing seldom found in marriage; but whereas I was free I must now place myself in bondage. Nevertheless I can see the sincerity of your intentions, and as I have always done I rely on your good sense. Therefore of my own free will I shall consent to marry as soon as ever I can. But as for your offer today to choose me a wife—let me release you from the burden of that choice; I beg you to give up the idea! Heaven knows that children often enough bear no resemblance to their parents; for goodness comes wholly from God and not from the stock of which they are born and begotten. I trust in the goodness of God, and therefore commend to Him my marriage, my rank, position, and peace of mind: let Him do as He pleases. Leave me alone in choosing a wife—I'll shoulder that responsibility. But I beg you—on your lives I enjoin you—to promise me you will honour whatever wife I may take, as though she were an emperor's daughter, in word and deed both here and everywhere as long as she lives. Furthermore you must swear you will neither oppose my choice nor murmur against it. Since it is at your request I am giving up my freedom, be sure of this: where my heart is set, there I mean to marry; and unless you agree to these terms I must ask you to speak no more of the matter.'

To all this they swore acceptance with heartfelt goodwill, none dissenting; only asking him before they left to be good enough to fix as soon as possible a definite day for his wedding. For even yet the people were somewhat afraid lest the marquis would not marry after all.

He named a day convenient to himself on which he would be married without fail, telling them he only did it at their request. For their part they all of them reverently knelt and humbly and submissively thanked him; and having thus achieved their object returned home. Thereupon the marquis commanded his officers to arrange the wedding-feast. He gave what orders seemed necessary to his personal knights and squires; which they obeyed, each doing his utmost to honour the occasion.

ii

Not far from the magnificent palace where the marquis was planning his marriage there stood a pleasantly situated hamlet, where some poverty-stricken villagers dwelt, kept their animals, and made what living they could from their toil, so far as the fertility of the ground allowed. Among these poor people lived a man who was considered even poorer than the rest—yet the Heavenly Father has been known to send His grace to a little ox-stall. The villagers called him Janicula. He had a daughter who was beautiful to look upon. The name of this young girl was Griselda.

But if I am to speak of the beauty of goodness, then she was the fairest under the sun. Having been brought up in poverty, no sensual desire had ever touched her heart; her drink came oftener from the well than from the wine-cask; loving virtue, she was better acquainted with hard work than idle comfort. Yet though the girl was of tender years her virgin breast enclosed a steadfastness and maturity of spirit. She looked after her aged and needy father with the greatest love and devotion: she would spin at her wheel while she watched over his few sheep in the fields, and was only idle when asleep. Coming home she often brought with her roots and other herbs which she would slice and boil for their meal; then she would make her bed—a hard bed, not at all soft; and so she kept her father alive, showing him all the devotion and care with which a child may honour its parent.

The marquis had often noticed this penniless creature when he rode out hunting. Yet when he happened to see Griselda it was not with the wanton glance of folly that he cast his eyes upon her. For he would often gravely contemplate her demeanour, appraising in his heart not only her womanhood but her goodness, in deed as in appearance far surpassing anyone so young. Although ordinary people have no great perception of virtue, for his part he justly assessed her qualities. He made up his mind that if ever he married he would wed her and her alone.

The wedding-day came but none could say who the woman would be. Many wondered at this singularity, saying privately among themselves, 'Won't our prince have done with his folly even now? Isn't he going to marry after all? Alas, the pity of it —why must he delude himself and us?'

Nevertheless the marquis had ordered for Griselda brooches and rings with jewels set in gold and lapis-lazuli. He had even had clothes made to fit her, measured upon another girl of about the same height, and all other furnishings that should go with so notable a wedding. The morning of the wedding-day approached: and the whole palace was festooned, the banqueting hall and the private rooms each in its proper style, while the kitchens and pantries were seen to be stuffed with abundance of the most delicious viands to be found throughout the length and breadth of Italy.

Richly dressed, accompanied by the lords and ladies who had been invited to the wedding, by the young knights of his retinue, and heralded by loud strains of music, the royal marquis took the shortest way to the village I spoke of, Griselda (Heaven knows she was quite unaware that all this pomp was intended for her) had gone to fetch water from the well. She was hurrying home as fast as she could, for she had heard it said that the marquis intended to be married that day and hoped to see something of the spectacle. 'I'll stand inside our door with other girls, my friends, and see the marchioness,' she thought, 'so I'll try to finish the work I have to do at home as soon as I can; then I'll have plenty of time to watch her if she takes this road to the castle.'

Just as she crossed the threshold the marquis arrived and called her. She at once put down her water-pot in an ox-stall near the threshold, fell upon her knees and stayed quietly kneeling with a solemn face to hear what the prince desired. Thoughtfully the marquis addressed the girl, speaking in a serious tone. 'Where is your father, Griselda?' he asked. And she replied in a humble and reverent manner, 'He is here and ready, my lord.' Without more delay she went inside and fetched her father to the marquis. He took the old man by the hand, and having thus drawn him aside said to him, 'Janicula, I may not, I cannot conceal my heart's dearest wish any longer. If you consent to it, then come what may, before I go I shall take your daughter to be my wife till death do us part. I am quite certain of your loyalty, since you were born my faithful vassal; I take it for granted that whatever pleases me must please you. Then give me a plain answer to the proposal I've just made—whether you will agree to take me for your son-in-law?'

Disconcerted and astonished at this abrupt offer, the old man reddened and stood trembling all over, scarcely able to utter more than this: 'My lord, my wishes are your wishes—never would I stand in your way—you are my beloved prince—arrange the business exactly as you please.'

The marquis gently replied, 'Still, I'd prefer that you and I and Griselda should confer together in your room, for this reason: I want to ask her if she is willing to be my wife and submit herself to my wishes; and this must be done in your presence, for I will say nothing out of your hearing.'

While they were in the room coming to terms (which you will hear about later) the people outside pressed round the house marvelling at the praiseworthy and attentive way she looked after her dear father. But Griselda, never having seen anything like it before, might well be more amazed than they—she was dumb-founded, and no wonder, at seeing so important a visitor in that place. Her face lost all its colour; she was unaccustomed to such visitors. But to continue the story, this is what the marquis said to that kind, true-hearted girl:

'Griselda,' said he, 'you must clearly understand that it is agreeable to your father and myself that I should marry you; and I imagine it may well be that you are willing. But I must first ask you these questions, since it must be done in such haste. Do you assent or would you like to think it over? I ask if you are prepared to carry out my every wish without demur; that I may be free to do whatever seems best to me whether it brings you happiness or pain; that you never at any time murmur or protest; that when I say "Yes" you do not say "No" by either a word or frown. Swear this, and I shall swear to our alliance here and now.'

Bewildered at these words and trembling with awe, she replied, 'My lord, I am unworthy and undeserving of the honour you offer me; but whatever you wish shall be my wish. And here I swear that I shall never wilfully disobey you in thought or in deed, though it cost me my life; and I have no wish to die.'

'My own Griselda, that will do!' said he. Gravely he stepped outside the door, followed by Griselda. Then he addressed the people: 'She who stands here is my wife,' said he. 'I ask whoever loves me to love and honour her also. That is all I have to say.'

And so that she should not bring any of her former apparel into his house he ordered the women to strip her there and then. The ladies were not exactly pleased to have to handle the garments in which she was clad. Nonetheless they dressed this fair maiden in new clothes from top to toe, combing her tumbled and disordered hair, setting a garland upon her head with their slender fingers and decking her in jewels of all kinds—but why make a long story of her adorning? And when she had been transformed by this magnificence the people could scarcely recognize her for her beauty.

The marquis married her with a ring brought for the purpose. Then he set her upon a snow-white ambling horse, and without more delay escorted her to his palace. Joyful crowds came out to meet and lead her there; and so they spent the day in revel until the sun went down.

To hasten my tale I will say that God so favoured the new marchioness with His grace that it seemed impossible she could have been born and bred a rustic in some hovel or ox-stall, but rather brought up in an emperor's palace. She became so loved and respected by all, that people from her native village who had known her from the day of her birth could hardly have believed —if they hadn't known—that she was the daughter of that Janicula I spoke of before, since she seemed to them to be a different creature.

For though she had always been virtuous, her naturally good qualities of mind, established as they were in the most charitable of hearts, soon reached the pitch of excellence. She was always so discreet and kind, her eloquence so enchanting, and herself inspired such respect, that she was able to secure the people's hearts till all who looked upon her face loved her. Nor was it only in the town of Saluzzo that her goodness was renowned, but in many a neighbouring region also; for whenever anyone spoke well of her, another confirmed it—and so the fame spread of her wonderful goodness till men and women, old and young, travelled to Saluzzo merely to look upon her.

Thus Walter, though humbly—or rather royally—wedded, had made a marriage both honourable and auspicious. He lived comfortably at home with God's peace about him, and his stock stood high among the people. And because he had perceived that virtue is frequently hidden in those of humble condition, people took him for a man of wisdom—which is a thing you don't often see.

Not only was Griselda adept in all the domestic arts: when circumstance required it she could retrieve the general good. For throughout the country there was no quarrel, rancour, or grievance that her wisdom might not appease and pacify. Were the nobles or others of the land at enmity she could reconcile them even though her husband were absent. Her sayings were so wise and thoughtful, her judgements so equitable, people thought she had been sent from heaven to save them and redress all wrongs.

Not long after Griselda's marriage she gave birth to a daughter. She would rather have had a son; however the marquis and the people were delighted, for though a girl came first, she was not barren; so there was every likelihood she would achieve a male child.

iii

While the child was still being suckled it happened (as it sometimes does) that the marquis conceived a longing to make trial of his wife's constancy. He was unable to get rid of this extraordinary desire to test his wife. God knows there was no necessity for him to frighten her. For he had assayed her often enough before and always found her sterling; what need to put her to the proof again and again? Some may applaud it as a shrewd notion: for my own part I say it ill becomes a man to put his wife to the test and subject her to needless anguish and terror. This is how the marquis set about it: one night he came alone with stern face and troubled brow to the room in which she lay and said, 'Griselda! I don't imagine you've forgotten the day when I rescued you from poverty and raised you to your high position? I am only saying, Griselda, that I don't believe this present dignity in which I've placed you makes you forgetful of the fact I found you in a most wretched condition. What happiness could you have looked for? Now mark every word I say: there is none to hear except the two of us. You yourself know perfectly well how it was you came into this house —it isn't so very long ago. Now, although to me you are most dear and precious, to my nobles you are nothing of the sort: they say it's a scandal and disgrace they should owe you allegiance and be subject to you, a mere villager! And there's no doubt whatever they've been talking like this, especially since your daughter was born. But I wish, as always, to live with them in peace and tranquillity. In these circumstances I cannot take any risks. I must dispose of your daughter as best I can—not as I would like but as my people wish. But God knows it goes very much against the grain! Nevertheless I'll not do anything without your knowledge. But,' said he, 'I wish for your consent in the matter. Now show your patience in practice, as you swore and promised to me in your village on the day we were married.'

All this she heard without the slightest alteration of face, voice, or bearing. To all seeming she felt no resentment, but replied, 'My lord, all things are at your disposal; my child and I are wholly yours and shall willingly obey. What is yours you may spare or destroy; do as you will. As heaven is my salvation, nothing that pleases you can displease me, nor is there anything I desire to have or fear to lose but you alone; this is and ever shall be my heart's wish. Neither time nor death may erase it, or turn my heart from you.'

Happy as this answer made the marquis, yet he dissembled it; for when he turned to leave the room his looks and bearing were grim. Soon after this—a very little later—he took into his confidence a fellow whom he sent to his wife. This trusty was by way of being a kind of attendant whom he had often found reliable in affairs or weight; and such fellows can be depended on to do one's dirty work. The prince was well aware that this officer was both loyal and feared his wrath. And when he understood what his master wanted he stepped quickly into Griselda's room.

'Madam,' said he, 'forgive me if I do what I am in duty bound to perform; but you are too wise not to understand that a prince's commands are not to be evaded, much as they may be lamented or deplored. But people must needs obey their wishes, and so must I, that's all there is to it. I am commanded to take away this child—' here he broke off, roughly seized the infant and made as if he would slay it on the spot. Griselda (who must put up with everything the marquis wished) remained sitting, quiet and gentle as a lamb, and let the cruel attendant do his worst. Ominous the ill repute of this man: ominous his face, ominous his speech, and ominous the hour of his appearance! Poor Griselda thought he would kill there and then the daughter she loved so tenderly; yet she neither sighed nor wept, but made herself acquiesce to the marquis' desire. At length, however, she spoke. Humbly she begged the attendant to have the goodness of heart to let her kiss her child before it died. Her face was filled with grief as she laid the tiny creature in her bosom. She rocked it in her arms and kissed it; and then she made the sign of the cross, saying in her gentle voice, 'Farewell, my child, I shall never see you again; but as I have signed you with the cross, may you be blessed by that Heavenly Father Who died for us upon the wooden rood. My little child, I commit your soul to His care, for tonight you must die because of me.'

Even for a nurse, I swear, the sight would have been past bearing; how much more excuse for a mother to cry out! But nevertheless she remained steadfast and unmoved, enduring all misfortune, and said gently to the officer: 'Take back your little maid. Now go and do your lord's command, but let me beg one favour: unless my lord has forbidden you, at least bury this little body in some place where birds and wild animals may not tear it to pieces.' To this request he returned not a word, but picked up the child and left.

The attendant returned to his master and gave him a short but complete account of Griselda's words and demeanour. Then he handed over his beloved daughter. The prince seemed somewhat remorseful; but nonetheless held to his purpose, as princes will when they mean to have their own way. He bade the fellow take the child secretly, and swaddle it round gently with the utmost care, that it might be carried in a box or wrap. And on pain of losing his head, none should know what he purposed, whence he came or whither he was going. He was to take it to Bologna, to the marquis' sister (who was at that time countess of Panago), explain the circumstances to her and beg her to do her best to bring up the child as befitted its noble station. But whose child it was he bade her conceal from everyone at all costs.

The officer went away and fulfilled his mission; but let us now return to the marquis. He was on the alert, wondering if he would be able to perceive any change towards himself in his wife's demeanour, or discover it from any word of hers. But he never found her other than consistently kind and unchanging. In every respect she was as cheerful, as meek, and as ready to serve and to love him; never did she say one word about her daughter. Misfortune had not changed her in the least, nor did she ever once mention her daughter's name in any circumstances.

iv

So matters stood while four years passed away and she was again with child; but this time God willed she should bear Walter a fine handsome boy. And when they told his father of it, not only he but the whole country rejoiced at the child, giving thanks and praise to the Lord. But one day, when it was two years old and weaned from its nurse's breast, the marquis again took a fancy to try his wife still further if he might. Yet how needless was it to put her to the proof! But married men know no restraint when they find a patient woman.

'My dear wife,' said the marquis, 'as you already know, my people take our marriage very badly; and now it is worse than ever, particularly since our son was born. Their mutterings pierce me to the heart; such cruel rumours have come to my ears that my spirit is almost broken. This is what they are saying now: "When Walter goes, the family of Janicula is bound to succeed him and become our overlord; we have no other choice." There can be no doubt that such is the common talk, and I ought to take good heed of murmurs of this sort, for, though they are not plainly declared in my hearing, I am truly afraid of such ideas. I mean to live in peace if I can, and therefore I am absolutely determined to dispose of my son in secret, just as I dealt with his sister that night. I'm giving you warning lest you should suddenly be beside yourself with grief. Be patient over this, I entreat.'

But she replied, 'I have said, and shall always say, that in truth I wish for nothing but what may please you; I am not grieved at all, though my daughter and my son be slain—at your command, that is. I have had no share in my two children but first sickness and then grief. You are our master; do just as you will with your own; ask no advice from me. For as I left all my clothing at home when first I came to you, so did I leave my will and freedom behind and took your apparel; therefore I pray you do as you wish, for I shall obey your pleasure. And indeed if I had fore-knowledge to know your will before you could tell me what your pleasure was, I should not fail to perform it; but now that I know your will and what you wish to have done, I shall be firm and constant to all that you desire; and if I knew that my death would give you ease, then to please you I would most gladly die. Death is nothing compared with our love.'

Perceiving the constancy of his wife, the marquis was ashamed and lowered his eyes. He marvelled how she could endure so much in patience. And away he went, a grim look on his face, though inwardly filled with joy.

His fearsome henchman took away her handsome son just as he had seized her daughter—or even more callously if possible. Yet she gave no sign of grief, so consistently patient was she; but kissed her son and made the sign of the cross over him, only begging the fellow if he could bury her little son in the ground to keep his tender delicate limbs from birds and beasts of prey. But she got no kind of answer. He went off as if it meant nothing to him; but he carefully brought the child to Bologna.

The longer he thought about it the more the marquis wondered at her patience; and if he had not already known for certain how absolutely she loved her children he would have suspected that it was from craft, or malice, or hard-heartedness she endured all this with an untroubled face. But he knew perfectly well that next to himself it was certain she loved her children best. And now I'd like to ask the ladies here if these tests were not enough? What more could the most relentless husband devise to prove her faithfulness and constancy to one so inexorable? But there is a kind of person who, once he has made up his mind to take a certain course, is quite unable to desist, but holds fast to his original purpose like a martyr bound to the stake. And this was the case with the marquis, who had every intention of putting his wife to the proof as he had first resolved.

He watched for a word or look to show she had changed towards him. But he could never find any alteration; her temper and demeanour remained always the same; and as she grew older she became, if possible, the more faithful and devoted. And in the end it seemed as if there were only one will between the two of them, for whatever Walter desired became her wish also—thank Heaven it all came right in the end. She showed how, despite all tribulations, a wife should have no wishes of her own apart from her husband's.

Now scandalous tales about Walter were current everywhere—that because he had married a pauper, in the cruelty of his heart he had wickedly and secretly murdered both his children. Such was the common talk. And no wonder; for no word reached people's ears to say that they had not been murdered. Thus, whereas up till then he had been much loved by his people, the opprobrium of his ill fame made them hate him; the name of murderer is odious. Nevertheless he would not desist from his cruel purpose for any consideration. His mind was wholly set upon proving his wife.

When his daughter was twelve years of age he sent his messenger to the court of Rome (which he craftily kept informed of his intentions) and instructed them to fabricate such documents as were necessary for his inhuman scheme. These were to say that the Pope, in order to set his people's minds at rest, had bidden him marry again if he wished. Indeed, he asked them to forge papal bulls to say he had permission, by the Pope's dispensation, to put aside his first wife, that the dissension and ill feeling between himself and his people might be restrained. So ran the bull, which they published in its entirety.

As you might expect, the common people believed it implicitly. But when the news reached Griselda I imagine it filled her heart with grief. Yet, steadfast as ever, she resolved, poor soul, to endure every adversity of fortune, ever waiting upon the pleasure of him to whom she had been given heart and soul as her true earthly solace.

Not to make too long a story of it, the marquis wrote a special letter to convey his plans and sent it secretly to Bologna. He earnestly besought the earl of Panago (who had married his sister) publicly to bring home his two children with an honourable escort. One thing he absolutely enjoined: that if inquiries were made the earl was to tell no one whose children they were, but say the girl was about to be married to the marquis of Saluzzo.

The earl did as he was asked and on the appointed day set forth upon the road to Saluzzo with a large retinue of richly-accoutred noblemen to escort the maiden and her young brother riding at her side. The budding girl was attired for her wedding and covered with glittering jewels, while her small seven-year-old brother was as brilliantly arrayed in his own fashion. Thus they rode daily upon their way with great magnificence and rejoicing, shaping their course towards Saluzzo.

v

In the meanwhile the marquis, in order that he might be absolutely convinced she was constant as ever, sought with his habitual ruthlessness to put his wife to the uttermost proof; and one day at a public audience addressed her in a loud voice: 'Indeed, Griselda, it has been pleasant enough having you for my wife, more on account of your faithfulness and obedience than your wealth and lineage. But when I come to think of it, I now realize it is perfectly true that the more exalted one's position the greater one's servitude. A ploughman is freer to please himself than I am, for my people are forcing me with their daily clamour to take another wife. And besides, I must tell you that the Pope has given his consent to this venture in order to restrain their ill-feeling. Indeed I will tell you this much: my new wife is already on her way here.

'Brace yourself to quit her place without delay. As regards the dowry you brought me, as a favour I shall allow you to take it back with you. Return to your father's house,' said he, 'nobody can be lucky all the time. Take my advice and bear the strokes of fortune with equanimity.'

Yet she answered him with fortitude. 'My lord, I knew and always have known that no one could possibly make any comparison between your splendour and my poverty; these things are undeniable. I never considered myself worthy to be your wife in any way—no, not even to be your chambermaid. And in this house of which you made me lady, I call on God to witness (and may He comfort my soul) that I never thought of myself as its lady or its mistress, but as a humble servant to your lordship above all other earthly creatures—and so I ever shall while my life lasts. I thank you, and Heaven, which I pray will reward you, because in your generosity you have so long honoured and exalted me in a position I was not worthy of; I can say no more. I will gladly go back to my father and live with him for the rest of my life. And there where I was brought up from a small child I'll live and die a widow, clean in body and soul and in all things. For as I gave you my virginity and without question am your faithful wife, God forbid the wife of so great a prince should take another husband or mate with another man! As for your new wife, may God in His grace grant you joy and prosperity; for I will gladly yield to her the place in which I have been so happy. Now, my lord, since it pleases you in whom my heart once rested that I should go, I will go whenever you please.

'But as to your offer to return whatever dowry I brought you, I am far from forgetting what it was; nothing splendid, but only my miserable rags; it would be hard for me to find them now. O blessed God! how noble and kind you seemed in your looks and speech on the day we were married! Yet they say truly—at any rate I find it so, for it proved true in my case—"Love changes when it grows old". But indeed, my lord, neither hardship nor death would ever make me in either word or deed repent that I gave you my whole heart.

'My lord, you know how you had me stripped of my miserable rags in my father's house, and graciously dressed me in splendid clothes. It is plain I brought you nothing except my faithfulness, my nakedness, and my virginity; and here I return to you your clothes, and also my wedding-ring, for evermore. I can assure you that the remainder of your jewels is in your chamber. Naked I came out of my father's house, and naked I must return. I will gladly submit to all your wishes; but hope you do not intend I should walk naked out of your palace. You could not do so dishonourable a thing as to allow that womb in which your children lay to be seen naked and uncovered before the people when I go; I entreat you, let me not walk naked as a worm upon the roads! My own dear lord, remember that I was your wife, though unworthy; and so, in recompense for the maidenhead that I brought to you but do not take back with me, vouchsafe to grant me in return a smock such as I used to wear, with which to hide the womb of her who was once your wife. And lest I anger you, my lord, I here take leave of you.'

'Keep the smock you are wearing,' said he, 'and take it with you.' Yet he could scarcely speak the words for pity and remorse, but turned away. She stripped herself in front of the people and set off in her smock towards her father's house, bareheaded and barefoot. The people followed her, weeping; and as they went they cursed Fortune; but she kept her eyes dry of tears, and all this time she did not speak one word.

But her father heard the news soon enough. He cursed the day and hour he was born. There is no doubt this poor old man had always had misgivings about her marriage. From the very beginning he had suspected that once the prince had satisfied his desire he would feel he had demeaned his rank by stooping so low, and then get rid of her as soon as he could.

The noise of the people gave him warning of her approach; he hurried out to meet his daughter. Weeping sadly, he covered her in her old coat as best he could, but could not get it round her because the cloth was poor, and older by many a day than it had been at her wedding.

So this pearl of wifely patience dwelt for some time with her father. Never did she show by word or look, in public or in private, that any injury had been done her; nor did her face betray the least hint she remembered her former high position. Nor was this any wonder, for while she was marchioness her disposition had always been entirely unassuming. She had no taste for delicate fare, no pleasure-loving spirit, but was full of patient kindness, discreet, without pretension, always honourable, and to her husband ever constant and submissive. People talk of Job, and particularly of his humility; when they wish, learned scholars are eloquent enough on the subject—especially humility in men—but although these scholars give little praise to women, the truth of the matter is that no man can be half as humble or as faithful as a woman; or if so it's news to me.

vi

When the earl of Panago came from Bologna the news of his arrival spread everywhere. It also reached the ears of all that he had brought with him a new marchioness in such pomp and splendour that throughout western Lombardy no human eye had seen a more magnificent spectacle.

Before the arrival of the earl, the marquis (who knew of it, having planned the whole thing) sent messengers for the poor innocent Griselda; and she, with humble heart and happy face, yet with no exaggerated hopes in her breast, came at his bidding. She went down upon her knees and gave him a respectful greeting.

'Griselda,' said he, 'I am absolutely determined that this girl I am going to marry shall be received as royally as possible in my house tomorrow; and that everyone shall be placed and served according to his rank and entertained as honourably as I can contrive. Of course I have no woman capable of ordering and arranging the rooms as I should like; and so I'd be glad if the management of it were in your charge. Besides you are familiar with all my tastes. Never mind if your clothes are mean and wretched, but do the job as best you can.'

'My lord,' she replied, 'not only am I happy to do as you wish, but it is also my desire to serve and please you as best I may in my humble station, till I am ready to drop—and this will always be so. For never, come weal or woe, shall the soul within my breast ever cease to love you with the truest loyalty.' And saying this she began putting the house in order, setting the tables and making the beds. She spared no pains, bidding the chambermaids for heaven's sake hasten, sweep and scrub, while she, busier than any, made ready the banqueting hall and the private rooms.

The earl arrived about mid-morning bringing the two noble children with him. The people ran out to see the costly spectacle; and now for the first time they began remarking to one another that Walter was no fool. If he wanted to change his wife it might be all for the best—for they all judged her fairer than Griselda, and far younger; the fruit of the marriage should prove finer, and, because of her high birth, more acceptable. Her brother had such a handsome face too! So the mob took a fancy to them, and now commended the marquis's conduct.

'O unstable crowd! always fickle, always faithless, flighty and changeable as a weathercock, always rejoicing in the latest rumour! Continually waxing and waning like the moon, and always filled with tattle not worth twopence! False in judgement, your constancy won't stand testing—whoever trusts in you is a complete idiot.'

That's what the graver citizens said while the crowd stared and gaped, happy to have a new marchioness of their town just for the novelty of it. Now I'll say no more upon the subject but turn again to Griselda and tell of her patience and industry.

Griselda busied herself tirelessly with everything to do with the wedding feast. Not in the least put out by her clothes, coarse and tattered though they were, she went happily to the gate with the others to greet the marchioness; after which she went on with her duties. She received the guests with such cheerful competence, each according to his rank, that far from anyone finding fault, they kept wondering who she might be that was so meanly dressed yet so polite and accomplished. And they gave her tact due praise.

Meanwhile she never stopped her wholehearted praises of the girl and her brother, which she gave in all kindness and sincerity; no one could have praised them more. But at last, when the nobles went in to take their places at the feast, the marquis called for Griselda while she was busy in the hall. In a bantering tone he asked her, 'How do you like the beauty of my wife, Griselda?'

And she replied, 'Very much indeed, my lord: believe me, I never saw a lovelier girl. May God grant her happiness; I hope that He may send you both all felicity for the rest of your lives. One thing let me entreat—and let me warn you too—do not put this gentle girl upon the rack as you have done others. She has been more delicately bred and reared; I do not think she could endure hardship so well as one brought up in poverty.'

Now when Walter saw her patience, her cheerful bearing that held no hint of malice while she herself remained always constant as a wall and free of resentment however often he had injured her, the obdurate marquis felt his heart take pity on her wifely steadfastness. 'My dearest Griselda, this will do!' cried he, 'be no longer afraid or distressed; I have put to the proof your faithfulness and kindheartedness in riches and in poverty as searchingly as any woman's ever was. My dearest wife, I am certain of your constancy.' With that he took her into his arms and kissed her. But in her amazement she took no notice of it, nor understood what he had said to her; she was as if suddenly startled from sleep. But at last she came to from her stupefaction. 'Griselda,' he cried, 'by the Lord who died for us you are my wife; I have no other wife nor ever had, as God shall save my soul! This is your daughter whom you have supposed to be my wife; and that boy there shall surely be my heir as I always intended—he is indeed the child of your body. I kept them hidden in Bologna: take them back, for now you cannot say you have lost either of your two children. As for those people who have said otherwise, let them take good note that I did not do this out of any malice or cruelty, but to test your faithfulness as a wife. God forbid I should slay my children! My idea was to keep them quietly hidden till I was sure of your resolution and strength of will.'

When she heard this she fell down in a faint, heartbroken with joy; and after recovering herself she called both her young children to her, and embraced them in her arms, weeping pathetically and kissing them tenderly like any mother, her face and hair bathed in salt tears. How heartbreaking it was to see her swoon away, and to hear her meek voice saying, 'A thousand times I thank you, my lord, for saving my beloved children! Now I care not whether I die here and now; so long as I am loved by you and have your favour, what matters death or when my soul departs! O my children! O my tender young ones! Your sorrowing mother always thought you had been eaten by cruel hounds or horrible creatures; but God in His mercy, and your kind father, have preserved you safe and sound.' And that very instant she suddenly slid to the ground, holding her two children so firmly in her first embrace that it was only with the greatest difficulty and effort they could tear them from her arms. The tears ran down the pitying faces of the bystanders, who could scarcely bring themselves to remain in the room.

Walter comforted her until her grief abated. When she recovered from her faint she felt ashamed; but everyone made much of her until she had recovered her composure. Then Walter treated her with loving consideration, till it was a joy to see the happiness between the two of them now they were again together. And when the ladies saw their chance they took her to her room and stripped her of her coarse garments; then, dressed in a glittering golden robe, and upon her head a crown set with many precious gems, she was led into the banqueting hall where due honour was paid her. And so this affecting day came to a happy end, for every man and woman put their best foot forward and spent the day in joy and festivity until the bright stars began to shine. To everyone there present, this banquet appeared more magnificent and lavish than the rejoicings at her wedding.

The two of them lived prosperously in peace and harmony for many a year. Their daughter made a rich marriage to one of the noblest princes in the whole of Italy; and Walter kept his wife's father at his court in peaceful retirement until his soul departed the body. When Walter's day was over his son succeeded to his inheritance in peace and tranquillity; he too was lucky in his marriage, though he did not put his wife to any severe test. The world isn't as tough as it used to be, and that's the truth.

Now listen to what Petrarch has to say about it: 'This tale has not been told that wives should imitate Griselda's meekness; it would be more than they could bear even if they wished; but so that everyone, whatever his condition, should be as constant as Griselda in adversity.' That's why Petrarch told this story, which he composed in his loftiest style.

For if a woman was so patient towards a mere mortal, how much more ought we to accept uncomplainingly all that God sends us? It is perfectly reasonable that He should put what He made to the proof. Yet, as St James says in his epistle, He will never try too highly those whom He has redeemed. Doubtless He is always testing us; for our own good He allows us to be scourged in various ways with the biting lash of adversity—not because He wishes to be sure of our strength of will, for indeed He was aware of all our weaknesses before we were born; His rule is for the best. Then let us live in virtue and fortitude.

But one word, sirs, before I go: nowadays it would be pretty hard to find three or even two Griseldas in the whole city. Their gold is now so debased with brass that were they to be put to such assays the coin (good as it looks) would be more likely to break in two than bend. And so, for the Wife of Bath's sake (may God maintain her and all her sex in their high authority, or it would be too bad!) I'll sing you a song which I hope will cheer you up, for I'm in excellent form. Let's have a rest from serious subjects. Now listen to my song—this is how it goes:

Griselda's dead, so is her patience,
And both are deader than a coffin nail;
I warn all husbands in the audience
Not to be too precipitate to assail
The patience of their wives, in hope to find
Griselda's; it is certain they shall fail.

You high-born wives, renowned for prudence,
Should you permit humility to nail
Your tongues, or give the scholars evidence
For an even more unimaginable tale
Than Griselda's, so patient and so kind,
Beware lest Chichevache* devour you all!

Take after Echo: she keeps no silence,
Her disposition is antiphonal;
Don't be made fools of by your innocence,
Be on your toes, take over the control,
And fix this lesson firmly in your mind;
The general good of all shall then prevail.

You archwives, stand up in your own defence!
Each is as huge and strong as a camel.
Then why permit a man to give offence?
You smaller wives, though feeble in battle,
Be fiercer than a tiger or a fiend,
Clack on and on like windmills, I counsel.

Why should you fear, or pay them reverence?
For if your husband armed himself in mail
The cutting arrows of your eloquence
Would pierce his breastplate and his tough ventail.

* A fabulous cow which fed only on patient wives, and as a result was half-starved.

Take my advice, be jealous and not blind,
And you shall make him cower like a quail!

If you be fair, when others are present
Show off your beauty and your apparel!
If you be ugly, use extravagance,
For this will win you friends so you prevail.
Be light and gay as a leaf in the wind,
Leave him to whine and worry, weep and wail!

'God's bones!' swore our Host, when the good Scholar had finished his story. 'I'd give a barrel of ale if only my wife could hear this legend! It's an excellent tale from my point of view, if you see what I mean; however it's no use worrying about what can't be helped.'

'Weeping, wailing, worrying, and trouble morning, noon, and night's a thing I know all about, like most other married men,' said the Merchant, 'or so I suppose because that's how it's with me, as I very well know. I've a wife, the worst you could find; if she were married to the Devil you can bet your boots she'd be more than a match for him. What's the use of giving you examples of her terrible spite—she's an all-round tartar! There's a wide, deep difference between the great patience of Griselda and my wife's unspeakable vindictiveness. I'm damned if I'd walk into that trap again if I were free! We married men live in trouble and sorrow —try it if you like and you'll find I'm telling the truth, by St Thomas of India! That goes for most of us—I don't say all, God forbid!

'Ah, good Master Host, believe me, I've been married no more than these two months, yet I'd say no lifelong bachelor could even begin to tell of anything like the sorrow I could relate here and now concerning the wickedness of my wife—no, not if they cut his heart out!'

'Well, God bless you, Merchant,' said our Host, 'since you know so much of the subject I most heartily beg you to tell us something about it.'

'Gladly,' replied the Merchant, 'but my heart's too heavy to speak any more concerning my own affliction.'

THE
MERCHANT'S
TALE

In Lombardy there once dwelt a noble knight, a native of Pavia, who lived in great prosperity. For sixty years he had been a bachelor, taking his bodily pleasure with the women he fancied, as is the way of these fools of laymen. Now, either from an access of piety or dotage—I can't tell which—when this knight had passed his sixtieth year he was seized by an overwhelming impulse to get married, and spent his days and nights looking for some woman he might wed. He prayed to the Lord to grant he might have a taste of that blissful existence which obtains between husband and wife, and live in that sacred bond with which God first united man and woman. 'No other life is worth a bean,' said he, 'the pure delights of wedlock make it a paradise on earth.' So spoke the old knight in his wisdom.

And certainly, as sure as God's in Heaven it's an excellent thing to marry, especially when a man is old and hoar, for then a wife is his choicest possession. Therefore he should take a young and pretty wife in order to beget an heir and live a life of joy and solace; whereas these bachelors whine and whimper when they meet any setback in love; which is just childishness. And really it's most fitting that bachelors should so often run into trouble and woe, for they build on shifting sands, finding instability where they look for security. Like the birds and beasts they live in freedom, under no constraint; whereas the married state compels a man to live a happy and ordered life, bound under the yoke of wedlock. And why shouldn't his heart abound in joy and delight —who can be so obedient as a wife? Who more faithful and diligent to look after him in sickness and in health? She'll not forsake him in weal or in woe, nor tire of loving and serving him even if he lie bedridden to the day of his death. And yet some learned men—of whom Theophrastus is one—say this is not so. And what's the odds if Theophrastus chose to lie? 'Don't take a wife for economy's sake, with the idea of saving your household expenses,' said he. 'A faithful servant will take more trouble to look after your possessions than your own wife, who'll claim a half share while she lives. And, as the Lord's my salvation, if you fall sick your real friends, or an honest servant, will look after you far better than a woman who's simply waiting, as many a day she's waited, to get hold of your goods! And if you take a wife into your keeping, you may pretty soon become a cuckold.' These sentiments, and a hundred worse, were set down by this fellow, God's curse on him! A fig for Theophrastus—take no notice of such nonsense, but listen to me.

Indeed a wife's a gift of God; all other boons—lands, revenues, pastures, common property or movables—are surely gifts of Fortune, and fleeting as a shadow on a wall. But never fear, let me tell you plainly that a wife's a lasting thing and will remain in your house a good deal longer than perhaps you bargained for.

Marriage is a cardinal sacrament; to my way of thinking a wifeless man's beneath contempt. His is a helpless and solitary life— I'm speaking of laymen of course. I'm not saying this lightly: if you'll listen to me I'll tell you why woman has been made man's helpmeet. When Almighty God created Adam, He saw him belly-naked and alone; whereupon the Lord in His great mercy said, 'Let us now make a helpmeet for this man; a creature like himself.' Then He made Eve. Hereby it is evident, and proof positive, that woman is man's help and comfort, his solace and terrestrial paradise. Obedient and virtuous as she is, how can they help but live in unity? One flesh they are; and one flesh, I take it, has but a single heart, come weal or woe.

A wife! Saint Mary bless us all, what hardship can afflict a man with a wife? I'm sure I can't say. No tongue can tell or heart imagine the bliss between the two. Should he be poor, she helps him toil; she watches over all his goods, never wasting a scrap; whatever pleases her husband delights her; when he says 'Yes' she never once says 'No'. 'Do this,' he says. 'At once,' she replies. O blessed and inestimable condition of wedlock, so joyous, and so virtuous too, so commended and approved! Any man who's not a mouse should spend his life thanking God upon his bare knees for granting him a wife—or else pray to be sent one to last him to the end of his days! For then his life's on a secure basis. In my view he can't go wrong so long as he follows his wife's counsel. He can hold up his head without fear; they are wise as well as faithful;—

always do what women advise if you want to follow the example of intelligent men!

Look how Jacob—as the scholars tell us—adopted the excellent suggestion of his mother Rebecca and tied the kid's skin round his neck, thus winning his father's blessing. History also relates how Judith saved the Chosen People with her sage counsel and slew the sleeping Holofernes. Think of Abigail and how she rescued her husband Nabal with sound advice when he was about to be executed; or take Esther, whose good counsel delivered the Chosen People from tribulation, and enabled Mordecai to earn advancement from Ahasuerus.

As Seneca says, nothing ranks superior to an obliging wife.

Bear with your wife's tongue, as Cato recommends; she must command, and you must put up with it; and yet, as a favour, she will obey. Your wife is keeper of the domestic purse; when you're sick, it's no use weeping and wailing if you haven't a wife to look after the house! If you want to act sensibly, I caution you to love your wife even as Christ loved His church. If you love yourself, then you love your wife, for no man hates his own flesh, but ministers to it while breath is in him; and so I tell you, cherish your wife or you'll never get on. In spite of the jokes they make about it, husband and wife have chosen the one secure path for people of this world; for they are united so closely no harm may befall either—especially the wife.

With this in mind, January (the knight I am speaking of) contemplated in his old age that life of happiness and virtuous tranquillity which is honey-sweet marriage. And one day he sent for his friends to tell them the result of his ruminations. Looking very serious, he began his account: 'My friends, I am old and hoar, and God knows I'm almost on the brink of the grave; I must think a little about my soul. My body I have foolishly dissipated; but blessed be God, this shall be remedied! For I have made up my mind to become a married man, and that as soon as possible. So will you kindly make preparations for my immediate marriage to some pretty young girl, as I'm not going to wait—and on my part I'll try to keep a look-out for someone I can wed without delay. But seeing that I am one and you are many, it's more likely you'll discover a suitable bride than I, and see where it would be best for me to ally myself.

'But a word of warning, my dear friends: nothing's going to induce me to take an old wife. She must not be over twenty; that's flat. My taste runs to old fish but young meat—a pike's better than a pikelet; tender young veal's better than beef. I won't have any woman of thirty—mere fodder, bean-straw—winter forage! And besides, God knows these old widows are up to as many tricks as Wade's boat, and can stir up so much petty trouble when they want, I'd never live in peace with one. Different schools make the clever scholar: it's the same when a woman has many husbands. But a young thing may be guided, no doubt, just as one can mould warm wax in the hands. And so, in a word, I tell you plainly I'll take no elderly wife for that very reason. Suppose I were unlucky enough not to find pleasure in her? Then I'd have to live the rest of my life in adultery and go straight to the Devil when I die. I'd beget no children upon her—and let me tell you this, I'd rather be eaten by dogs than have my heritage fall into the hands of a stranger. I'm not talking nonsense: I know why men should marry; furthermore, I'm perfectly aware that many people who talk of marriage know less than my stable-boy of the reasons why a man should take a wife. If a man can't live in chastity, then he must reverently take unto himself a wife, not merely for concupiscence or love, but for the lawful procreation of children to the glory of God; and so avoid fornication, paying their debt when it's due, each helping the other in trouble like brother and sister, and living in holy continence. But, gentlemen, I'm not that sort, if you don't mind. God be thanked, I think I may boast my limbs feel strong and able to do all a man should—for I'm the best judge of that. Though I be hoar I'm like a tree that blossoms before the fruit ripens; and a tree in blossom is neither dead nor dry. It's only my head feels hoary; my heart and limbs are green as a laurel all the year round. Now that you've heard what's in my mind, I beg you to fall in with my wishes.'

Different people told him different stories about marriage. Some condemned it, and some, of course, praised it; but in the end (you know how controversies arise during an argument among friends) a dispute began between his two brothers. The name of one was Placebo; the other was called Justinus.

Said Placebo, 'Brother January, there wouldn't be the least need for you to ask the advice of anybody here were it not for the

consummate sagacity and prudence which make you, my dear
sir, so unwilling to set aside that proverb of Solomon which ap-
plies to us all: "Do nothing without advice"—that's what he said
—"and then you'll not repent." But, my dear sir, my own dear
brother, though Solomon himself said it, as sure as God's my
salvation I think your own opinion's best. For, brother, you can
take it from me, as I've been all my life a courtier and heaven
knows I've been in considerable standing (unworthy as I am)
among lords of high rank, yet never quarrelled with any. The fact
is I never contradicted them—I always bore in mind that a lord
knows better than I, so whatever he says goes as far as I'm con-
cerned: I say the same as him, or something like it. There's no
bigger ass than a counsellor in the service of some great lord who
dares presume or even think his advice better than his master's
ideas. No, take it from me, lords are no fools! You yourself have
here displayed such solid judgement, piety, and ability today, I
can only agree with your opinion and confirm every single word
you've said. By God, there's not a man in town, or in Italy for
that matter, could have spoken better! It'd satisfy Christ Himself
to hear you! Truly it shows great spirit in a man of advanced
years when he takes a young wife. Upon my soul, your heart's in
the right place! Do exactly as you please in this business, for I
think that's the best thing when all's said and done.'

Justinus, who had been sitting and listening quietly, made this
reply to Placebo: 'Now, brother, please be patient; having had
your say, you can listen to mine. Seneca, among his other wise
sayings, has remarked that one ought to be very careful to whom
one gives one's land or property. Now if I ought to be most careful
to whom I give away my property, how much more careful ought
I to be to whom I yield my body in perpetuity? I warn you
seriously, it's no child's play to pick a wife without due reflection.
In my view it's essential to inquire whether she's discreet, tem-
perate or given to drink, whether she's vain, or in any way a
tartar, or a scold, a spendthrift, rich, poor, or a virago. And al-
though one never discovers a horse whose action is quite perfect
—in this world the ideal is not to be found in man or beast—it
should nevertheless be enough if a wife has more good qualities
than bad; but all this takes time to investigate. And many's the
secret tear I've shed, God knows, since I got myself a wife. Any-

body who cares to can sing the praises of wedlock; but the fact is I find in it nothing but trouble, duties, and expense; quite bare of blessing. Still, Lord knows my neighbours—and in particular womenfolk in droves—tell me I've the most constant and obliging wife that breathes. But I know best where my shoe pinches. As far as I'm concerned you can do what you please, but reflect seriously—you're an old man—before you enter into marriage, especially with a wife that's young and pretty. By the Lord who made water, earth, and air, the youngest among us here has quite enough to do to have his wife to himself. Trust me, you won't please her—give complete satisfaction I mean—much longer than three years on the outside. Wives require all sorts of attentions. Now please don't take offence at what I've said.'

'Well,' replied January, 'have you finished? A straw for your Seneca and your proverbs—scholars' jargon, not worth a basket of weeds. Just now you heard wiser folk than you agree with me. What do you say, Placebo?'

'I say that only a villain would put obstacles in the way of matrimony, that's a fact,' said he.

And with that they immediately got up, being wholly agreed that he should marry whoever he pleased whenever he wished.

From day to day January's soul was filled with extravagant fancies and busy conjectures about his marriage; night by night ravishing figures and faces passed through his mind, as if somebody had taken a brightly-polished mirror and set it up in the public market to watch the throng of figures walking by in the glass. In this way January envisaged in his thoughts the girls who lived near him. He didn't know which to settle on. For if one had a pretty face, then another stood so high in people's favour for kindness and equanimity that the general voice was for her; and some were rich, but had a bad name. At last, between earnest and jest, he dismissed from his heart all others and fixed on one whom he chose entirely on his own. Love is ever blind and cannot see. He pictured her in his heart when he went to bed—her gay beauty and tender years, her slim waist and long slender arms, her sensible conduct and noble blood, her womanly bearing and sedate ways. Having decided upon her he felt he couldn't have made a better choice; and once he'd made up his mind he lost faith in others' judgement; and he could see no possible objection—or so he deluded himself. Then he sent an invitation to his friends requesting the pleasure of their company with all speed, as he intended to cut short their labour on his behalf. There was no more need for them to ride hither and thither on his account; he had found his haven.

Soon Placebo and his friends arrived. First of all he asked them as a favour to offer no arguments against the course he had taken, for it was not only pleasing to God, he explained, but the true basis of his happiness.

There was, he said, a maiden in the town celebrated for her beauty; and though not of high rank, for him her youth and beauty was enough. He declared he would take this maiden for his wife and live in ease and sanctity; and he thanked God he could have her wholly, that no man would share in his delight. Next he begged them to give him the help he needed so that his enterprise should not fail; when, said he, his heart would be at rest. 'Now I've nothing to worry about,' he declared, 'except one matter that pricks my conscience, which I'll disclose to you now you're here. A long time ago I heard it said that no man can have two paradises—I mean the one on earth and the one in heaven. For even if he keeps clear of the seven deadly sins and all their ramifications, yet there's such perfect delight, and so much comfort and pleasure in marriage, that I keep worrying lest in my old age I may be leading a life so pleasant and delicious and free of grief and trouble that I'll have had my heaven here on earth. For if the real heaven's bought with infinite suffering and tribulation, how then shall I (living in delight like all married men with their wives) enter into bliss with Christ Eternal? That's what worries me, and I ask you both to resolve me the question.'

Justinus, who detested his nonsense, gave him a light-hearted answer (but without adducing any authorities, for brevity's sake). 'Sir,' said he, 'so long as this is the only obstacle, it may be that God in His wonderful mercy shall so dispose matters that you may repent of married life, in which you claim there's neither grief nor trouble, even before Holy Church weds you. God forbid a married man shouldn't be granted occasion to repent a good deal oftener than a single man! Therefore, sir—it's the best advice I can offer —don't give way to despair, but bear in mind that she may perhaps be your purgatory. She may be God's instrument, God's scourge—and then your soul shall skip straight up to Heaven faster than an arrow from a bow! I hope to God you'll realize, later, that there isn't and never will be enough happiness in marriage to stand in the way of your salvation, always provided you regulate the pleasures of your wife as is seemly and reasonable, that you don't give her too much amatory satisfaction—and keep from other sins of course. That's all I have to say—I'm a stupid fellow—but don't worry about it, brother; let's drop the subject. The Wife of Bath—if you have followed her—has already expounded her views most ably and concisely on the matter in hand —that is, marriage. Now farewell, and God preserve you.'

And with this Justinus took leave of his brother. When they saw there was no help for it, by dint of much astute bargaining they so arranged matters that this girl—her name was May— should be married to January as soon as possible. But I think it would be a waste of time if I were to detail all the deeds and documents by which she was endowed with his land, or tell you of her rich and elaborate trousseau. At length the day came when the two of them went to church to receive the holy sacrament. Out came the priest, the stole about his neck; he bade her be like Sarah and Rebecca in wisdom and in fidelity to the marriage-vow; he then said the customary prayers, signed them with the cross and asked God's blessing upon them, and made all sure with holy rites.

Thus they were married in due form, and took their seats with other notables upon the dais at the wedding-feast. January's palace was filled with music, joy and merriment, and the most delicious eatables in all Italy. Instruments of sweeter tone than any music ever made by Orpheus or by Amphion of Thebes played before them, and each course was heralded by a blare of ministrelsy louder than the trumpet-blast of Joab, and clearer than the horn sounded by Thiodamas in Thebes when that city was in peril. On every side Bacchus poured the wine, while Venus smiled on all, for January had become her knight and was about to test his mettle in wedlock, as he had while free; and so she danced, a flaming torch in her hand, before the bride and the whole company. Indeed I'd go so far as to say that Hymen, god of weddings, never in his life saw a happier bridegroom. Hold your tongue, you poet Marcian, you who wrote of the gay wedding between Philology and Mercury, and of the songs the Muses sang! Both your tongue and pen are too feeble to portray a marriage such as this. When tender youth weds stooping age, the joke's beyond description. Try yourself, and you'll see if I'm lying or not!

May looked charming sitting there; to behold her was like a fairytale—Queen Esther never turned on Ahasuerus such a glance, or a regard so demure. I can't describe the half of her beauty, but this much I can tell you—she looked like a clear May morning brimming with beauty and delight. And every time January looked at her face he fell into a trance of ravishment and began inwardly anticipating how he would that night hug her in an even closer embrace than Paris clasped Helen. But nevertheless he still felt compunction when he thought how he must offend her that night: 'Alas! the tender creature! God grant you may be able to stand up to my lust for you, it's so hot and sharp! I'm afraid you mayn't be able to bear it—Lord forbid I do all that I might! I wish to God the night would come and last for ever, and all these people had gone.' And in the end he did everything in his power (as best he could without actual rudeness) to manoeuvre them discreetly from the table.

When in due time they rose from the board they danced and drank freely, then went through the house scattering spices. Everybody was filled with happiness and high spirits, all save one: a squire named Damian, who had long carved the meat at the knight's table. His lady May so ravished him he almost went out of his mind with the pain of it. Dancing torch in hand, Venus singed him so cruelly that he all but swooned and perished on the spot; and he hastily took to his bed. For the moment I'll say no more about him but leave him there to weep and bemoan himself until smiling May shall take pity on him.

O perilous fire, bred in bedstraw! Household foe making show of service! O treacherous servant, faithless domestic, like a sly treacherous adder in the bosom—God shield us all from knowing you! O January, drunk with the joy of marriage, see how your Damian, your own squire and liegeman born, plans to dishonour you—God grant you discover the enemy in your home, for there's no worse plague in all the world than a household foe ever in one's presence.

Now the sun had completed his daily arc and was about to descend; he could no longer stay above the horizon in that latitude. Night spread his coarse dark mantle over the hemisphere: and so, with thanks on all sides, the gay crowd began to take leave of January. They rode joyously home to their houses, where they attended to their affairs at leisure and in due course went to bed. As soon as they were gone the impatient January insisted on going to bed; he could wait no longer. First he drank hot spiced wine to fortify his courage—hippocras, clarry, and vernage—for he had a good store of strong aphrodisiacs like those which the accursed monk Constantine has noted in his book *De Coitu*. January swallowed the lot without the slightest hesitation. 'For the love of God hurry up,' said he to his bosom friends, 'be polite, but get everybody out of the house.' They did as he requested. A last toast was drunk, the curtains drawn, and the bride brought to bed as silent as a stone. When the bed had been blessed by the priest and everyone had left the room, January hugged his lovely May—his paradise, his mate! close in his arms, fondling and kissing her over again, rubbing the bristles of his gritty beard (which was like the skin of a dogfish, and sharp as briars, for after his fashion he was freshly shaved) against her tender face. Said he, 'Alas, my wife, I must take a few liberties and offend you greatly before I again descend! But nevertheless remember this: there's no workman whatever that can do a good job in a hurry; so we'll take our time and do it properly. It doesn't matter how long we make merry; the two of us are linked in holy wedlock—blessed be that yoke, for nothing we do is a sin! A man cannot sin with his wife —it would be like cutting yourself with your own dagger—for the law permits our frolic.' So he laboured away until day began to break, when he took a sop of bread soaked in strong spiced wine. Next he sat straight up in the bed and carolled loud and clear; then he kissed his wife and began to play the goat. He was as randy as a colt; he jabbered like a magpie. As he sang and yodelled, creaking away like a corncake, the slack skin round his neck was ashake—God knows what May thought in her heart when she saw him sitting up in his shirt with his nightcap on and scrawny neck; she didn't give a sixpence for his fun and games. At last he said, 'I'll go to sleep now the day has come; I can't keep awake any longer,' and laid down his head and slept till nine. Afterwards, in due course, January got up and dressed; but lovely May kept to her room until the fourth day, which is the best thing for new-married wives. For every workman must sometimes rest, or he won't last long—and that goes for every living creature, fish, bird, beast, or man!

Now I'll return to the miserable Damian and tell how he pined away for love. But this is what I'd like to say to him: 'Alas, poor Damian! Now answer my question if you can: How are you going to declare your passion to your lady, the lovely May? She'll only say "No". Besides, if you speak, she'll give you away. All I can say is, God help you!'

The lovesick Damian burned in the flames of Venus till he almost perished with desire; and so, unable to go on suffering like this, he put all to the hazard. Surreptitiously borrowing a writing case, he wrote a letter in which he poured out all his grief in the form of a complaint or song addressed to his fair lady May. This he placed in a silk purse that hung under his shirt, and laid it next his heart.

The moon, which had been in the second degree of Taurus at noon on the day January married pretty May, had now slid into the sign of Cancer, but May still kept to her room, as is the custom among gentlefolk. A bride should never eat in the banqueting-hall until four, or at least three, days have passed; then she may dine in public. And the fourth day had been completed—counting from noon to noon—when January and May took their seats in the banqueting-hall after High Mass. She looked as fresh as a bright summer's day. It chanced that the good knight thought of Damian and exclaimed, 'St Mary! How is it that Damian isn't in attendance? Is he still sick? What's the matter?' The squires standing beside him made his excuses, saying that his illness prevented him from performing his duties; no other reason could have kept him away.

'I'm sorry to hear it,' said January, 'for upon my soul he's a good squire, and were he to die it would be a calamity. He's as sensible, discreet, and trustworthy as any man of his rank that I know; a manly, useful, and most capable fellow besides. But I'll visit him as soon as possible after dinner, and take May with me, and cheer him up as much as I can.' This won him general approbation for his kindness and magnanimity in wishing to console his squire in his illness; they thought it a gentlemanly act. 'Madam,' said January, 'immediately after dinner, when you leave the hall for your chamber with your women, mind that you all go to see Damian. Keep him amused—he's a gentleman—and tell him I'll pay him a visit as soon as I've had a little rest. Don't be long, for I'll be waiting for you to come and sleep in my arms.' And having said this he called the squire who was marshal of the hall over to him, and began to give sundry instructions.

Lovely May, attended by her women, went straight to Damian, and sat down by his bedside to cheer him as well as she was able. Damian, seeing his chance, with no more sign than a remarkably long and heavy sigh, surreptitiously placed in her hand the purse that contained the paper on which he had set down his yearnings. And he gently whispered, 'Mercy! Don't expose me, for I'm a dead man if this should be known.' She hid the purse in her bosom and left him—and that's all you'll get from me! But she returned to January, who was sitting comfortably on the side of his bed. January took her into his arms, kissed her over and over again, and soon lay down to sleep. As for May, she pretended she had to visit a certain place where, as you know, everybody has to go at times; and when she'd read the note she finally tore it into shreds and threw it into the privy.

And now whose thoughts were busier than those of pretty young May? She laid herself down beside old January, who slept on until awakened by his cough. Presently he begged her to strip quite naked: he said he wanted a bit of fun and her clothes got in his way; and willy-nilly she obeyed. I daren't tell you how he acquitted himself, or whether to her it seemed paradise or hell, in case I should vex persons of refinement; so I'll leave them to it till the bell for evensong rang and they had to get up.

Whether it was due to destiny, or chance, or nature, or the influence of the stars, or whether the constellations stood in a favourable position in the heavens for petitioning any woman to play Venus' game, and for winning her love (as the scholars say there's a time for everything), I really cannot say; but let God above—He knows nothing happens without a cause—be the judge, for I'll keep silence. But the truth is, that day the sick Damian made such a sympathetic impression upon the lovely May that she could not rid her heart of the idea of making him happy. 'One thing's sure, I don't in the least care who it may upset,' thought she, 'for I can promise Damian here and now that I love him more than any living creature, though he had no more than the shirt to his back.' How quickly pity flows in to noble hearts!

This shows the wonderful generosity that is in women when they give their minds to it. Some—and they are many—are tyrants with hearts of stone who would have allowed Damian to perish on the spot sooner than grant him their favours, all the while rejoicing in their proud cruelty, caring nothing if they should be his murderers!

Filled with pity, compassionate May wrote with her own hand a letter in which she granted him her whole heart. Nothing was wanting save the time and place where she might satisfy his desire, for he was to have everything he wanted. And one day, when she saw her chance, May paid Damian a visit and dexterously thrust the letter underneath his pillow—let him read it if he likes! Bidding him recover, she took his hand and squeezed it hard, yet so secretly nobody noticed; and off she went to January when he sent for her.

Next morning Damian arose, his sickness and despair completely banished; and having combed and trimmed and prinked, and done all he could to make himself attractive in his lady's eyes, he came into January's presence like a huntsman's dog, all eager obedience. He made himself pleasant to everybody (flattery's the thing if you know how to manage it) till all were disposed to speak well of him; and so he stood high in his lady's favour. Here I'll leave Damian to go about his affairs and get on with my story.

Some scholars believe the purest happiness is to be found in enjoyment; and if so, the excellent January certainly did his utmost to lead a life of luxury, and live in a creditable manner as befitted a knight. His house, furnishings, and equipage were as suited to his rank as a king's. Among his other fine things he had made a garden walled round with stone. I know of no prettier garden anywhere. Indeed I really believe that even the author of *The Romance of the Rose* would not find it easy to depict its charm; even Priapus, god of gardens though he is, might be unequal to describing this garden and its well which stood beneath an evergreen laurel. They say that round this well Pluto and his queen Proserpine and her troop of fairies used often to amuse themselves with music and dancing.

This worthy old knight took great delight in walking and pass-
ing the time in this garden. He permitted nobody but himself to
keep the key; for he always carried a small silver latchkey with
which to unlock the little wicket-gate at pleasure. And when, in
the summertime, he felt like doing his duty by his lovely wife, then
he would visit it with May, and none but they two; and those
things they had not done in bed he would perform with advantage
in the garden. January and his wife spent many a happy day in
this manner. But for January, as for other living men, earthly
happiness cannot last for ever.

O sudden Chance! O unstable Fortune! Deceitful as the scor-
pion whose head fascinates the prey it means to sting, and whose
venomous tail is death! O insecure joy! O sweet strange poison!
Monstrous Fortune, that subtly tricks out its gifts with the hue of
stability till one and all are taken in! Why, having wholly be-
friended January, did you deceive him so? For now you have
robbed him of both his eyes; and such is his grief, he wishes he
were dead.

Alas, that noble, generous January! In the midst of all his hap-
piness and prosperity he suddenly went blind. How piteously he
wept and lamented! And to cap it all the fire of jealousy burned
his heart—for he feared his wife would fall into some folly—till he
wished somebody would slay both himself and her. Alive or dead,
he couldn't bear the idea of her being a lover or wife of someone
else. He wanted her to live for the rest of her life clad in black like
a widow, solitary as a turtledove that's lost its mate. But after a
month or two, in the end his grief began to abate. Realizing there
was no help for it he patiently accepted his misfortune. But one
thing he certainly couldn't give up, and that was his continual
jealousy. This jealousy was so overriding he wouldn't allow May
to go anywhere—his own hall, the houses of others, any place
whatsoever—unless he kept his hand upon her all the time. The
lovely May shed many tears over this, for she loved Damian so
dearly that she felt she must either have him as she wished or die
on the spot. And so she waited for her heart to break.

As for Damian, he became the saddest man you ever saw—at no
time could he say a word to pretty May about anything to the
purpose without January hearing it, for his hand was always in
hers. Nevertheless, what with secret signals and the writing of

notes back and forth, he was able to communicate with May, and she to know what schemes he had in mind.

Ah, January, what good would it be to you could you see as far as the furthest horizon? As well be blind and deceived as have eyes and still be deceived. Argus had a hundred eyes, but was blind for all his peering and prying—like many another, Lord knows, who's convinced to the contrary! All I say is, what the eye doesn't see the heart doesn't mourn for.

Lovely May, whom I spoke of just now, took a wax impression of the latchkey January carried for the little wicket-gate by which he used to enter his garden; and Damian, knowing exactly what she had in mind, forged a counterfeit key in secret. There's no more to be said—but soon enough some remarkable developments will take place connected with this wicket-gate, which if you wait you'll hear about.

Noble Ovid, the Lord knows you speak very truly when you say that however ingenious and elaborate the strategem, Love will somehow find a way. Take a lesson from Pyramus and Thisbe: though closely guarded on every side, they reached an understanding by whispering through a wall—now who could have found out a trick like that?

But to my theme: in the first week of June it happened that January, egged on by his wife, took a fancy to amuse himself alone with her in the garden; and so one morning he said to her, 'Rise up, my wife, my lady and my love! Sweet dove, the voice of the turtle is heard, the winter is past, the rains are over and gone! Come forth, with thy dove's eyes! Thy breasts are sweeter than wine! The garden is enclosed all about—come then, my snow-white bride! My sweet wife, you've stricken me to the heart, that's sure. I can find no spot in thee! Then come and let us take our pleasure; for I chose thee for my wife and my solace.'

Such were the lewd old tags he used. May signalled Damian to go in front with his latchkey. So Damian unlocked the wicket-gate and slipped inside in such a way that nobody saw or heard him. Then he crouched quietly beneath a bush.

January, blind as a stone, took May by the hand and went alone with her into his enchanting garden. Smartly he clapped the wicket-gate to and said, 'Now, wife, there is none here but me and you who of all creatures I love best. Heaven's my witness, I'd sooner stab myself to death than give offence, my dear and faithful wife! For God's sake remember how it was I chose you—certainly for no mercenary considerations, but simply for the love I bore you! Be true to me, even if I'm old and blind; and I'll tell you why. Three things you will certainly gain by it: first, the love of Christ; second, honour to yourself; and third, my entire estate, town and castle—I give it you; draw up the deeds as you like; and as sure as God's my salvation it shall be settled before tomorrow sunset. First kiss me to seal our covenant. Don't blame me if I'm jealous. My thoughts are so bound up with you that whenever I think of your beauty—and then of my unpleasing old age—even if I were to die I really can't bear to be out of your company: I love you so, and that's the plain truth. Now kiss me, my dear wife, and let's roam about.'

To these words lovely May returned a gentle answer—but first of all burst into tears. 'I've a soul to look after as well as you, not to mention my honour, that delicate bud of wifehood I entrusted into your hands when the priest bound my body to yours. So if you don't mind, my dearest lord, this is my reply: I pray God the day will never dawn when I shame my family and impair my good name by faithlessness, or let me suffer a death as terrible as ever woman suffered; and should I ever commit that crime, strip me and put me in a sack and drown me in the nearest river! I'm a lady, not a trollop! Why say such things? But men are always faithless and never tire of casting reproach upon women. That's what you're always doing—distrusting and upbraiding us women.'

As she spoke, she caught sight of Damian squatting behind his bush. She coughed and signed him with her finger to climb a tree laden with fruit, and up he went. Indeed he understood her, and any signal she could make, far better than her own husband January. For she had explained everything to him in a letter, and what he was to do. Here I'll leave Damian sitting in the pear-tree while January and May roam happily about.

Bright was the day and blue the sky, and Phoebus—then by my reckoning in Gemini, not far from his maximum northern declination (Cancer, which is the exaltation of Jupiter)—was sending down his golden rays to cheer the flowers with his warmth. Now it happened on that bright morning Pluto, the King of Faery, accompanied by many ladies in the train of his wife, Queen

Proserpine (whom he had carried off from Aetna while she was gathering flowers in the fields—you can read in Claudian the story of how he bore her away in his grim chariot) was sitting upon a bench of fresh green turves on the farther side of the garden and speaking to his queen.

'My dear wife,' he was saying, 'nobody can deny it; daily experience goes to show the treacheries you women practise upon men. I could give you ten hundred thousand notorious instances of your dishonesty and fickleness. O wisest Solomon, richest of the rich, full-fraught with wisdom and glory, how memorable are your sayings for anyone who has wit and intelligence! For thus he appraises the goodness of men: "One man among a thousand have I found; but a woman among all those have I not found." Thus spoke the king; and he was acquainted with the wickedness of you women. Nor, I believe, does Jesus the son of Sirach usually speak of women with respect. Now plague and brimstone upon your bodies! Do you not see that honourable knight about to be cuckolded by his own squire just because the poor man's old and blind? See that lecher perching in the tree! Now I will grant a royal boon: the moment his wife begins to deceive him, this good old blind knight shall receive his eyesight back again. Then all her harlotry shall be made plain to him—a reproach to her and others like her.'

'You will, will you?' said Proserpine. 'Well, then, I swear by Saturn, my mother's father, that I'll provide her with a complete answer, and not only her but all women ever afterwards for her sake, so that when they're caught out in any misdemeanour they'll excuse themselves with a straight face and bear down all accusers —not one shall perish for want of an answer! Though a man should see everything with both eyes, yet we women shall put a bold face on it with tears and vows and cunning recriminations till you men look stupid as geese!

'What are your authorities to me? I'm quite aware this Jew, this Solomon of yours, came across plenty of fools among us women; yet though he found no good woman, there are dozens of other men who have found women that were completely faithful, good and virtuous—for example those who now dwell in Heaven with Christ, who proved their constancy by their martyrdom. And be-

sides, Roman history preserves the memory of many a true and
faithful wife. Now, sir, don't lose your temper: even if Solomon
did say he found no good woman, pray consider the man's drift:
he meant that sovereign goodness resides only in God, who dwells
in the Trinity.

'Well! Then why in the name of the one true God do you make
so much of this Solomon? What if he did build a temple to the
Lord and was rich and glorious? He also built temples for false
gods—how could he do a thing more forbidden? Excuse me, you
can gild his reputation as much as you like, yet he remains a
lecher, an idolator who forsook the true God in his old age! And
had God not spared him (according to the Bible) for his father's
sake, he would have lost his kingdom sooner than he expected! I
don't give a rap for all the slanders you men write of women, but
I must speak or burst—I am a woman! If he calls us spitfires, good
manners aren't going to stop me from reviling a man who tries to
slander us—I'd sooner have my hair cut off!'

'Calm down, madam,' said Pluto, 'I give it up! But seeing that
I swore upon oath to give him back his sight, my word must be
kept, I warn you plainly: for I'm a king and it doesn't do for me
to lie.'

'And I am Queen of Faerie!' she retorted. 'She shall have her
answer, I guarantee that. Let's bandy no more words about the
matter: I really don't wish to argue with you any longer.'

Now let us turn again to January, sitting in the garden with his
lovely May and singing 'I'll always love you and you alone' as
merrily as a popinjay. He wandered so long in the garden walks
till at last he came to the pear-tree where Damian gaily perched
high overhead among the fresh green leaves.

Bright-eyed and glowing, the lovely May sighed and said, 'Oh,
my poor side! Come what may, I've got to have some of those
pears I see up there—I've such a craving to eat those little green
pears I feel I'll die if I don't. For heaven's sake do something! Let
me tell you, a woman in my condition can have such an appetite
for fruit she may easily die if she doesn't get it.'

'Alas!' cried he, 'if only I had a boy here to climb up! If only I
wasn't blind!'

'That doesn't matter,' she replied, 'for goodness' sake, if you'd only vouchsafe to put your arms round that pear tree—for I know you don't trust me—I'd climb up easily enough if I might set my foot on your back.'

'Of course,' said he, 'I'll do that and more—you could have my heart's blood if it was any good.'

He bent down and she stood upon his back, caught hold of a branch, and up she went! Please don't take offence, ladies; I'm only a rough fellow and don't know how to beat about the bush— Damian lost no time but yanked up her smock and in he thrust.

When Pluto saw this shameful wrong he gave back January his sight and made him see as well as ever. Nobody was gladder than January when his sight was restored. But his thoughts were still fixed upon his wife, and he cast his eyes up into the tree where he saw Damian investing his wife in a manner I find impossible to express without being rude; at which he set up a roaring wail like a mother whose child is dying: 'Help! Murder! Stop thief!' he yelled. 'What are you up to? You big brazen strumpet.'

'What's the matter with you?' she returned. 'Have a bit of patience and use your brains! I've cured your blindness. Upon my soul, I'm not lying, they told me the best thing I could do to heal your eyes and make you see again was to wrestle with a man in a tree—God knows I was only trying to help!'

'Wrestle!' cried he, 'Oh yes! It went in at any rate! May God bring you both to a shameful death! He plugged you, I saw it with my own eyes—hang me if I didn't!'

'In that case my medicine isn't working,' said she, 'for if you could see you certainly wouldn't speak to me like that—you see only by glimpses, and not properly at all.'

'Thanks be to God, I see as well as ever I did in both eyes,' he replied, 'and on my word of honour that's what he seemed to be doing with you.'

'You're muzzy, quite muzzy, my dear sir,' said she. 'This is the thanks I get for helping you to see. I wish to God I hadn't been so kindhearted!'

'There, there, my dear,' he replied, 'put it all out of your head; come down, my dearest, and if I spoke amiss, why, God help me, I'm punished enough. But by my father's soul! I thought I saw Damian right up you, and your smock against your breast.'

'Well, sir, you can think what you like. But a man waking from sleep doesn't take things in all at once or see properly until he's quite awake; and in the same way a man who's long been blind and has just begun to see again isn't all at once going to see as well as a man whose vision's been back for a day or two. Before your sight's had time to settle you may pretty often be misled by what you think you see. Be careful, I beg you; for by the Lord in heaven there's many a man thinks he's seen a thing and it isn't so at all. Misapprehensions lead to misjudgements.' And with this she jumped down from the tree.

Who so happy as January? He kissed and embraced her over again and gently stroked her belly; then he led her home to his palace. Now, gentlemen, I wish you happiness; for here ends my tale of January. God and His Mother Saint Mary bless us all!

Then our Host cried out, 'Well! Mercy of God, may the Lord keep me from a wife like that! Look what tricks and dodges women get up to—always busy as bees diddling us poor fellows and always twisting the truth, as this Merchant's tale plainly shows. I've a wife, certainly, and though a poor one, she's true; but she's a rattling spitfire with her tongue; she's got plenty other faults besides—no matter, let it go! But do you know what? Between ourselves, I wish to God I wasn't tied to her. Yet I'd be a damn fool if I reckoned up her faults—and why? It would get back to her; someone in this company would be bound to tell— who, I needn't say; women know how to spread such matters around; anyhow I haven't the brains to tell the whole, and so my tale's over.'

'Come over here, Squire, if you please, and tell us something about love—surely you must know as much about it as any man.'

'No, Sir,' he replied, 'but I'll do what I can with all my heart, for I don't want to go against your wishes. I'll tell a story, but if I tell it badly I hope you'll excuse me. I'll do my best; and here's my tale.'

THE SQUIRE'S TALE

At Tsarev in the land of Tartary there dwelt a king who warred on Russia; and thereby many a brave man met his death. Cambuscan was the name of this noble king; he was greatly renowned in his day, for nowhere by land or sea was there so excellent a lord in all respects. He lacked no quality a king should have. He kept his sworn allegiance to the faith in which he was born; in addition he was powerful, rich, wise, merciful and just always; true to his word, honourable, benevolent, in disposition steadfast as the pole; lively, young, and strong; in arms as mettlesome as any young knight in his household. Handsome and fortunate, he lived in such royal splendour there was none to compare with him.

This great king, Cambuscan the Tartar, had two sons by his wife Elpheta. The eldest was called Algarsyf and the other Cambalo. He also had a daughter named Canace, the youngest of the three. But I have neither tongue nor skill to tell you the half of her beauty, nor would I dare undertake so high a task—in any case my English is unequal to it. To describe her fully would require a great poet skilled in the rhetoric which belongs to that art, and none such am I—I can only speak as best I may.

It came about that when Cambuscan had worn his diadem for twenty years he commanded (as I believe was his yearly custom) his birthday celebrations to be proclaimed throughout his city of Tsarev for the exact day on which the Ides of March fell according to the calendar. Phoebus the sun shone joyous and clear, for he was near his point of exaltation in the house of Mars in the first ten degrees of the hot and fiery sign of Aries. Pleasant and benign was the weather, so that the birds, what with the season of the year and the young greenery, sang loudly of their loves in the bright sunshine; for it seemed to them they had won protection from the keen cold sword of winter.

Now this Cambuscan of whom I spoke sat in his royal robes and diadem high on the dais in his palace, holding high festival with a splendour and magnificence such as the world had never seen.

It would take a whole summer's day were I to describe all the spectacle. However it isn't necessary to detail the order of the serving of the courses: I won't speak of their exotic soups, nor of their roasted swans and herons, for in any case, as old knights tell us, in that land there are some foods which are prized as great delicacies but for which people care little in this country. No one could report it all. The morning is wearing on, so I shan't delay you; in any case it would be no more than fruitless waste of time. So I'll go back to where I began.

Now after the third course had been brought in, while the king was sitting in the midst of his nobles and listening to his minstrels playing delightful music before him at table, suddenly a knight riding upon a brazen horse burst in at the door of the hall. In his hand he carried a great mirror of glass, and on his thumb he wore a golden ring, while a naked sword hung from his side. So great was the astonishment at this knight that not a word was spoken as he rode up to the high table. Young and old looked on and watched him intently.

This strange knight who had so suddenly made his appearance was fully armed in rich armour, but bareheaded. He saluted first the king and queen, then all the nobles in order as they sat in the hall, with such deep respect and deference, both in words and bearing, that Sir Gawain with his antique courtesy could hardly improve on it were he to come again from the land of faery. Then in ringing tones he delivered his message before the high table (not missing a thing out, according to the style fashionable in his language). In order to lend point to his meaning he fitted his manner to his words as the art of speaking directs those who study it. And though I cannot imitate his style—which is far too high for me to climb over—I can say that what follows is the general gist of what he intended to convey, if I remember right:

He said, 'My liege lord the King of Arabia and India proffers you his best salutations on this illustrious occasion. In honour of your festival he sends you, through me, who am entirely yours to command, this horse of brass. Come rain or shine it can take you in ease and comfort wherever you wish within the space of a natural day—that is to say twenty-four hours—and transport you bodily without the least harm to yourself through fair or foul to any spot you have a mind to visit. Or should you wish to fly into the air as high as a soaring eagle, this same horse will carry you wherever you want to go even though you fall asleep on his back; and at the twirling of a pin he'll return again. He that made it was skilled in machinery and knew many magic seals and spells, and watched long for a favourable combination of the planets before he finished making it.

'And this mirror which I hold in my hand is of such power that those who look in it can see when danger threatens your kingdom or yourself; it will reveal who is your friend and who your foe. Over and above this, should any fair lady have set her heart on any kind of man, this mirror will show her his treachery if he be false; and also his new love, and all his guile, so plainly that nothing shall be hidden. Wherefore, against the coming of the pleasant summer season, he has sent this mirror and this ring that you see to your excellent daughter, my lady Canace here.

'Should you wish to learn the power of the ring, it is this: if she cares to wear it upon her thumb or carry it in her purse, there's no bird that flies under heaven but she shall perfectly understand its song, and know its meaning plain and clear, and answer it again in its own speech. And she shall also know the properties of every herb that grows, and whom it will benefit, no matter how deep and wide his wounds.

'This naked sword that hangs by my side has power to cleave and bite through the armour of whatsoever man you strike, be it thick as a branching oak; and whosoever is wounded by the blow may never be healed until it pleases you out of compassion to stroke with the flat the place where he has been hurt—that's to say you must stroke the wound with the flat of the sword, when it will close up. This is plain unvarnished truth: and it will never fail while it remains in your possession.'

Having thus given his account, the knight rode out of the hall and dismounted. His horse stood stock-still in the courtyard, gleaming like the sun. Then the knight was led to his chamber, unarmed, and taken to his seat at the banquet.

The gifts—that's to say the sword and mirror—were immediately borne with royal pomp to the high tower by special officers appointed to the task, while the ring was ceremoniously brought to Canace where she sat at the high table. But as for the horse

of brass—and this is fact, not fable—it could not be shifted but
stood as if glued to the earth. None could budge it from the
spot, even with the aid of windlass or pulley, for the simple
reason they didn't know how it worked. So they had to leave
it there until the knight showed them how to move it, as you
will hear in a moment.

A great crowd swarmed hither and thither to gaze upon the
stationary horse. For it stood as high, and was as broad and long
and as well-proportioned for strength as any Lombard steed; more
than that, it was so quick-eyed, and so much what a horse should
be that it might have been a thoroughbred Apulian courser. All
agreed it was perfect from head to tail, that it plainly could not
be improved on by either art or nature. But still their greatest
wonder was how it could go, being made of brass; it was magic,
they thought. Different people had their different notions—there
were as many ideas as heads. They murmured like a swarm of
bees, constructing theories according to their fancies; they quoted
the ancient poets, and said it was like Pegasus, the flying horse,
or perhaps the horse of Sinon the Greek, which brought Troy
to destruction, as you may read in old romances. Said one, 'Fear
keeps nibbling at my heart, for I feel certain there are armed
men inside who plan to overthrow the city. It would be best if
such things were looked into.' Another whispered quietly to a
friend, 'He's wrong, it's more like one of those magic illusions
jugglers work at great banquets.' Thus they argued, discussing
their various misgivings, always ready to put the worst con-
struction on things, as uneducated people generally do when
passing opinions on matters too subtle for their ignorance to
comprehend.

Some wondered how marvels could be seen in the mirror
which had been carried into the master-tower. Another had the
answer, saying it might well have some natural explanation and
work by means of a deft arrangement of angles and ingeniously
contrived reflections—there was one like it in Rome as he pointed
out. Alhazen, Vitello, and Aristotle were mentioned, for as those
who have read their books know, they wrote in their lifetimes of
curious mirrors and the science of optics.

Yet others marvelled at the sword that could pierce everything:
they began discussing King Telephus and Achilles' wonderful

spear that could both wound and heal, just like the sword you have heard about. They debated the different methods of tempering metal (sometimes by the use of potions) and how and when the tempering should be done—all of which is a mystery, to me at any rate.

Then they discussed Canace's ring: all agreed they had never heard of so wonderful a specimen of the ring-maker's craft, save that Moses and King Solomon were said to be skilled in this art. Thus people talked, drawn aside in small groups. Some nevertheless pointed out it is remarkable that glass should be made from the ash of ferns, yet does not resemble fern-ash; but because this has been known for so long, people had stopped talking and wondering about it. Many had speculated just as earnestly upon the cause of thunder, the ebb and flow of tides, mist, gossamer, and all sorts of things, until the answers were known. So they chattered and argued and theorized till the king rose from the high table.

Phoebus had left the tenth mansion at noon; the royal beast, the noble Leo, with the star Aldiran between his paws, was still ascending, making it two hours past the meridian when the Tartar king Cambuscan rose from the table where he sat in state. Loud strains of music went before him till he came to the presence-chamber where various musical instruments played in celestial harmony. Now the worshippers of gay Venus began to dance, for their Lady was in her exaltation in Pisces and looked upon them with a friendly eye.

When the noble king was seated on his throne the stranger knight was quickly brought to him. He led Canace to the dance. Here all was gaiety and revel, such as no dull dog may dream of; it would take a man acquainted with love and the service of love—some gay fellow as fresh as May—to picture to you the spectacle.

Who could describe their exotic style of dancing, their beautiful faces, the subtle glances, the coverings-up lest they be perceived by the jealous? None but Lancelot, and he is dead. So I will pass over all this gaiety and say no more, but leave them to their revelry till it is time to dine.

Music plays, the steward bids them hurry with the wine and spices, which ushers and squires run off to fetch; they are soon brought in, when all eat and drink. And when this was at an end they proceeded to the temple, as was meet and proper. What need to describe what they had? Everyone knows perfectly well that at a king's banquet there's plenty for everybody, high and low; besides more delicacies than I know of.

When the dinner was over the noble king accompanied by his whole troop of lords and ladies went to see the horse of brass. There was more amazement at this brazen horse than at the siege of Troy, when a horse was also an object of wonder. In the end the king asked the knight about the strength and capabilities of the horse and begged him to explain how he was controlled.

When the knight laid hand on the rein, the horse immediately began to frisk and curvet. 'There's nothing to it, Sire,' he said. 'When you wish to ride anywhere you must twist a wire that's fixed inside his ear, which I'll show you when we are by ourselves. You must also tell him the name of the place or country to which you wish to ride. Then when you reach the place where you want to stop, tell him to descend and twist another wire—for this is what works the whole mechanism—when he'll obey you and descend. He'll stand rooted to the spot, and no one on earth will be able to drag him away or carry him off. Or if you wish to bid him go away, twist this wire and he'll vanish from everyone's sight in an instant; but he'll return at any time, night or day, whenever you want to call him back. I'll show you how presently, when we're alone together. Ride him whenever you like; that's all you have to do.'

Having clearly grasped the principle of the thing when he had been instructed by the knight, the noble valiant Cambuscan returned delightedly to his revels. The bridle was carried off to the tower and kept among his most precious and treasured jewels, while the horse vanished from sight—how, I don't know, and that's all you'll get from me! Now I'll leave Cambuscan feasting his nobles in merriment and delight till day was near dawn.

ii

Sleep, nurse of the digestion, gave them a wink and a warning: deep drinking and exercise call for rest. With yawning mouth he kissed them all, saying it was time to lie down because it was the hour when the hot, moist humour of blood was in domination: 'Look after your blood, it's Nature's friend,' said he. Yawning, they thanked him in twos and threes, and everyone began to retire to his rest as Sleep had bidden; they knew it was for their good.

Their dreams are not going to be related as far as I'm concerned; for their heads were full of the fumes of drink, which means they had no significance. Most of them slept late, except for Canace; like most women she was very temperate, and had taken leave of her father to go to bed early in the evening. She had no wish to appear looking pale and jaded in the morning, so she took her first sleep, and then awoke. Both the magic mirror and the ring had so delighted her heart that a dozen times her colour came and went; and the mirror had made so deep an impression that she dreamed of it in her sleep. And so before the sun had stolen up into the sky she called her duenna to her side and told her she wished to get up.

The duenna, inquisitive as old women usually are, answered at once, 'Where in the world can you want to go as early as this, madam, when everyone's asleep?'

'I wish to get up and go for a walk, as I don't want to sleep any longer,' said she.

Her duenna summoned a large retinue of women, and some ten or twelve of them arose. Then up rose Canace herself, as fair and fresh and rosy as the new-risen sun which by the time she was ready stood no higher than four degrees above the horizon. She went forth at a leisurely pace, lightly dressed as was in keeping with freedom in walking and the sweet and pleasant season of the year. With no more than five or six in her train she followed an alley through the trees in the park.

The mist rising from the ground made the sun appear huge and ruddy, yet the scene was so beautiful it delighted their hearts, what with the early morning and the season of the year and the singing of the birds. For from their songs she at once understood what they meant and what their feelings were.

If one delays coming to the point of a story till after the interest of those who have long been listening has cooled, the more it's spun out the less savour is there in its prolixity—and for this reason, it seems to me, it's high time I condescended to come to the point myself, and brought this walk of Canace's to an end.

As she sauntered idly along she came upon a dried-out tree, white as chalk; and there, perched high overhead in it was a falcon crying out so piteously that the whole wood resounded with her lament. She had beaten herself so pitilessly with both wings that the red blood ran right down the tree to which she clung. And ever and again she shrieked and lamented, stabbing herself with her beak and wailing so loud that no tiger, nor other cruel beast that dwells in wood or forest, but would have wept if weep it could for pity of her. If only I were good at describing falcons! For no living man ever heard of one more beautiful in plumage, nobility of form, and all other attributes worthy of note. She seemed to be a peregrine falcon from some foreign land. Every now and then she fainted on her perch for lack of blood, until she was on the point of falling from the tree.

As the lovely princess Canace was wearing upon her finger the magic ring that enabled her to understand perfectly the language of every bird and to answer it in its own tongue, she could understand what this falcon was saying; and for the pity of it almost dropped down dead. She hastened to the tree. Looking pityingly at the falcon, she spread out her lap; for it was clear to her the falcon must fall from her twig when next she fainted for loss of blood. She stood watching her a long time, till at last she thus addressed the hawk:

'What is the cause—if it may be told—of your being in this fierce torment of Hell?' said she to the hawk overhead. 'Is it for grief at death, or loss of love? For these are the two things, as I believe, that cause most grief to a noble heart; other misfortunes are not worth mentioning. For you are inflicting punishment upon yourself, which clearly proves either bitterness or despair must be the occasion of your cruel agony, since I see no one hunting you. I pray you take pity on yourself, for God's love, or say how I can help you. Nowhere in the world have I ever seen bird or beast maltreat itself so pitifully. I feel such compassion for you that truly your grief is killing me. For God's love come down from the tree, and as I am true daughter of a king, when I know the real cause of your sorrow, I'll put it right before the day is over if it lies in my power—as surely as the great God of Nature may give me aid! And I'll find plenty of herbs that will quickly heal your wounds.'

Then the falcon shrieked even more piteously than before and suddenly fell to the ground in a dead faint, where she lay like a stone. Canace took her into her lap until she began to regain consciousness. And when the falcon had recovered from her swoon, she said something like this in hawk-language:

'That pity quickly flows in noble hearts, which feel the sharp pangs of another's like their own, is proved every day as one may see in both books and real life; for a noble heart declares its nobility. My fair Canace, I can plainly see you have compassion on my distress because of the truly womanly kindheartedness that Nature implanted in your character. With no hope of bettering my condition but only to obey your generous heart and to let others take warning from my case—as a lion is daunted when a dog is beaten in front of it—for that reason and to that end I'll tell you my troubles before I go, while I have time and opportunity.'

And ever, while the one told her sorrow, the other wept as if she would turn to water, till the falcon bade her cease, and, with a sigh, began her story thus:

'I was born—alack the day!—in a rock of grey marble, and fostered so tenderly that nothing troubled me; and I did not know the meaning of adversity till I was able to soar high under the heavens. Close by me there dwelt a tercel who seemed a very fountain of nobility. Though he was filled with perfidiousness and treachery it was shrouded under a modest demeanour, a colour of honesty, an eager attentiveness and desire to please, and this in such a way that none could have guessed it was all pretence—so deep in grain had he dyed these colours. Just as a snake hides itself under flowers biding its time to strike, so did this hypocrite, this paragon of lovers, pay his gallant courtesies and deferential homage, keeping up an appearance of the attentiveness that goes with a noble love. And as a sepulchre is beautiful above while you know that underneath there is a rotting corpse, so was this hypocrite—warm outside but cold within. And he pursued his end in such a way that none—unless it were the Devil himself—knew what he intended. He wept and complained for so long, and for so many years pretended his service to me that, believing in his oaths and promises, my too tender and too foolish heart (all innocent of his consummate wickedness, being afraid also that he might die, for it seemed to me this might happen) granted him love on the condition that my honour and good name would always be kept inviolate, both in public and private. In other words, as he seemed worthy I gave him my whole heart and soul—else, God knows, and he knows, I would never have given them—and I exchanged my heart for his for all eternity. But there's a true old saying, "An honest man and a thief never think alike." So when he saw that things had gone so far, and that I'd wholly granted him my love in the way I've described, and yielded him my faithful heart as freely as he swore his had been given me, then, filled with duplicity, this tiger fell upon his knees with such humble devotion and deep reverence, in aspect and behaviour so much the noble lover, so ravished, it seemed, for joy, that never Jason nor Trojan Paris—Jason, did I say? surely no man since Lamech who (as his been written) was first to love two women—never since the first man was born could anyone have imitated a twenty thousandth part of his skill in deceits and sophistries, or have been worthy to unlatch his shoe where double-dealing and pretence are concerned—or so thank a creature as he thanked me! No woman, however prudent, could resist his heavenly graces, so exquisitely groomed and polished was he in both conversation and demeanour. And I so loved him for his deference and the honesty I thought was in his heart, that if the slightest thing gave him pain and I knew of it I seemed to feel death wring my heart. In short, things went so far that my will became the instrument of his—I mean that in everything within the bounds of decorum and my honour my will obeyed his will. God knows, I never had anything so dear as he nor ever shall!

'My imagining nothing but good of him lasted for a year or two or longer. But in the end this is how things stood: Fortune willed it that he must depart from the place where I lived. No question but that it was grief to me—I cannot begin to describe it; but one thing I will say: for certain it taught me what the pain of death is like, I felt such torment at his having to go. So one day he took leave of me, and so sorrowfully that when I heard him

speak and saw how changed was his colour I really supposed
he felt as much pain as I did. However, I thought he was faithful,
and that he would indeed return again within a little while; and
there were also reasons of honour, as so often happens, for his
going; so that I made a virtue of necessity and took it well, seeing
it had to be.

'Hiding my sorrow from him as best I could I took him by
the hand and swore by St John: "See, I am wholly yours; be
you to me as I have been and ever shall be to you."

'There's no need to repeat what he said in reply—who could
speak better than he, or behave worse? He'd speak with eloquence
—and do nothing. "Whoever sups with the devil has need of a
long spoon"—or so I've heard. So at last he had to set out and
flew whither he wished to go; and when he decided to halt I
imagine he had in mind this adage: "Everything rejoices at re-
turning to its natural bent"—or so, I believe, they say. Men have
a natural love of novelty, just like birds one feeds in cages. For
you can look after them night and day, strewing their cages with
straw as soft and fine as silk, giving them sugar, honey, milk
and bread, yet, such is their love of novelty in diet, the moment
the door's open they'll kick over the cup with their feet and be
off to the wood to feed on worms—they have a natural love of
anything new, and no nobility of blood can restrain them. So it
was with this tercel, alas the day! Nobly born, lively, gay, hand-
some, modest and generous as he was, one day he saw a kite
upon the wing and suddenly fell so deeply in love with her that
all his love for me was clean gone. And in this way he broke
his troth; and so my love became the servant of this kite—and
I'm forsaken with no remedy!'

And with these words the falcon gave a cry and fainted again
in Canace's bosom. Great was the sorrow of Canace and all her
women for the hawk's misfortune; they did not know how
they might comfort her. But Canace brought her home in her lap
and gently bound her in plasters where she had hurt herself with
her beak. All Canace could now do was dig the ground for
medicinal plants and make new salves from rare and brightly-
coloured herbs to heal the hawk. She busied herself with all her
might night and morning. At the head of her bed she made a
mew for the hawk, covering it with blue velvet—blue stands for

the fidelity that is found in women—painting it green on the outside, with pictures of all faithless birds such at titmice, tercelets, owls; while beside them, for scorn, were painted magpies scolding and crying out upon them.

So I leave Canace nursing her hawk; and for the present I'll say no more about her ring, till the time comes to relate how the falcon won back her lover—repentant, according to the story—through the mediation of the king's son Cambalo of whom I told you. From henceforth my story shall tell of adventures and battles and greater marvels than have ever yet been heard of. First, I'll tell about Cambuscan, who captured so many cities in his time; then I'll explain how Algarsyf won Theodora for his bride. He was many times in peril of his life for her, had he not been helped by the horse of brass. And after that I'll speak of another Cambalo who fought in the lists with the two brothers for Canace before he could win her. Now I'll begin again where I left off.

iii

So high had Apollo whirled his chariot that it had entered the mansion of Mercury, the cunning god—

[*The Squire's Tale breaks off here; Chaucer never finished it. D.W.*]

What the Franklin said to the Squire
and what the Host said to the Franklin

'Upon my word, Squire, you've acquitted yourself honourably and well, and I compliment you on your talents,' said the Franklin. 'Considering your youth you speak with so much feeling I can only applaud. If you keep on, in my judgement none here will equal you in eloquence—God grant you luck, and may your powers continue to develop! I take the greatest delight in your conversation. I have a son, and by Trinity, I'd rather he were a man of discrimination like yourself than have twenty pounds' worth of land, though you were to give it me on the spot. What's the use of possessions if a man has no abilities? I've rated my son often enough, and shall again, because he has no taste for such accomplishments—all he does is play dice and throw money around and lose everything he has. And he'd rather talk to a servant-lad than converse with some gentleman from whom he could learn true good breeding—'

'A fig for your good breeding!' cried our Host. 'What's all this, Franklin? Sir, for heaven's sake, you know perfectly well that each of you must tell at least a tale or two, or break his promise.'

'I'm quite aware of that, sir,' replied the Franklin; 'but please don't think the worse of me if I have a word or two with this young man.'

'Not another word, but get on with your story!'

'Gladly, Master Host,' he answered. 'I bow to your will; so listen to what I shall tell. So far as my wits may serve, I'll not oppose you in any way. I pray to God it may please you, for if it does I'll know it's good enough.'

In their time those noble old Bretons used to make lays from all kinds of adventures, versified in the original Breton tongue. They either sang these ballads to the accompaniment of musical instruments or read them for their own pleasure. I have one in mind which I shall willingly relate as best I can.

But, gentlemen, as I am a simple fellow, before I begin I must first beg you to excuse my homely style. To be sure, I never studied the art of rhetoric; so what I say must be bare and plain! I never slept on the Parnassian mountain, nor studied Marcus Tullius Cicero. Make no mistake, I know nothing of rhetorical devices for colouring language—the only colours I know are those which grow in the fields, or those which people dye or paint with; the colours of rhetoric are too difficult for me—my heart has no feeling for that kind of thing.* But, if you wish, you shall hear my tale.

---

* This is an ironic disclaimer; the tale which follows is in fact full of rhetorical devices; which Chaucer seems to be gently guying, as in the long speech by Dorigen towards the end.

THE FRANKLIN'S TALE

In Armorica, as Brittany was called, there was a knight who loved a lady. He served her to the best of his ability and before winning her performed many a labour and many a great undertaking. For she was the fairest of women under the sun. Moreover she came of a family so exalted that the knight scarcely dared reveal to her his grief and pain and longing. But in the end, because of his worth and especially his humble attentiveness, she took pity on his suffering and tacitly consented to take him for her husband and master—such mastery as men have over their wives. And in order to live the more happily together, he voluntarily swore upon his knighthood that so long as he lived he would never exercise his authority against her will, nor exhibit jealousy, but obey her and follow her wishes in all things, as any lover ought with his lady. But for the honour of his status as husband, he would appear to be the master.

She thanked him, saying with great humility, 'Sir, since in your magnanimity you offer me so free a rein, God forbid there shall ever be either strife or discord between the two of us through my fault. And I here give you, Sir, my word of honour: I shall be your true and humble wife till I die.' So they lived together in peace and tranquillity.

For, gentlemen, there is one thing I may safely assert: lovers who wish to live together for any length of time must submit to one another. Love will not be constrained by mastery: when mastery appears, then the God of Love claps his wings, and presto! he's gone! Love is a thing as free as any spirit. Women by their nature desire liberty, not to be constrained like bondslaves; and if I'm not mistaken so do men. In love whoever is the most patient has the advantage. Patience is surely a sovereign virtue: for according to the scholars it conquers where severity achieves nothing. You cannot scold or grumble at every harsh word. Learn forbearance; or you will have to learn it, I swear, whether you will or no; for surely there is nobody in the world who does not behave badly on occasion. Anger, illness, the influence of the stars, wine, grief, or a change of mood very often make one act or speak amiss. You cannot take revenge for every wrong. Everyone who knows how to govern himself must exercise restraint according to circumstances. And therefore, that they might live in harmony, this wise and worthy knight promised forbearance, while she promised him most faithfully that in her there should never be any fault to find.

Here one may see a modest and sensible bargain: thus did she take her servant and master—in love her servant, her master in marriage. And so he was both master and servant. No, not servant, but in mastership above, since he has both his lady and his love; she was his lady, certainly, but his wife also; and this is in accordance with the law of love.

Having attained this felicity, he went home with his wife to his own land, not far from Penmarch Point where his dwelling was; and there he lived in happiness and delight. Who but a married man could tell the joy, the ease and comfort that is between husband and wife? This happy state lasted a year or more, till this knight of whom I speak (his name was Arveragus of Caerrud) made up his mind to go and live for a year or two in England—which was also called Britain—to seek honour and renown in deeds of arms, for his whole heart was set upon such feats; and there, so the book says, he dwelt two years.

Now I will leave talking about Arveragus and tell of his wife Dorigen, who loved her husband with all her heart. She wept and sighed for his absence, as noble wives do when they feel like it. She mourned, she watched and wailed, fasted and lamented, and was so tormented by longing for his presence that nothing in the whole wide world meant anything to her. Realizing her sorrowful mood, her friends comforted her in every way they might; they exhorted her night and day, saying she was killing herself for no reason. They busied themselves giving every possible consolation in the circumstances to make her leave off her melancholy.

As you all know, if you carve away at a stone for long enough, in the course of time some image will be impressed on it. They comforted her for so long that with the help of hope and common sense she received the imprint of their consolation; and thus her great sorrow began to assuage. She could not have endured so violent a grief for ever.

And besides, in all this unhappiness Arveragus sent home letters to her saying he was well and would quickly return; otherwise this sorrow must have broken her heart.

Seeing her grief begin to abate, her friends knelt down and begged her for heaven's sake to go walking with them to drive away her gloomy thoughts. And finally she granted their petition, plainly seeing it was for the best.

Now, her castle stood hard by the sea. To amuse herself she often walked with her friends upon the cliff above, where she saw many ships and barges sailing on their courses wherever they wished to go. But this became part of her grief, for often and often she would say to herself, 'Alas! Is there no ship of all the many I see will bring my husband home? For then my heart would be quite cured of its bitter pangs.'

At other times she would sit there and think, casting her eyes downward from the edge of the cliff. But when she saw the black forbidding rocks her heart would quake from sheer terror till she could hardly keep upon her feet. Then she would sit down on the grass, gaze sadly upon the sea and say with many a sorrowful and heavy sigh:

'Eternal God, that through Thy providence guidest the world with sure control, it is said that Thou hast made nothing in vain. But, Lord, these fiendish, black, forbidding rocks that seem rather the work of a foul chaos than any fair creation of a God so perfect, wise, and unchangeable—why hast Thou made so irrational a creation? For neither man nor bird nor beast is benefited by them in any quarter of the world; they do no good that I know of, nothing but harm. Do you not see, Lord, how mankind is destroyed by them? Rocks have slain the bodies of a hundred thousand men, unremembered though they be. Yet mankind is so fair a part of Thy creation that Thou madest it in Thine own image. *Then,* it seemed as if Thou hadst great love towards mankind—so how can it be that Thou fashionest such means to destroy it, things that do no good, nothing but harm? I know well enough the scholars will say what they like and prove by logic that all is for the best, even though I cannot understand the reasons. May God who made the wind to blow preserve my husband! That's my conclusion; I leave all disputing to scholars. But would to God that all those grim rocks were sunk in Hell for his sake! Those rocks kill my heart with fear.' Thus would she speak, weeping sadly.

Her friends, seeing it was no pleasure for her to wander by the sea but rather a distress, determined to find amusement elsewhere. They led her to rivers and springs and other delightful places, where they danced and played chess and backgammon.

So one fine morning they went to a nearby garden where they had made arrangements for a provision of food and other necessaries, and there diverted themselves the livelong day. It was the sixth morning of May: and the month had painted the garden with its gentle showers and filled it with leaf and blossom. Skilful hands had so exquisitely arrayed this garden that there was never another of such beauty, unless indeed it were Paradise itself. So full it was of beauty and delight that the scent of the flowers and sight of their brilliant hues would have lightened any heart that ever lived, unless burdened with a too great sickness or a too heavy sorrow.

After dinner they began to dance and sing, save only Dorigen, who kept sighing and lamenting. For among the dancers she might not espy him who was to her husband and lover both. Nevertheless she had to stay on for a while and let her grief allay with hoping.

Among others at this dance there danced a squire before Dorigen. He was, to my thinking, more spirited and gaily apparelled than the month of May; he danced and sang better than any man that ever was since the beginning of the world. To give some idea of what he was like, he was one of the most gifted of living men besides: young, strong, talented, rich, intelligent, popular and well thought of. And in short, if I'm not mistaken, it so happened that for over two years this gallant squire, servant to Venus, (Aurelius was his name) had loved Dorigen more than any living creature, wholly without her knowledge; but had never dared to tell her of his grief. He suffered inward torment beyond measure. He was in desperation; afraid to say anything; though he used to reveal something of his passion in his songs, for example in a general complaint that he loved and was not loved in return. Round this theme he composed many songs, lyrics, complaints, roundels, lays and virelays: how he dared not tell his grief but suffered torment like one of the Furies in Hell. He must die, said he, as Echo for Narcissus, who feared to tell her woe. This was the only way in which he ventured to disclose his grief to her; except, perhaps, sometimes at dances where young people are courting it may well be that he gazed upon her face like one who asks for mercy; but she was unaware of what he meant. Nevertheless, before they left the garden it chanced—for he was her neighbour, a man of honour and repute, and she had known him a long time—that they fell into conversation; and little by little Aurelius steered it towards his purpose. And when he saw his opportunity, he said:

'Madam, by that God that made this world, had I been sure that it might have made you happy, I wish that on the day your Arveragus crossed the sea I, Aurelius, had gone whence I should never return. For I well know that my devotion is in vain and my reward no more than a broken heart. Madam, have pity on my cruel sufferings, for with one word you may either slay or save me—would to God I were buried here at your feet! There is no time now to say more. Have mercy, love, or you will make me die!'

She turned and stared at Aurelius. 'Do you really mean what you're saying?' said she. 'Before this I never suspected what you meant; but now, Aurelius, that I know your intentions, I swear by the God who gave me life and soul that so far as in me lies I'll never be an unfaithful wife, either in word or deed. I mean to be his to whom I am wedded. Take that for my final answer.' But afterwards she said, banteringly, 'Lord in heaven, Aurelius, since I see you lament so pitifully, I would consent to be your love—on the day you remove all the rocks, stone by stone, from one end of Britanny to the other till they no longer hinder the passage of any boat or ship! This I say: when you have cleared the coast so free of rocks that no stone is to be seen, then will I love you more than any other man. I give you my word, so far as I can promise anything. For I know it can never happen. Let these foolish notions slip from your heart. What satisfaction could anyone find in loving the wife of another, who can possess her whenever he pleases?'

Aurelius sighed heavily. 'Is that all the mercy you can offer?' said he.

'Yes, by the Lord that made me!' she answered.

Hearing this, Aurelius was stricken with grief, and with sad heart replied:

'Madam, that would be an impossibility! It means I must now die a miserable death.' And with that he turned away.

Then came a crowd of her friends, wandering up and down the garden walks, quite unaware of what had just taken place; for they at once renewed their merrymaking. This went on until the bright sun lost its colour, having been robbed of its light by the horizon—that's as much as to say night had fallen —when, with the sole exception of poor Aurelius, they went home happy and contented. He returned to his house with a heavy heart, for he saw no way of avoiding death—he seemed to feel his heart grow cold. Raising his hands to heaven he fell down upon his bare knees and in frenzy began a prayer. He was out of his wits with sheer grief and did not know what he said. But thus he spoke when with breaking heart he began his lament to the gods, and to the Sun in especial:

'Apollo, lord and governor of every plant, herb, tree and flower; you who give, according to your distance from the celestial equator, to each its time and season, as your lodging in the ecliptic alters from high to low: Lord Phoebus, cast your merciful eye on miserable Aurelius who is all but lost. Behold, Lord, for no fault of mine my lady has vowed my death, unless in your magnanimity you take some pity on my dying heart. For I well know, Lord Phoebus, that if you will you can help me best of all, save only my lady. Vouchsafe that I may tell you how I can be helped, and in what manner.

'Your blessed sister, bright Lucina, queen and paramount goddess of the sea (though Neptune be its god, yet is she empress over him)—Lord, you well know that just as she desires to be lit and kindled at your fire and therefore follows you eagerly, just so does the sea by nature desire to follow her; for she is goddess not only of the sea but of all rivers great and small. Therefore, Lord Phoebus, this is my request—O perform this miracle, or let my heart break!—that when next the sun is in the sign of Leo and at the height of his power in opposition to the moon, you pray her to bring a tide so high it will rise at least five fathoms above the tallest rock in Armorican Britanny; and let this tide continue for two years. Then I may safely say to my lady, "The rocks have gone: now keep your word."

'Lord Phoebus, perform this miracle for me. Beseech the moon to keep pace with you as you go on your course; beseech your sister, I say, for two years to go no faster in her course than you. Then she shall always be uniformly at the full and the spring tide shall continue night and day. But if she will not vouchsafe to grant me my dear sovereign lady in this way, then beseech her to sink every rock into her own dark underground region where Pluto dwells; else I shall never win my lady. Barefoot I'll make a pilgrimage to your temple in Delphi. Lord Phoebus, see the tears streaming down my cheeks, and take some pity on my pain!'

Saying this he fell down in a swoon and lay for a long time in an unbroken trance.

His brother, who knew of his misery, picked him up and carried him to bed. I shall leave the unhappy creature lying there in this desperate torment and distress of mind; he can live or die as he chooses, for all I care.

Arveragus, the flower of chivalry, returned home with other distinguished knights, prosperous and covered with honours. Now Dorigen is in the seventh heaven: her valiant husband is in her arms, her bold knight and worthy warrior who loves her dearer than life itself. He was not in the least given to suspicious imaginings as to whether anybody had spoken of love to her while he was away. Of that he had no fear. Instead he danced, jousted, and made merry with her. So I leave them living in happiness and delight, and return to sick Aurelius.

The wretched Aurelius lay ill in furious torment for two years and more before he was able to set foot upon the ground. During this time his only comfort was his brother, a scholar, who knew of all this trouble and grief; for you may be sure he dared not breathe a word about the matter to any living soul. He hid it in his bosom more secretly than Pamphilus did his love for Galatea. Outwardly his breast appeared unwounded, but the sharp arrow remained in his heart; and in surgery, as you well know, the cure of a wound healed only on the surface is hazardous unless one can reach the arrow or get at it. In secret Aurelius' brother wept and lamented, till at last he recalled that, when he was at Orleans in France seeking knowledge of out-of-the-way sciences in every nook and cranny (being eager like other young students to read the occult arts) he remembered seeing one day in his study at Orleans a book on white magic which a friend of his (although there to learn another profession and at that time reading Law) had privately hidden in his desk. This book had a good deal of information touching the workings of the eight and twenty mansions of the moon, and nonsense like that which isn't worth a fly nowadays, for the faith of Holy Church and our creed will not allow us to be harmed by such chimeras. And when he remembered this book his heart danced with joy, and he said quietly to himself: 'My brother will shortly be cured, for I'm sure there are arts by which various illusions can be produced, like those created by expert magicians. For I've often heard tell that at banquets these magicians can make water and a barge appear and row up and down the great hall; sometimes a fierce lion has seemed to come; sometimes flowers blossoming as if in a meadow; sometimes a vine with grapes white and red; some-times a castle built all of stone and lime; and they made them instantly vanish whenever they pleased. Or so it seemed to all men's eyes.

'So I've come to the conclusion that if I can find at Orleans some old friend who has these mansions of the moon stored away in his head, or some other white magic besides, he might well make my brother have his love.

'For by means of some illusion a magician could make it appear to human eyes that every one of the black rocks of Brittany had been removed, that ships were coming and going along the coast; and he could keep up the illusion for a week. Then my brother would be cured of his grief, for she'd have to keep her word or at least be put to shame.'

Why make a long story of it? He went to his brother's bed and so warmly urged him to go to Orleans that he immediately arose and was soon on his way there, hoping to be released from his misery.

When they had almost come to the city and were within two or three furlongs of it they met a young scholar strolling by himself who greeted them politely in Latin and then astonished them by remarking, 'I know why you've come.' Before they'd gone a step further he told them all they had in mind to do.

The Breton scholar asked after friends he had known in the

old days, but the other replied that they were dead; at which he shed many tears.

Then Aurelius alighted from his horse and went home with the magician to his house, where they made themselves comfortable. There was no lack of delicious food; Aurelius had never seen a house so well appointed in all his life.

Before they went in to supper the magician showed him forests and parks filled with wild deer. There he saw harts with towering antlers, the largest ever beheld by human eye; he saw hounds slay a hundred of them while many others bled from cruel arrow-wounds; and when these wild deer were done away with, he saw upon the banks of a river falconers whose hawks had just killed a heron. Then he saw knights jousting on a plain; after which the magician delighted him by showing him his lady in the midst of a dance in which it seemed he was himself taking part.

When the master who had made this magic saw it was time he clapped both hands together, and lo! the whole show vanished. Yet they had never once left the house while they watched this marvellous spectacle, but sat quietly in the study where he kept his books, with no other person there except the three of them.

The astrologer called his squire and said: 'Is our meal ready? I declare it's almost an hour since I told you to prepare our supper when these gentlemen came with me into the study where my books are.'

'Sir, it is ready whenever you please,' said the squire, 'even should you wish it to be served at once.'

'Then let us go and sup,' said he, 'I think that would be best. People who are in love must sometimes have refreshment.'

After supper they fell to bargaining about the amount of the fee the astrologer should be paid for removing all the rocks of Britanny from the Gironde to the mouth of the Seine. He held off at first, swearing he'd not take less than a thousand pounds, God help him. Nor was he too eager to do it for that sum.

But Aurelius, whose heart was bursting with happiness, soon replied, 'A fig for a thousand pounds! Were I lord of it I'd give the wide world, which they say is round—the bargain's struck, and we're agreed. You'll be paid in full, on my word of honour! But see to it that you don't delay us here later than tomorrow through any slackness or negligence.'

'No,' replied the astrologer, 'I pledge you my word.'

Aurelius went to bed when he felt like it and slept almost the whole of the night. What with his tiring day and hope of happiness, his sad heart found relief from suffering.

At daylight next morning Aurelius and the magician took the shortest route to Britanny and alighted at their destination. This was—so the books remind me—in the cold and frosty season of December.

Phoebus had grown old and copper-coloured, who had earlier, in his burning summer solstice, shone like burnished gold with glittering rays; but now, being descended into Capricorn, I daresay he shone palely enough. In every garden bitter frosts had destroyed the greenery with sleet and rain. Now double-bearded Janus sits by the fire drinking wine from his great ox-horn; the flesh of tusked boars stands in front of him, and every stout fellow cries 'Nowel!'

Aurelius made his astrologer feel an honoured and welcome guest in every way he could, and then begged him to do his utmost to deliver him from his cruel agony, or he'd cut his heart open with a sword.

That skilled astrologer so pitied the fellow he made all possible haste. Night and day he watched for a favourable hour for his astrological experiment—that's to say, producing by some conjuring trick (I don't know the proper astrological terminology) some illusion by which Dorigen and everyone else should think —and say—that the rocks of Britanny had disappeared or sunk underground. And at last he found the right time for the performance of his wretched, diabolical mumbo-jumbo. He brought out his newly corrected Toledan tables of astronomy and everything he needed—tables for the motions of the planets for round periods, and tables for subdivisions of periods, and longitudes for given dates to furnish bases for calculation; and all his other paraphernalia, such as his centres and angles of calculation, and his tables of proportionals for computing planetary movements so that he could make all his equations. By the motion of the eighth sphere he knew exactly how far Alnath had moved from the first point of the sign Aries overhead, which is deemed to be in the ninth sphere; all this—the exact amount of the precession of the equinoxes—he had expertly calculated.

Having found the moon's first mansion he was able to compute the rest proportionally, and tell when the moon would rise and in what relation to the planets and their places in the zodiac, and all the rest of it. He knew exactly which mansion of the moon was appropriate for his experiment, also all other ritual ceremonies necessary for such illusions, and other evil practices employed by heathen folk in those days. Therefore he delayed no longer. And by means of his magic for a week or two it seemed as if all the rocks had disappeared.

Aurelius, still on tenterhooks whether he was going to win his love or miss his chance, waited for this miracle night and day. And when he realized that all obstacles had gone and all the rocks had vanished, he fell at the astrologer's feet and said, 'I, the sorrowful wretched Aurelius, thank you, Master, and my lady Venus, who have helped me out of my grievous troubles.' And he made his way to the temple where he knew he would see his lady. Then, seeing his chance, forthwith he greeted his beloved sovereign lady with humble demeanour and tremulous heart.

'My own true lady, whom with all my heart I most dread and love, than whom there is no one in the whole world I am more reluctant to displease,' began this unhappy man, 'were it not that I suffer such distress for you that I am on the point of dying at your feet here and now, nothing would induce me to reveal to you how oppressed with misery I am; but the truth is I must either speak or die. For no fault of mine you are killing me with the most utter torment. But even if you have no pity of my death, reflect a moment before you break your pledged word. By that God that reigns on high, think better of it before you kill me because I love you. For, Madam, you well know what it is that you have promised—not that I claim anything as of right from you, my lady, except your consent—but in that spot in yonder garden, well you know what you promised me; in my hand you pledged your word to love me best. God is witness you said so, unworthy though I be of your love. Madam, I am now speaking more for the sake of your honour than to save my heart's life. I have done as you commanded, as you will see if you vouchsafe to go and look. Do as you like; remember your promise; for, dead or alive, you will find me here. It lies entirely with you whether I live or die—but this I know: the rocks have gone.'

He took his leave while she stood there dumbstruck without a drop of blood in her cheeks. She had never thought to fall into such a trap. 'Alas that ever this should happen!' cried she, 'for I never dreamed there was any possibility of such a monstrous prodigy or marvel. It's against the course of nature.'

And she went home an unhappy woman, so dismayed she was hardly able to walk. For the whole of the next day or two she wept and lamented, often fainting away; it was pitiful to see. But she told no one the reason, for Arveragus had gone out of town. With a pale face and dejected countenance she communed with herself, and in this manner made her lament:

'Alas!' cried she, 'it is against you, Fortune, I make my complaint: you who have entangled me unawares in your chain, from which I know of nothing that can help me escape save only death or dishonour. One of these two I am forced to choose. But nonetheless I would rather lose my life than dishonour my body, know myself unfaithful, or lose my good name. And surely by my death I may be freed from this dilemma. Have not, alas! many honourable wives and virgins slain themselves rather than transgress with their bodies? Indeed they have—and lo, these stories bear witness. When the Thirty Tyrants, their hearts filled with iniquity, had slain Phidon at a banquet in Athens they ordered his daughters to be arrested; who, to gratify their filthy pleasure, they maliciously commanded to be brought stark naked before them; when they made them dance upon the pavement in their father's blood. God's curse on them! And so, according to the books, these terrified unhappy virgins slipped away and leapt into a well where they drowned themselves rather than lose their maidenheads.

'The people of Messene, also, inquired and sought out fifty Lacedemonian virgins, meaning to satisfy their lust upon them; yet there was not one of the whole band but killed herself, willingly choosing to die rather than consent to be robbed of her virginity. Why then should I fear to die?

'Consider, again, the tyrant Aristoclides who loved a virgin called Stymphalis. When her father was slain one night, she ran straight to the temple of Diana and clasped the statue with both hands: and from this statue she would not go—nobody could wrest her hands from it till she was killed in that very spot.

'Now if virgins have such abhorrence of being sullied by a man's filthy pleasure, how much more, it seems to me, ought a wife to choose to slay herself rather than be defiled.

'And what shall I say of Hasdrubal's wife, who took her own life at Carthage? For when she saw the Romans had won the city she took all her children and leapt into the fire, choosing to die rather than let any Roman violate her. Did not poor Lucretia kill herself in Rome after she had been raped by Tarquin, because she thought it shameful to go on living when she had lost her honour? And the seven virgins of Miletus slew themselves in grief and despair, rather than suffer the Gauls to rape them. I suppose I could relate over a thousand stories touching this theme. For example, after Abradates had been killed his beloved wife slew herself and let her blood flow into his gaping wounds, crying, "At least no man is going to pollute my body if I can help it!"

'Why should I rehearse any more instances when so many have killed themselves rather than be violated? All things considered it is better I should slay myself than be thus defiled. I'll be true to Arveragus, or else kill myself in some way, as did Demotion's beloved daughter, because she didn't want to be deflowered. O Scedasus, how piteous it is to read how your poor daughters died, who slew themselves for a like reason. It was as piteous, if not more so, when the Theban virgin killed herself on account of Nicanor when she was in the same kind of trouble. Another Theban virgin did exactly the same thing because a Macedonian had raped her; and with her death redeemed her lost maidenhead. And what shall I say of Niceratus' wife, who made away with herself in like circumstances? How true, also, was Alcibiades' love, who chose to die rather than suffer his body to remain unburied! Think what a wife Alcestis was!' said she. 'What does Homer say of the good Penelope? All Greece knows of her chastity. Of Laodamia, indeed, it is written that when Protesilaus was slain at Troy she refused to live a day beyond his death. I can tell a similar story of the noble Portia who could not live without Brutus to whom she had given her whole heart. And the perfect fidelity of Artemisia is honoured throughout barbarian lands. And as for you, Queen Teuta, your wifely chastity may serve as a mirror for all wives. I can say the same of Bilyea, of Rhodogune, and of Valeria.'

Thus for a day or two Dorigen lamented, all the while making up her mind to die; however, on the third evening the worthy knight Arveragus came home and asked her why she was weeping so bitterly. At this she wept even more. 'Alas!' she cried, 'I wish I had never been born! I have said—I have promised—' and she told him all, just as you've heard; no need to repeat it all over again.

But it was with a serene countenance and friendly tones that the husband answered, as I shall relate:

'Is there anything else, Dorigen, but this?'

'No, no,' cried she, 'as God is indeed my help! And it is too much, even if it be God's will!'

'Ah, wife,' said he, 'let sleeping dogs lie. Perhaps all may yet be well. You shall keep your word, I swear it! For as I hope for heaven, so great is the love I bear you I had rather be stabbed to death than you should fail to keep your promise. Nothing is more sacred than the keeping of one's word.' But saying this, he burst out weeping; then cried, 'While life and breath is in you I forbid you on pain of death ever to tell anyone of this affair—I will endure my grief as best I may—and do not look sad, lest people guess or suspect something is wrong.'

Then he summoned a squire and a maidservant. 'Go with Dorigen,' he said, 'and take her at once to whatever place she wishes to go.' They took their leave and set out, but without knowing why she was going there. He did not wish to tell anyone what was in his mind.

Many of you, perhaps, will surely think him a fool to put his wife in jeopardy like this; but listen to the story before you cry out upon her. She may have better luck than you think; judge for yourselves when you've heard the tale.

Aurelius, the squire so much in love with Dorigen, happened by chance to meet her right in the middle of the busiest street of the town as she was preparing to go straight to the garden where she had given her promise. And he also was going to the garden, for he kept a good watch and knew when she left her house to go anywhere. But thus it was that they met, whether by chance or providence. He greeted her gladly, and asked where she was going. And she replied, almost as if crazed, 'To the garden as my husband bade me, to keep my promise, alas! alas!'

At this Aurelius began to wonder; and in his heart felt great compassion for her and for her sorrow, as well as for Arveragus, the noble knight who had bidden her fulfil her promise because he could not endure that his wife should break her word. And this so touched his heart that, taking everything into consideration, he thought it best rather to deny himself his pleasure than commit so mean and wretched an act in the face of such generous magnanimity. So he said briefly:

'Madam, tell your husband Arveragus that having seen his great magnanimity towards you, and having seen your distress also, and knowing he would prefer to be shamed—which would be a thousand pities—rather than you should break your pledged word to me in this way, I would far sooner suffer eternal torment than break up the love between the two of you. Madam, I remit into your hands every pledge and bond you have ever made me since the day you were born. I give you my word I shall never reproach you with any promise. And here I take my leave of the best and truest woman that ever I knew in my whole life.'

But let all women beware of making promises! Or at any rate let them think of Dorigen! And so there's no question but that a squire can behave as nobly as a knight.

On her bare knees she thanked him, then went home to her husband and told him all, as I've related. And you may be sure he was so well pleased it's impossible for me to describe it. Why should I protract the tale?

Arveragus and his wife Dorigen lived in perfect happiness for the rest of their lives; never again was there any difference between them, then or later. He cherished her as if she were a queen, and she was true to him for evermore. And that's all you'll get from me about those two.

Having forfeited his entire capital, Aurelius began to curse the day he was born. 'Alas!' he cried, 'I wish I'd never promised that astrologer a thousand pounds weight of pure gold! What shall I do? So far as I can see I'm completely ruined; I'll have to sell my inheritance and turn beggar. I cannot live here and bring disgrace on all my kindred in this town, unless I can persuade him to leniency. However, I'll try him with the proposal that I make him an annual payment on fixed days; and I'll thank him for his great kindness. And I shan't fail to keep my promise.'

With heavy heart he went to his treasure-chest and brought gold

to the value of five hundred pounds or thereabouts to the astrolo-
ger, beseeching him to be generous enough to give him time to pay
the remainder. Said he, 'Master, I may claim that I've never failed
to keep my word as yet. My debt to you will certainly be paid off
whatever happens, even if I have to go a-begging in nothing but
my jacket. But if you'd grant me—on security—a respite of two
or three years, then I'd be all right—but otherwise I must sell my
heritage; I can say no more.'

Hearing these words, the astrologer replied gravely, 'Have I not
kept my bargain with you?'

'Yes indeed: both well and truly.'

'And have you not enjoyed your lady as you wished?'

'No,' he answered, 'no.' And he sighed sadly.

'Why not? Tell me the reason if you can.'

Then Aurelius began his story and told him all; as you've al-
ready heard it there's no need to tell it again.

Said he, 'Arveragus, in his magnanimity, would rather have died
in sorrow and distress than that his wife should be false to her
pledged word.' Also he told him of the grief of Dorigen, how loath
she was to be an unfaithful wife; that she would rather have died
on the spot; that she had pledged her word to him in all innocence,
never having heard before of magic illusions. 'This made me take
such pity on her that as freely as he sent her to me, as freely did I
send her back to him. That's the sum total of it; there's no more
to say.'

The philosopher replied: 'Dear friend, each of you behaved
nobly to the other. You are a squire, and he is a knight. But God
Almighty forbid a scholar should not behave as nobly as any of
you. Never fear!

'Sir, I remit you of your thousand pounds as much as if you had
but now come into existence and had never set eyes on me before.
Sir, I will not take a penny from you for all my skill, nor anything
for my labour. You paid generously for my board. It's enough—
farewell, and good day to you!' And he mounted his horse and
went on his way.

Now, gentlemen, I'd like to put to you this question—which of
them seems to you the most generous? Tell me before you ride
any further. I can do no more; my tale is over.

We should do all that is in our power to eschew that nurse and servant of the vices, portress at the gate of pleasure, whose English name is Idleness: we should beat her down with her opposite—that's to say lawful industry—lest the Devil get hold of us through our indolence. For, once he sees an idle man, he who is continually watching to entrap us with his thousand subtle snares can so quickly snap him up in his net that the man doesn't know he's in the grip of the Fiend till he's fairly caught by the lapel. We should work earnestly, thus resisting Idleness; for even though we only take this present life into consideration, it plainly stands to reason that Idleness is a rotten torpidity from which nothing good or profitable ever comes; that Sloth holds Idleness in a leash, only to sleep and eat and drink and devour the product of others' labour. To put from us the sort of idleness that's the cause of so much calamity, I have here done my faithful endeavour in translating from the Legenda Aurea thy glorious life and passion, O thou whose garland is woven of the lily and rose—it is thee I mean, virgin and martyr, St Cecilia.

Invocation to the Virgin Mary

Thou that art flower of all virgins, thou of whom St Bernard so loved to write, thee I first invoke at my beginning. Enable me to celebrate, O thou who comfortest us miserable sinners, the death of thy maiden who through her merit won eternal life and victory over the Fiend, as in her story may hereafter be read. Thou Maid and Mother, daughter of thy Son, thou fount of mercy, balm of sinful souls, in whom God in His goodness chose to dwell: lowly, yet exalted above all creatures, thou didst ennoble our nature to such a degree that the Maker did not disdain to clothe and bind His Son in flesh and blood of human nature. Within the blessed cloister of thy womb the eternal love and peace—of the threefold world the Lord and Guide, whom earth and sea and heaven praise forever without cease—took man's shape. And thou, un-

spotted Virgin, bore of thy body the Creator of all creatures, yet retained thy maiden purity.

In thee is magnificence united with mercy, goodness, and so much of compassion that thou, who art the sun of excellence, dost not only help those who pray to thee, but even before men beseech thy help dost often, of thy benignity, freely anticipate their prayers and become the physician of their lives. O fair Virgin, meek and blessed, help me now, a banished exile in this desert of bitterness. Remember the woman of Canaan who said, 'The dogs eat of the crumbs which fall from their masters' table', and though I, unworthy son of Eve, be sinful, yet accept my faith. And because faith without works is dead, give me the wit and opportunity so to work that I may escape from that most dark region! O thou who art so fair and highly favoured, mother of Christ, dear daughter of St Anne, be my advocate in that high place where Hosanna is sung without end. Illumine with thy light my prisoned soul, troubled by the contagion of my body and by the weight of earthly lust and false affections: O haven of refuge, O salvation of those in sorrow and distress, help me now, for I am about to begin my task.

Nevertheless I pray you who read what I write to forgive me if I take no pains to ornament the story, for I am presenting the words and sense of one who wrote it in reverence of the saint. I merely follow the account of her life, and beg you to improve upon my work where necessary.

Interpretation of the Name of Cecilia

First I should like to expound the etymology of the name of St Cecilia in the light of her history. In English it means 'heaven's lily' (coeli lilia) signifying the pure chasteness of virginity; or perhaps she was called 'lily' since she had the whiteness of honour, the green of conscience, and the sweet savour of good fame. Alternatively, Cecilia is as much as to say 'a path for the blind' (caecis via) because of the example she set by her teaching. Or again, as I have read, 'Cecilia' is made up of a kind of compound of 'heaven' (coelum) and 'Leah'. Here, figuratively, 'heaven' signifies her holy contemplation and 'Leah' her ceaseless activity. Cecilia can also be interpreted in the following manner: 'wanting in blindness' (caecitate carens) *because of the great light of her wisdom and her shining virtues. Or yet again, this radiant virgin's name comes from 'heaven' (coelum) and 'leos', for she may well be called, and quite rightly, 'a heaven to people'—an exemplar of all wise and good deeds. For 'leos' means 'people' in English, and just as in the heavens one sees the sun and moon and all the stars, so in the spiritual sense one sees in this noble virgin the magnanimity of faith, the perfect clarity of wisdom, and many bright and excellent works. The learned have written that the heavenly spheres are swift, and round, and burning; even so was the white and lovely Cecilia ever swift and diligent in good works, round and entire in her perseverance, ever burning with the radiant flame of charity. I have now explained her name.*

THE
SECOND NUN'S
TALE

According to her Life, the fair virgin Cecilia was born of a noble Roman family and brought up from her cradle in the faith of Christ, whose gospel was never absent from her thoughts. And I find it written that she never ceased to love and fear God or to pray Him to preserve her maidenhood. Now when she was to be married to a youth named Valerian, and the day came of her wedding, such was the humbleness and piety of her spirit, she wore a haircloth next her skin under the golden robe which so well became her. And while the organ played its music she sang in her heart to God alone: 'O Lord, keep both my soul and body spotless, lest I perish.' (Every second and third day she fasted and gave herself up to continual and fervent prayer, for the love of Him who died upon the tree.) Night came, when according to custom she must go to bed with her husband; but she spoke privately to him, saying, 'Sweet and dearly beloved husband, there is a secret you may wish to hear, and which I will gladly tell you if you swear not to reveal it.'

Valerian bound himself with an oath that he would never betray her under any circumstances, come what may; and then at last she said, 'I have an angel who loves me with a love so great that waking or sleeping he is always at hand to watch over my body. If he perceives you touch me or make carnal love, he will slay you in the act without hesitation, and you will die in the flower of youth. But if you protect me with a pure love, for your purity he will love you as myself and reveal his radiance and his joy.'

Thus chastened according to God's will, Valerian replied, 'If I am to trust you, let me see this angel and look upon him. If it should prove to be a real angel I will do as you have asked; but believe me, if you love another man I'll slay you both on the spot with this sword.' To this Cecilia at once replied, 'You shall see the angel if you wish on condition you believe in Christ and are baptized. Go forth to the Appian Way, which is only three miles from this city,' said she, 'and speak to the poor people who live there as I shall direct you. Tell them that I, Cecilia, sent you to them to show you the good old man Urban for secret reasons and a holy purpose. And when you see St Urban, tell him what I have told you; and when he has baptized and purged you from sin, then before you go you shall see that angel.'

So Valerian went to this place. And he found this holy old man Urban just as he had been directed, hiding among the catacombs of the saints. He lost no time delivering his message. Having received it, Urban lifted up his hands for joy and let the tears fall from his eyes. 'Almighty Lord, O Christ Jesus,' he said. 'Thou Sower of the chaste ideal and Shepherd of us all, take to Thyself the fruit of this seed of chastity Thou hast sown in Cecilia! How like a bee, busy and innocent, Thine own handmaid Cecilia serves Thee ever! For this husband whom she took but now was like a lion rampant, yet here she sends him to Thee as gentle as a lamb!' And as he spoke an old man clad in clothes of white radiance, carrying in his hand a book written with letters of gold, suddenly appeared and stood before Valerian. Seeing him, Valerian fell down in terror like one dead, whereupon the other caught hold of him and began to read from the book: 'One Lord, one Faith, one God alone; one Christendom, one Father of us all, omnipresent and supreme.' These words were all written in gold. When they had been read the old man cried, 'Do you or do you not believe these sayings? Answer yes or no.'

'All this I believe,' said Valerian, 'for I dare maintain no man may conceive of anything more true under heaven.' Upon this the old man vanished, he knew not where; and Pope Urban christened him on the spot.

Valerian went home and found Cecilia standing in his room with an angel. This angel carried in his hands two garlands, one of roses and one of lilies; I understand he gave the first to Cecilia, then took the second to her husband Valerian. 'Cherish these garlands always, with bodily purity and spotless mind,' said he. 'I have brought them to you from Paradise; I assure you they will never decay nor lose their sweet odour, nor shall any person set eyes on them unless he is chaste and hates wickedness. As for you, Valerian, because you responded so quickly to good advice, you may ask what you please and the boon shall be granted.' To this Valerian replied, 'I have a brother I love more than any living man: I pray you let my brother be granted grace to know the truth as I do here.'

Said the angel, 'Your request is pleasing to God; both of you shall attend His blissful feast bearing the palm of martyrdom.' And as he spoke Valerian's brother Tiburce arrived. Perceiving the odour that spread from the roses and lilies, he wondered much in his heart and said: 'Where can this sweet odour of rose and lily which I smell in the room come from at this time of year? The perfume could hardly be stronger were I holding them in my hands. The sweet scent that I feel in my heart has changed my whole nature.'

Valerian told him, 'We have two bright and shining garlands, snow-white and rose-red, that your eyes have no power to see. And as it is at my prayer that you can smell them, dear brother, so shall you see them—if only you hasten to believe aright and know the truth itself.'

Tiburce answered, 'Are you really saying this to me or do I hear it in a dream?' 'Surely, brother, we have been dreaming up till now,' replied Valerian, 'but now for the first time we inhabit the truth.' 'How do you know—and in what way?' asked Tiburce. 'I shall explain it to you,' said Valerian. 'The truth was taught me by the angel of God, whom you shall see if you renounce the idols and be clean, but not otherwise.'

(St Ambrose has elected to speak concerning the miracle of these two garlands in one of his prefaces. The excellent, beloved Doctor solemnly commends it thus: 'In order to receive the palm of martyrdom, St Cecilia, filled with the Grace of God, forsook the world and even her marriage-bed; witness the conversion of Tiburce and Valerian, to whom God in His goodness apportioned two garlands of sweet-smelling flowers and sent them by His angel. The maiden brought these men to bliss on high. The world has indeed learned the reward of chaste devotion to spiritual love.')

Then Cecilia plainly showed Tiburce that all idols were manifestly vain, for they are not only dumb but deaf; and enjoined him to forsake them. 'He who does not believe this is truly no more than a beast of the field,' said Tiburce. Hearing this she kissed his breast, overjoyed that he could see the truth. 'From today I take you for my comrade,' said this blessed maiden, lovely and beloved.

Then she continued: 'For as the love of Christ made me your brother's wife, by that same token, since you are willing to condemn your idols, I take you for my comrade here and now. Go now with my brother and be baptized, and purify yourself, so that you may behold the face of the angel of whom my brother told you.'

And Tiburce answered, 'Dear brother, first tell me where I should go and to whom?' 'To whom?' exclaimed Valerian. 'Come, be of good cheer, for I will take you to Pope Urban.' 'To Urban, brother Valerian!' cried Tiburce. 'That would be a miraculous feat, it seems to me. Don't you mean the Urban who has been so often condemned to death and lives in holes and corners—here today, gone tomorrow—and dares not once stick his head out? Were he found, or could they spy him out, they'd burn him in a red-hot fire, and ourselves as well to keep him company. And while we seek this Deity hidden away in heaven, in this world, at any rate, we shall be burned!' But Cecilia answered him bravely, 'My dearest brother, men might well fear, and with reason, to lose their lives if there were no other life than this. But fear you not, there is a better life elsewhere which shall never be lost. Through His mercy the Son of God has told us of it. The Son of that Father made all things; and indeed the Spirit which proceeded from the Father has endowed with souls all creatures which have been given intelligence and reason. In His sayings and miracles while He was in this world God's Son showed us that there is another life where men may dwell.'

To this Tiburce replied, 'Dear sister, did you not just now say something like this: there is but one God, one true Lord? How is it you now speak of three?'

'I shall explain that to you before I've finished,' said she. 'Just as a man has three faculties—memory, imagination, and reason, so there may well be three Persons in one Divine Being.' Then she began earnestly preaching to him about Christ's coming, and taught him concerning His suffering and many particulars of His passion—how, for the redemption of mankind fettered in deadly grief and sin, the Son of God was constrained to dwell in this world. All these matters she explained to Tiburce. After this, filled with holy aspiration, he went with Valerian to Pope Urban who gave thanks to God and christened him with a glad and joyful heart. There and then he completed his instruction and made him God's knight. And after this Tiburce achieved such grace that every day he saw the angel of God in our temporal world; and whatever boon he asked of God was speedily granted.

It would be very difficult to list the many miracles that Jesus performed for them; but in fine, the officers of the city of Rome at length sought them out and fetched them before the prefect Almachius, who examined them till he understood their aims and intentions. Then he sent them to the image of Jupiter, saying, 'This is my sentence: whosoever does not sacrifice to Jupiter, strike off his head!' Then one Maximus, a subordinate officer of the prefect's, arrested the martyrs of whom I speak; but felt compassion and wept as he led the saints away. And when Maximus heard their teaching, he obtained permission from the executioners and immediately brought them to his house. Before evening, with their teaching they stripped not only Maximus and all his people, but also the executioners, of their false beliefs and made them believe in the One God.

At nightfall Cecilia came with priests who christened them all together. Later, when the light of day began to grow, she spoke to them with great earnestness: 'Now, dearly beloved soldiers of Christ, cast away all the works of darkness and arm yourselves in the armour of light. You have fought a great battle for the truth; your course is run, and you have kept faith. Go, receive the unfading crown of light which the righteous Judge, whom you have served, shall give as you have merited.'

And when she had thus spoken they were led forth to perform the sacrifice. However, when they were brought to the place they absolutely refused either to sacrifice or offer incense, but went down on their knees with humble hearts and steadfast devotion. Both their heads were struck off on the spot; their souls went up to the King of Grace. Maximus, who had seen it all, bore witness forthwith, and weeping sadly announced that he had seen their souls soar to heaven attended by angels of clarity and light. His words converted many, and for this Almachius had him beaten so severely with a leaden whip that the life forsook him.

Then Cecilia took him and secretly buried him beside Tiburce and Valerian beneath a stone in her own burial-ground. Upon this Almachius immediately ordered his officers to fetch Cecilia publicly that she might perform sacrifice and offer incense to Jupiter before him. But, converted by her wise teaching, they wept bitterly, giving full credence to her sayings, and crying again and again: 'Christ, the Son of God and His Co-Equal, who is served by so good a servant, is the true God—this is our whole belief, and this we maintain with one voice, though we perish!'

Hearing of these events, Almachius ordered Cecilia to be brought that he might see her. Now this was the very first thing he asked her: 'What kind of woman are you?'

'I am a noblewoman born,' said she.

'I am asking you about your faith and religion, though this may get you into trouble.'

'You have begun your examination stupidly,' she retorted. 'You expect two answers to one question; you asked like a fool.'

To this rejoinder Almachius returned: 'Where do you get such contemptuous replies?'

'Where? From conscience and unfeigned good faith.'

'Have you no respect for my authority?'

'Your power is nothing to be afraid of; the power of mortal men is no more than a bladder full of wind. A needle's point can deflate its blown-up pride.'

'You began by being wrong and you persevere in wrong,' said he. 'Do you not know that our noble and mighty princes have commanded and ordained that every Christian shall suffer punishment unless he renounces his Christianity, but go free if he abjures it?'

'Your princes are wrong, and so are your nobles,' said Cecilia. 'You make us guilty through a crazy law, but the truth is we are not guilty: it is you, who are perfectly aware of our innocence, who impute crime and odium upon us because we revere Christ and bear the name of Christian. But we who know the power of that name may never abjure it.'

'You have two choices,' Almachius replied. 'Either perform sacrifice or renounce Christianity; in that way you may escape.'

At this the blessed and lovely maiden began to laugh, and to the judge she said, 'Stand convicted in your folly! Would you have me renounce innocence and make myself a criminal? Just look at him, he's making a fool of himself in open court—his mind's wandering, he stares like a madman!'

'Unhappy wretch!' cried Almachius, 'do you not realize the extent of my power? Have not our mighty princes given me both power and authority over life and death? How dare you address me with such arrogance?'

'I do not speak with arrogance but steadfastness,' said she. 'For my part I can say we Christians have mortal hatred of the sin of pride. And if you are not afraid to hear the truth I will publicly and convincingly demonstrate that you have uttered a monstrous lie. You say that your princes have given you power of life and death over the people—you, who can only destroy life; you have no other authority or power! But you can say your princes have made you the servant of death—if you claim to be more you lie, for your power is scant.'

'Enough of your impudence,' cried Almachius, 'and before you go, sacrifice to our gods! I care not what insult you fling at me, for I can bear it like a philosopher; but I will not endure the contumely you heap upon our gods.'

'You stupid creature!' answered Cecilia. 'Ever since you first opened your mouth your every word has proclaimed to me your stupidity and shown you up in all ways for an ignorant officer, an impotent judge! You might as well be blind for all the good your bodily eyes are to you; for a thing which we can all see is a stone —as is indeed perfectly obvious—that same stone you call a god. Take my advice, since you can't see out of those blind eyes of yours. Place your hand upon it and test it: you'll find it stone. Shame it is that the people should hold you in derision and laugh at your folly! For it's common knowledge everywhere that Almighty God is in the heaven above, while these idols, as you can plainly see, are of no use whatever either to you or to themselves; in fact they're not worth a brass farthing.'

These and words like these she spoke to him till he grew furious and ordered her to be led home. 'Burn her in a bath of flames in her own house,' said he. As he commanded, it was done; for they sealed her in a bath, and lit a great fire underneath which they kept going night and day. There she sat throughout the long night and the next day, but for all the fire and the heat of the bath she stayed quite cool and felt no pain; she did not even sweat. But in that bath she was to lose her life, for in the iniquity of his heart Almachius sent a messenger with orders to slay her in it. The executioner struck her three blows on the neck but could not contrive to sever it completely; and because at that time there was a law that none should suffer the penalty of a fourth stroke, be it light or heavy, he dared do no more but went away and left her lying there half dead with her neck cut open. The Christians who were around her carefully caught the blood in sheets. In this torment she lived three days, never ceasing to teach and preach the faith to those she had converted; and she gave them her goods and movables to deliver to Pope Urban, saying, 'I asked Heaven's King for three days' respite and no more, that I might commend these souls to you before I go, and that my house might be converted into a church for evermore.'

St Urban and his deacons secretly fetched away the body and buried it honourably by night among the other saints. Her house is called the Church of St Cecilia; St Urban, as was fitting, consecrated it; and there Christ and His saint are worthily honoured to this day.

*When the life of St Cecilia was ended, we hadn't ridden five
miles before a man overtook us at Boughton-under-Blean. He was
dressed in black clothes and wore a white surplice underneath. It
seemed as if he'd spurred hard for the last three miles, since his
hackney, a dapple-grey, sweated fearfully, while the horse his Yeo-
man rode was in such a lather it could scarcely keep going. Foam
lay thick upon the breast-harness and spotted him all over till he
looked like a magpie. Upon his crupper lay a doubled-over leath-
ern bag; he seemed to be carrying little and travelling light as if
for summer. I began wondering to myself what he was, till I
noticed how the hood was sewn to his cloak; from which, after
reflecting for a while, I judged him to be a Canon of some kind.
His hat hung down behind him on a string, for he had ridden at
more than a walk or trot—he'd been galloping like a madman.
He had a burdock-leaf under his hood to keep the sweat off and
cool his head. And it was something to see him sweat—his fore-
head dripped like a still filled with plaintain or pellitory. As he
came up with us he called out, 'God bless this jolly company; I've
been galloping hard on your account—I wanted to catch you up
and ride with this happy band.'*

*His Yeoman was also full of politeness and said, 'Sirs, I saw you
when you rode out of your hostelry this morning; so I told my
lord and master here, for he's very keen to ride with you for the
fun of it—he loves to chat.'*

*'Good luck to you for telling him, my friend,' said our Host,
'for it certainly looks as if your master were a man of parts—or so
I judge—and full of high spirits, I'll be bound. Perhaps he can tell
a pleasant tale or two and entertain our party?'*

*'Who, sir? My master? Why, surely! He knows more than
enough about fun and games! Trust me, sir, if you knew him as
well as I do you'd be amazed at the skill and ability he has in all
sorts of matters. He's taken on many big projects which would be
pretty difficult for any of you here to bring off, unless he showed
you how! Though he looks ordinary enough as he rides among*

you, you'd find it would pay to get to know him—and I'd go so far as to wager all I have in my possession that you wouldn't forgo his acquaintance for a tidy sum. I give you good warning, he's a man of great distinction, a really remarkable man.'

'Well, then,' said our Host, 'will you please tell me if he is a cleric or not? Explain what he is.'

'No, he's much more than a cleric, to be sure,' said the Yeoman, 'and I'll tell you something of his trade in a few words. Let me tell you that my master knows such secret arts—but you'll not all learn his secrets from me; I still help a bit with his work—he could turn all the ground over which we are riding as far as the town of Canterbury clean upside-down: and pave the whole with gold and silver!'

When the Yeoman had made this statement our Host exclaimed, 'God bless us! Then it seems rather wonderful to me—seeing your master is so very ingenious and entitled to respect—that he should think so little of his appearance. For such a man, his coat isn't worth a brass farthing, or I'll be damned. It's filthy and all tattered. May I ask why your master is so bedraggled when he has power to buy much better cloth—supposing he can do as you say? Kindly tell me that.'

'Why ask me?' said the Yeoman. 'So help me God, he'll never come to any good (but I won't admit saying this, so please keep it under your hat). It's my belief he's too clever by half. Enough is as good as a feast, as they say; too much is a mistake. That's why I think him a fool and an idiot; when a man has too many brains it often happens he misuses them, which is the case with my master, and a sore plague to me, God mend it! And that's all I can tell you.'

'Never mind that, good Yeoman,' said our Host, 'but as you know about your master's accomplishments, let me press you to tell us what he does, since he's so skilled and ingenious. Where do you live, if it may be asked?'

'In the outskirts of a town,' he replied, 'lurking in corners and blind alleys where thieves and robbers naturally gather, living in fear and concealment like all who dare not show their faces—that's how we live, if the truth must be told.'

'Can I ask you something else?' our Host went on. 'Tell me, why is your face so discoloured?'

'St Peter!' exclaimed the Yeoman, 'it's been unlucky, that's why. I'm so used to blow the fire, I suppose it's changed my colour. I don't spend my time peering into mirrors, but working myself to death and learning how to transmute metal into gold! We make ourselves giddy poring into the fire, but for all that, fail of our hope and never reach our goal. We delude any number of folk, and borrow, say, a pound or two, or ten, or twelve, or even bigger sums of gold, and make them believe we can double their money at least. But it's all lies, though we have good hopes it can be done and keep groping after it. However, the science of alchemy* is so far beyond us we can't catch up with it, whatever we say; it slips away so fast—and it'll beggar us in the end.'

While the Yeoman was chattering away the Canon drew near him and heard everything he said. This Canon was always suspicious of people talking. For as Cato says, the guilty suppose themselves the subject of every conversation. This was the reason he edged closer to the Yeoman to hear what he said. Then he shouted at his Yeoman: 'Hold your tongue! Don't say another word! If you do you'll pay dearly for it! You're slandering me in front of these people, and what's more you're revealing what you ought to keep dark.'

'That's right,' said the Host, 'tell away, no matter what—don't give a sixpence for his threats!'

'My faith, no more I do,' replied the Yeoman.

And when the Canon saw there was no help for it, but his Yeoman meant to tell all his secrets, for sheer vexation and shame he turned and fled.

'Ah,' cried the Yeoman, 'we'll get some fun out of this; now I'll tell you all I know, seeing he's gone—the devil choke him! From now on I promise you I'll have no more to do with him, no matter if he offers pence or pounds. Sorrow and shame fall on him! He was the first to drag me into this game—no game for me, I tell

---

* In Chaucer's time the interest in alchemy was widespread. Charles VI of France is said to have patronized the famous alchemist Nicholas Flamel, who (so it was claimed) in 1382 turned quicksilver into silver and some months later succeeded in transmuting the same metal into gold. Chaucer shows such considerable knowledge of alchemical technique and jargon it has even been suggested he may have been duped by an alchemist, but this is unlikely. Edward II and Henry IV of England are also said to have patronized alchemists.

you straight! That's what I feel, whatever you may think. Yet for all the misery, grief, toil and misfortune it brought I could never bring myself to break away from it. Would to God I had the brains to tell you everything that belongs to this science! Still, I'll tell you a bit about it; and as my master has gone I'll hold nothing back—what I know I shall reveal.'

THE CANON'S YEOMAN'S TALE

I've lived with this Canon for seven years and am none the better for his science. By it I've lost all that I ever had, like many another besides myself, God knows. There was a time when I used to be gay and spirited with good clothes and other fine trappings; now an old sock does duty for my cap. My colour was fresh and ruddy; these days it's leaden and wan. Take up alchemy and bitterly you'll rue it! All that work—my eyes water still from the wool that's been pulled over them! See what you get from alchemy! That slippery science has stripped me bare. I've nothing left whichever way I turn. And on top of this, the fact is I'm so in debt on account of the gold I've borrowed, as long as I live I'll never pay it off. Let me be a warning for evermore! Whoever takes it up is done for if he goes on, if you ask me; for all he'll get, so help me God, is an addled head and an empty purse. And when his own goods have been hazarded and lost through his madness and folly, he eggs on others and they lose their property as he himself has done. Rascals find it a joy and comfort to have companions in misery, or so a scholar once taught me. But of that no matter; I'll tell you what we do.

Very wise we seem (our jargon's so weird and technical) in the laboratory where we practise this recondite science of ours; me, I blow the fire till my heart gives out. Why should I give all the proportions of the ingredients—for example, of silver five or six ounces or so, or some such quantity; or busy myself with telling you their names—orpiment, burnt bones, iron filings ground to fine powder—and describing how they're all placed in an earthenware pot (salt and pepper are put in before the powders I spoke of) tightly covered with a glass plate, together with much else; how glass and pot are sealed with clay so that no air whatever can escape; how the fire's regulated—moderate to hot; of the worry and trouble we have vapourizing our ingredients, in the amalgaming and calcining of quicksilver, or crude mercury as we call it? For all our ingenuity we never attain a result. Nothing's any good, not orpiment nor mercury sublimate nor lead protoxide ground in a porphyry mortar, so many ounces of each—our labour's in vain. Neither the risen gases, nor the solids stuck to the bottom of the pot are the least use in the job we're doing—all our labour and drudgery lost—and all our capital as well, devil take it!

There's any number of things appertaining to this science of ours, though being uneducated I can't rehearse them in order—still, I'll list them as they come to mind, even if I can't put them in their proper categories: Armenian clay, verdigris, borax, sundry glass and earthenware vessels—urinals, retorts, phials, crucibles, vapourizers, gourd-retorts, alembics and stuff like that not worth a leek. No need to reckon up the lot—rubeficated water, bull's gall, arsenic, sal ammoniac, brimstone; and if I wanted to waste your time I could recite any number of herbs: agrimony, valerian, moonwort, and so on; our lamps burning day and night trying to get results; our furnaces for calcification, and for the albification of water; unslaked lime, chalk, white of egg; various powders; ashes, dung, piss, clay, waxed receptacles, saltpetre, vitriol; the different firings of wood and charcoal; potash, alkali, prepared salt, combusts, coagulates, clay mixed with horse-hair or human hair, oil of tartar, rock alum, yeast, wort, argol, ratsbane, and other absorbent or incorporative substances; our citronized silver, and substances in fermentation or hermetically sealed; our moulds, assaying instruments and all the rest.

I'll repeat to you, just as I myself was taught, the four spirits and the seven bodies in their order, as I so often heard my master name them. The first spirit is called quicksilver, the second orpiment, the third sal ammoniac, and the fourth brimstone. Now here are the seven bodies: gold for the sun, silver for the moon, iron for Mars, quicksilver for Mercury, lead for Saturn, tin for Jupiter, and copper for Venus, so help me God!

Nobody who takes up this confounded science will ever make enough to live on—he'll lose every penny he spends on it. Of that I haven't the slightest doubt. Anybody want to make a fool of himself? Then go study alchemy. If you've money, come on, you too can be an alchemist! Maybe you think it's easy to learn? No, no, a hundred times no—be you monk, friar, priest, canon, no matter what, and sit day and night over your books to study this weird and wonderful science, God knows it will all be in vain and worse than vain, by God! As for teaching it to an uneducated man

—pooh, don't talk about it, it can't be done. But whether they've booklearning or no it's all the same in the end; on my salvation, if they study alchemy when all's done both wind up in exactly the same situation—that's to say, they get nowhere.

But I forgot to list the acids, metals filings, ways of softening and hardening substances, the oils, ablutions, and fusible metals— the full list would transcend any book there is; it would be best if I gave myself a rest from all these names, for I swear I've re- peated enough to raise the grimmest fiend from hell.

Ah, no, let it go; each of us desperately seeking the Philosopher's Stone, or Elixir as it is called. If only we had it we'd be safe enough. But I declare to God in heaven that for all our skill and ingenuity, when we've done all it won't come to us. It's made us squander everything we have, a thought which would almost drive us crazy were it not that hope creeps into our hearts with the constant expectation, even in the bitterest moments, that the Philos- opher's Stone will rescue us in the end. Hard and painful are such hopes and suppositions; I give you good warning, it's a never-end- ing quest. Trust in the future tense makes men part with every single thing they ever had! Yet of this science they never have enough; it seems to carry a fatal enchantment. For if they had no more than a sheet to wrap themselves in at night and an old clout to their backs to walk abroad by day, they'd sell both to spend on this alchemy. They can't stop till there's nothing left. And wher- ever they go you can always tell them by the smell of brimstone. They reek like goats; take it from me, their stink's so hot and ramlike you can smell it a mile off. And so, if you want to, you can tell these people by their stench and threadbare clothes. And if you take them aside and ask them why they're so shabbily dressed, they'll whisper in your ear that were they spotted they'd be put to death for their alchemy. That's how they take innocent folk for a ride!

Enough of this; I'll get on to my story. Before the pot is placed upon the fire my master, and none but he, heats up a certain quantity of metals (I can speak out now he's gone) for he's said to be an expert—at least I know he's got that reputation. And yet he's always running into trouble. You ask me how? What gener- ally happens is, the pot explodes—so goodbye to the lot! These metals are so combustible our walls could stand up to them only if they were built of stone and mortar—as it is they go straight through the wall, and some of the stuff buries itself in the earth (we've lost pounds like this), some gets scattered all over the floor and the rest shoots up into the roof. Though the Devil never shows himself in our sight, I bet the old villain is with us: in Hell, where he's lord and master, there can hardly be more wrath and woe and rancour. For when our pot blows up as I've said, then everyone begins scolding and feeling badly done by.

Says one, it was because of the way the fire was built; another says no, the bellows were the trouble (and then I'm scared, for that's my job). 'Stuff!' cries a third, 'you don't know what you're talking about; it wasn't properly regulated.' 'No,' says a fourth, 'shut up and listen to me: it was because the firing wasn't beech —that's the one and only reason, or I'm a Dutchman!' Myself, I've no idea what the trouble was—all I know is we're in the middle of a row.

'Well,' says my master, 'it can't be helped; I'll guard against these risks in future. I'm pretty sure the pot was cracked—but be that as it may, don't stand there gaping! Look alive, sweep the floor as usual, and cheer up, don't lose heart!'

Then the debris is swept into a heap, a canvas laid upon the floor, and all this rubbish thrown in a sieve, sifted, and picked over again and again.

'By God,' says one, 'there's still some of our metal here, though we haven't got it all. Even if things went wrong just now, they'll come right another time, perhaps. If you don't speculate you won't accumulate. Lord save us, a merchant can't always be prosperous, believe me. Sometimes his goods go to the bottom, and sometimes come safe to land.'

'Quiet!' says my master, 'next time I'll find a way to bring our ship home in different style; and if I don't, gentlemen, put the blame on me. There was something wrong somewhere, I know.'

Another says the fire was too hot—but whether too hot or too cold I'll say this much: it works out wrong every time. We fail of our object yet go on with our raving lunacy. When we're all together each one of us seems as wise as Solomon; but as I've heard tell, all that glisters is not gold, nor every apple good that delights the eye, whatever people say. And that's exactly the case with us: the one who seems the wisest is the biggest fool when it comes to the test, and the most honest-seeming a thief, by Jesus! This will be plain to you by the time I've finished my story.

ii

There is among us a canon regular who could contaminate a city the size of Nineveh, Rome, Alexandria, Troy, and any three others put together. If he lived a thousand years no man could record all his tricks and bottomless deceit. In the whole wide world there's nobody to touch him as a swindler: when he talks with someone it's in so involved a jargon, with a delivery so subtle, that in two minutes he's got the fellow completely humbugged—unless he happens to be another fiend of hell like himself. He's taken in hundreds of people before now, and will again so long as the breath is in him. Yet people travel miles to seek him out and make his acquaintance, knowing nothing of his true character—which, if you care to listen, I'll reveal here and now.

You honourable canons regular, don't think I'm slandering your fraternity, even though my tale is of a canon. Heaven knows some rascal's always to be found in every religious body; but God forbid an entire fraternity should pay for the folly of a single individual. I haven't the least intention of slandering you; I merely wish to castigate what's amiss. This tale isn't directed at you in particular, for it's applicable to many others also. As you well know, none of Christ's twelve apostles was a traitor but Judas himself—why, then, should that stigma attach to the rest, who were innocent? I tell you it's the same in your case, except for one thing, if you'll listen to me: should there be any Judas among you, take my advice and get rid of him in good time if you stand in dread of ruin or disgrace. Please don't be vexed, but listen to what I'm going to say about this particular case.

There was a chantry priest who had lived for many years in London. He had made himself so agreeable and attentive to the landlady of the house where he lodged and boarded that she wouldn't let him pay a penny for either board or clothing, no matter how well he dressed; and so he had plenty of spending money. Never mind that; I'll now proceed with my story of the canon who brought this priest to ruin.

One day this rascally canon visited the priest in the room where he lodged and begged him to lend a certain sum of gold, promising to pay it back in full. Said he, 'Lend me a gold mark, just for three days, and I'll pay it back on the day—if I let you down, another time you can have me hanged by the neck!'

The priest handed him a gold mark on the spot. The canon thanked him over and over, then took his leave and went. On the third day he brought the money and handed it back to the priest; upon which the priest was so highly delighted he said, 'Really, I've no objection at all to lending a man a noble or two, or even three, or whatever I have on me, if he's the honest sort who always pay back on the nail whatever happens. I never can say "No" to a man like that.'

'What!' exclaimed the canon, 'me dishonest! That would be something new indeed! So help me God, my word is a thing I'll always keep till the day I crawl into my grave! Believe that as you believe your Creed! God be thanked—and I think this is a good time to say it—no man was ever the worse for lending me gold or silver, for there has never been the smallest deceit in my heart. Now, sir,' he went on, 'since you've been so generous and shown me such kindness, I'll reveal something of my secret knowledge in partial repayment for your goodness; and if you'd like to learn, I'll give you a clear demonstration of my skill in alchemy. Now watch: with our own eyes you'll see me perform a miracle before I leave.'

'Indeed!' said the priest. 'Will you really? By St Mary! Go ahead by all means, I beg you.'

'As you wish, then,' said the canon. 'God forbid I should do otherwise.'

How well that thieving canon could tender his services! Very true it is that 'proffered service stinks' as the old authorities testify —and very soon I shall prove it in the case of this canon, father of all fraud, whose greatest joy and delight lay ever in bringing Christian folk to destruction—for his heart was filled with fiendish schemes. God keep us all from his lying humbuggery!

The priest knew nothing of the man he was dealing with, nor had he the least suspicion of what was in store for him. Ah, simple priest! Poor innocent, about to be blinded by your own covetousness! Luckless fellow: your understanding is completely clouded over; you've not the slightest idea of the deception this fox has planned; you can't escape his wily stratagems. And so, unhappy man, the sooner to reach the consummation of your ruin, I'll make haste to relate, so far as my skill affords, your brainless folly and the duplicity of that other wretch.

You take this canon to be my master? Master Host, I swear by the Queen of Heaven it was not he, but another, a hundred times more cunning, who'd swindled people time and again—it numbs my wits to speak of his double-dealing. Whenever I talk of his dishonesty my cheeks grow red for shame of him—or at any rate begin to burn, since, as I should know, I've no colour in my face because the various fumes from the metals you've heard me speak of have consumed and wasted it. Now mark this canon's villainy!

Said he to the priest, 'Now, sir, let your man go for some quicksilver that we may have it at once; let him bring us two or three ounces, and as soon as he comes back you'll see a marvellous thing, such as you never saw before.'

'It shall be done without fail,' said the priest, and ordered his servant to fetch the metal. He readily obeyed, went out and returned with three ounces of quicksilver, no less, which he handed over to the canon, who laid it down carefully, then told the servant to bring some charcoal that he might set to work at once.

The charcoal was fetched without delay. The canon took from his bosom a crucible which he showed the priest. 'Do you see this instrument? Take it in your hand, and yourself put in an ounce of this quicksilver—and now begin your training as an alchemist, in the name of Christ! There are very few to whom I'd offer to reveal this much of my science. For you'll now see an experiment by which I'll transform or reduce the quicksilver and make it malleable—without deception, and under your very eyes—and turn it into silver as sterling and fine as any in my purse or yours, or anywhere else. Or you can call me a fraud and unfit ever to show my face among honest folk! I've a powder here that cost me a lot; it will do the trick, for it's the foundation of my power —which I'm about to reveal to you. Send your man away and let him stand outside; keep the door shut while we're busy with secret matters, so that nobody spies on us while we're at work in this science.'

All was done as he asked. The servant went out at once; his master then shut the door and they quickly got down to work. At the request of this scoundrelly canon the priest placed the stuff upon the fire, which he diligently blew, while the canon sprinkled into the crucible a powder—I don't know what it was, chalk or glass or something else not worth a curse—so as to hoodwink the priest. Next he asked him to make haste and pile charcoal on top of the crucible. 'As a mark of my regard for you,' said the canon, 'everything we have to do shall be done with your own two hands.'

'A thousand thanks,' exclaimed the delighted priest, piling on charcoal as the canon requested. And while he was busying himself, that damned scoundrel, that rascally canon, the foul fiend fetch him!—took a beechwood coal in which a hole had been skilfully pierced, and put therein an ounce of silver filings, stopping the hole with wax to keep the filings in. Understand this: the fraudulent device was not made on the spot, but prepared beforehand like other things he'd brought with him and which I'll tell you about later. The canon had planned to trick the priest before he came, and so indeed he did before they parted; he couldn't lay off until he'd skinned him. When I speak of him my mind feels numb. I'd pay him out for his lies if I knew how; but he's here today and gone tomorrow; he's so restless he never stays in any one place.

Now mark this, gentlemen, for the love of God! Taking the piece of charcoal I spoke of above, the canon held it concealed in his hand and while the priest was busily stacking the coals as I told you, he remarked: 'Friend, you're doing it all wrong, it's not properly bedded; but I'll soon put it right. Just let me fiddle with it for a bit—by St Giles, I feel sorry for you, you're so hot! I can see you're dripping with sweat—take this cloth and wipe it off.' And while the priest mopped his face the canon, devil fetch him, took his piece of charcoal and placed it over the centre of the crucible, then blew hard until the coals began to glow briskly.

'Let's have a drink now,' said the canon. 'Trust me, all will be well in a moment. Let's sit down and refresh ourselves.' And when the canon's beechwood coal had burned away, all the filings fell out of the hole and into the crucible, as would naturally happen since they had been placed exactly above it. But of this the poor priest knew nothing. He had no notion of the trick that was being played on him but thought all the coals were equally sound. When he saw the time had come, the alchemist said: 'Get up now, Master Priest, and stand beside me. As I'm pretty certain you haven't a mould, step outside and get me a piece of chalk, and with luck I can cut it to the shape of a mould. While you're about it, bring a bowl or pan full of water, and then you'll see how well our work turns out. And so that you shall have no disbelief or wrong suspicion of me while you're away, I'll not leave your side but go and return with you.'

In short, they opened the chamber door, locked it, took the key with them, went out and came back forthwith—why take all day telling of it? The canon took the chalk and cut it in the shape of a mould as I shall describe. Listen: from his sleeve he took a small bar of silver—hanging's too good for him—no more than an ounce in weight. Now mark his damned juggling! He cut the mould to the same length and breadth as this bar, but so adroitly that you may be sure the priest never noticed; then once more hid it up his sleeve. Next he took the stuff from off the fire and, with a satisfied expression, poured it into the mould; then, when he was ready, threw it into the vessel of water, at the same time bidding the priest: 'See what's there—put your hand in and grope around. You'll find silver I should think. What the devil else would it be? A silver shaving's silver, isn't it?' The priest plunged his hand in and fished out a bar of pure silver; and when he saw what it was, joy thrilled through his veins and he cried, 'God's blessing, and His Mother's too, the blessing of all the saints upon you, Master Canon! Only vouchsafe to teach me this noble art and science and I'll be your man so far as I'm able, or their curse upon me!'

Said the canon, 'All the same, I'm going to have a second try so that you can watch closely and become expert in it. Another time, if need be, you can try your hand without me in the practice of this ingenious science. Now don't argue,' he went on, 'take another ounce of mercury and do the same with it as with the other one that's now silver.'

The priest then set to work and did his best to do all that this villainous canon commanded, furiously blowing upon the coals in hope to win his heart's desire, while in the meantime the canon got ready to trick the priest yet again. As a blind he carried in his hand a hollow stick—now mark this carefully—in the end of which (as in the case of the piece of charcoal) a bare ounce of silver filings had been placed, well stoppered with wax to keep in every scrap of the filings. While the priest was fully occupied the

canon came up to him with his stick and sprinkled powder into
the crucible as before—for his lies, God grant the devil flays him
out of his skin! His every thought and act was a lie! And he
stirred the coals above the crucible with this loaded stick until the
wax began to melt (as anybody but a blockhead knows it must)
when its contents poured out and fell straight into the crucible.

Gentlemen, it couldn't have been bettered. When he'd been
fooled again like this the priest (who indeed suspected nothing)
was overjoyed. I can't begin to describe his happiness and delight;
once more he offered himself body and soul to the canon. 'Well,'
said the canon, 'poor I may be, but you'll find I know a thing or
two: I warn you there's more to come. Is there any copper here?'

'I think so, sir,' said the priest.

'If not, go and buy some without delay. Now off with you, my
dear sir; make haste.'

Away he went, returning with the copper. This the canon took
into his hands, and weighed out an ounce.

My tongue is too inadequate an instrument to utter what I think
of the humbuggery of this canon—father of all villainy! To those
who didn't know him he seemed a friend—and was a fiend in
heart and mind! It wearies me to tell of his knavery; nevertheless,
for no other reason, truly, than to warn others I must make it
known.

He put the ounce of copper in the crucible, quickly set it upon
the fire (which, as before, he made the priest blow, bending double
to perform the task) and sprinkled in the powder. It was nothing
but tomfoolery. He made a monkey of the priest just as he pleased.
Next he poured the melted copper into the mould and finally put
it in the pan of water. Then he plunged in his hand, for as I told
you earlier he had a bar of silver up his sleeve; this he deftly shook
out—the damned scoundrel!—and left in the bottom of the pan.
The priest knew nothing of his legerdemain. The canon fumbled
about in the water, and with wonderful adroitness palmed the bar
of copper (still unperceived by the priest) and hid it.

Then he took the priest by the shoulder and said banteringly,
'Lord, this will never do! Bend down and help me as I helped you
a moment ago—plunge your hand in and see what's there.'

The priest soon fished out the bar of silver, upon which the
canon said, 'Let's go to some goldsmith with these three bars we've

made and find out if they're anything. I swear they're sterling silver—if not I'll eat my hat! But we'll soon put it to the proof.'

They took these three bars to a goldsmith and had them assayed with fire and hammer. Nobody could deny they were the real thing.

Who happier than that besotted priest? No bird more glad at break of day, no summer nightingale more apt to sing, no lady readier to dance, or—speaking of lords and ladies—no knight more keen to win his lady's favour with feat of arms, than that priest to learn this miserable art. And this is what he said to the canon: 'If I may deserve it of you, for the love of Him who died for us all, how much does the formula cost? Now tell me!'

'By our lady,' said the canon, 'I give you fair warning, it's expensive. Apart from one friar and myself, there's no man in England that knows it.'

'No matter,' cried the other, 'now, sir, for God's sake, how much? Tell me, I implore you!'

'Seriously,' he replied, 'I tell you it's pretty expensive. In one word, sir, if you wish to have it, you must pay forty pounds, so help me God! And were it not for the friendship you showed me a while ago you'd have to pay more, that's certain.'

Upon this the priest fetched the sum of forty pounds in nobles and paid over the whole to the canon for this same formula. The whole business was nothing but fraud and deceit.

'Sir Priest,' said he, 'I look for no praise for my skill, but would prefer it kept dark; if you love me, keep it secret. For did people know of my powers, by God they'd be so envious of my alchemy it would cost me my life—no two ways about that.'

'God forbid!' exclaimed the priest. 'You don't say! Sooner than see you in trouble I'd go crazy and sell all I have!'

'Thanks for your good wishes, sir,' returned the canon. 'And now goodbye, and a thousand thanks!' And off he went; as for the priest, he never set eyes on him again from that day to this. And when, in his own good time, the priest came to try out the formula—alas! it wouldn't work. And so he was diddled and done. It was in this way the canon used to introduce himself and bring folk to ruin.

Consider, gentlemen, how in every rank of life men struggle for gold till there's hardly any left. So many are taken in by alchemy that I truly believe it's the chief reason for this scarcity. Those who practise the art of transmutation speak in such cloudy terminology none can understand it—if indeed they have the wit nowadays. Let them chatter away like jackdaws and devote their enthusiasm and energy to polishing up their jargon, for they'll never attain their object. It's easy enough for a man to learn to transmute his property, if he has any, into nothing!

This tomfoolery offers such glittering prizes it will turn a man's happiness into despair, empty the biggest and heaviest purse, and earn the curses of those who have given their goods. They should be ashamed—can't people with burnt fingers keep away from fire? If you go in for alchemy, take my tip, give it up lest you lose all. Late is better than never; and never to thrive's too long a time. You can hunt for ever, but you'll never find the Philosopher's Stone. You're as bold as blind Bayard, the old horse that blunders on and doesn't give a damn for danger. He'll walk into a boulder as boldly as step aside. You alchemists are the same, I tell you! If you can't see straight, take care your minds are not blinded. For though you should keep your eyes open and look never so wide-awake, you'll never win anything at this trade, but squander whatever you can beg or borrow. Damp the fire lest it burn too fast—by that, I mean meddle with alchemy no more; for if you do your luck's clean out. And here and now I'll tell you what the real alchemists say on the subject.

Here is what Arnold of Villanova says in his *Rosarium Philosophorum*—these are his very words: 'The mortification or reduction of mercury cannot be accomplished without the aid of its brother.' But the first to lay this down was Hermes Trismegistus, the father of alchemy, who says, 'The dragon will not die unless his brother is slain with him', that's to say, by the dragon he meant mercury, and by the dragon's brother, brimstone; for the latter comes from Sol—which is gold—and the former from Luna—which is silver. 'And therefore,' said he—now mark this precept—'let no man trouble himself to pursue this science unless he can understand the aims and terminology of alchemists; otherwise he's a fool. For this art and science is indeed of the mystery of mysteries.'

There was also that disciple of Plato who once asked a question of his master (as his book *Senioris Zadith Tabula Chimica* records). This is what he asked: 'Tell me the name of the Philosopher's Stone.' And Plato answered, 'It is the stone people call Titan.' 'And what is that?' said the other. 'The same as Magnesia,' replied Plato. 'Well, really, sir! This is *ignotum per ignotius.** Pray, what is Magnesia, my dear sir?' 'Let us say it's a liquid made of the four elements,' said Plato. 'Dear master, if it please you, tell me the essential principle of this liquid.' 'Certainly not,' answered Plato. 'All alchemists were bound by an oath never to disclose it to anyone or even write it in a book. For it's so dear and precious to Christ that He does not wish it to be revealed except when it pleases His Godhead to inspire men; to others He forbids it, as He wills. That's all.'

So I conclude: since God in Heaven does not wish alchemists to explain how this stone is to be discovered, to my way of thinking the best thing one can do is forget it. He will surely never prosper who makes God his adversary, by working against His will—not if he alchemizes to the end of his days. Here I stop; my tale is ended. God send all good men a cure for sorrow!

* Explaining the unknown by the more unknown.

Do you not know the spot where stands a little village called Bob-up-and-down, under Blean Forest on the Canterbury Road? That's where our Host began cracking his jokes: 'Well, gentlemen! Dobbin's stuck in the mud—who'll haul him out? Will nobody wake up our friend at the back, for love or money? Some thief might easily rob him and tie him up. See him snoozing away—cock's bones, he'll fall off his horse in a moment! Is it that confounded London Cook? Make him come forward—he knows the penalty; I swear he's got to tell us a tale, even though it isn't worth a bundle of hay. Wake up, Cook, God damn you,' cried he, 'what's the matter with you—asleep in the morning? Were the fleas at you all night—or are you drunk? Or did you spend the whole night sweating over some slut till you can't lift up your head?'

All pale and colourless, the Cook answered our Host, 'God bless my soul, such a heaviness is come over me—I don't know why—but I'd sooner have a sleep than a gallon of the best wine in Cheapside.'

'Well,' said the Manciple, 'if it's any comfort to you, Master Cook, I'll excuse you from your tale for the nonce—that is, if nobody riding in our party objects and our Host is good enough to assent—for upon my soul it seems to me your face is uncommonly pasty; your eyes are dazed too, and your breath, as I ought to know, is stinking sour—a plain sign you aren't in good fettle. You'll not get any flattery from me, that's certain. Look how he yawns, the drunken lout, as if he'd swallow us up on the spot! Keep your mouth shut, man, for Christ's sake! May the Devil from hell shove his foot in it! Your horrible breath will poison us all. For shame, you stinking pig, for shame—plague take you! Ah, sirs, have a good look at this fine fellow. Would you like to take a crack at quintain, sweet sir, and dodge the sandbag? I'd say you were in splendid shape for it. You've been drinking monkey-wine, I bet—and when people do that they're finished.'

At this speech the Cook grew furious with rage. Unable to speak, he shook his head violently at the Manciple, when his horse threw him; and there he lay until they picked him up again. Fine horsemanship for a cook—pity he didn't stick to his ladle. What grief and trouble, what shoving and heaving, before they got him back into the saddle; for that pale unhappy wraith was somewhat unwieldy.

Then our Host turned to the Manciple and said, 'Upon my soul, the man's so overcome with drink he'd probably have made a botch of his tale. I don't know if it's wine he's been drinking, or new ale or old, but he's talking through his nose and snorting as though he'd a cold in the head. And it's more than he can do to keep himself and that carthorse of his out of the mud. If he falls off his nag again we'll have our work cut out lifting up his heavy drunken carcass. Begin your story, I've had enough of him! All the same, Manciple, I'd say you were a bit of a blockhead to twit him for his failings in public like that. Another day, perhaps, he'll lay a trap for you and bring you to book— I mean he'll touch on one or two little matters, by way of picking holes in your accounts, which wouldn't be to your credit if they came to the proof.'

'No, it would be pretty awkward,' agreed the Manciple, 'he could easily trip me up like that. I'd sooner pay for the mare he's riding than start feuding with him—I mustn't make him angry if I can help it! What I said was only my joke. But do you know what? I've got a drink of wine in this gourd here—yes, a good vintage—and I'll show you a rare joke in a moment. I'll see if I can get the Cook to drink some—he won't say no, I'll stake my life.'

And as it turned out, the Cook drank deep from the gourd, more's the pity. What need for it? He'd drunk enough already. Having played a tune on the gourd he handed it back to the Manciple. The Cook seemed remarkably pleased with the drink, and thanked him as best he could manage.

Then our Host began to roar with laughter and said, 'I can plainly see it's necessary to carry good drink with us wherever we go, for it turns grievance and rancour into love and harmony and appeases so many wrongs. O Bacchus, who canst thus turn earnest into jest, blessed be thy name! Honour and thanks to thy divinity! That's enough from me on the subject: now, Manciple, pray begin your story.'

'All right, sir,' he replied, 'now listen to me.'

THE
MANCIPLE'S
TALE

When Phoebus lived down here upon earth (as ancient books report) not only was he the most mettlesome young knight in the world but the best archer: for one day he slew the serpent Python as he lay sleeping in the sun. And you may read of many another eminent exploit he performed with his bow. He could play any instrument; it was music to hear the clear tones of his voice when he sang. Surely Amphion, King of Thebes, who built the walls of that city with his singing, never sang half so well as he. Moreover he was the handsomest man on earth—but what's the point of describing his features? for there was no better-looking man alive. And besides he was endowed with nobility, honour, and excellence in perfection. Phoebus, that paragon of youth in his generosity and knightly accomplishment, used to carry in his hand a bow, both for sport and as an emblem of his victory over Python. Or so the story goes.

Now in his house Phoebus kept in a cage a crow which he had reared a long time and had taught to speak, just as one teaches jays. This crow was white as a snow-white swan, and knew how to mimic anybody's voice when telling a story; besides which no nightingale in all the world could sing a hundred thousandth part as well and joyously as he.

And Phoebus had also a wife in his house; he loved her more than life itself. He was solicitous to please and do her honour night and day, one thing excepted. To tell the truth, he was jealous and too inclined to keep his eye upon her; for he was loth to be made a fool of—like everyone in the same case—but what's the use, there's nothing you can do about it. A good wife—one that's pure in thought and deed—ought never be kept under surveillance; equally certainly, mounting guard over a trollop is labour in vain—it won't work. I think it's plain foolishness to lose one's labour watching over wives—the old scholars have said as much in their books.

But to get back to my theme. This excellent Phoebus did everything he could to make her happy, supposing his agreeable behaviour, manliness and conduct sufficient guarantee none would oust him from her favour. But, God knows, there's one thing nobody may compass: the alteration of any instinct naturally implanted in a creature.

Take any bird: put it in a cage, keep it as clean as you can and set your whole heart and mind upon tenderly fostering it with the most delicious food and drink you can think of—yet the bird, though kept in the gaiest of golden cages, will twenty thousand times rather fly to the cold harsh forest and eat worms and like filth; it will never stop trying to escape from its cage, but continually longs for liberty. Take a cat: feed him well with milk and tender meat, give him a silken bed—but let him see a mouse run along the wall and he'll at once abandon milk, meat, and the rest—every luxury in the house—such is his appetite for mice. You see, instinct has the upper hand and appetite banishes prudence. A she-wolf has a base nature too: when in heat she'll take the roughest, most disreputable wolf she can find. But all these instances I am giving refer to men who are unfaithful, and not by any manner of means to women—for men never lack a lecherous appetite to take pleasure in inferior creatures sooner than their wives, no matter how beautiful and faithful and gentle they may be. So greedy for novelty is this confounded flesh of ours, we cannot for long take pleasure in anything that's consonant with virtue.

For all his great merits this Phoebus, who suspected nothing, was deceived. She had another man in tow, a man of little note, worth nothing in comparison. More's the pity! This often happens, and results in much trouble and grief. And it so fell out that when Phoebus was away his wife at once sent for her fancy man. Fancy man? It's a coarse way of putting it, and really I beg your pardon.

But the wise Plato has said, as you may read in his works, that it's necessary for the word to suit the deed—if one is properly to express a thing the word must be related to the action. Now I'm a blunt man; what I say is, between a lady of rank who is bodily unfaithful, and a common woman—granted they both do wrong —there's in fact no difference other than this: the gentlewoman, being of higher station, is said to be a 'lady-love' whereas the other, being a poor woman, is called his 'woman' or 'girl-friend'. And God knows, my dear fellow, the one is laid as low as the other.

Likewise I claim there's no difference between an usurping tyrant and an outlaw or roaming brigand. This definition was given to Alexander: Because a tyrant, having an army, has the greater power to massacre and burn down house and home and raze all flat, they call him a general; but because an outlaw has only a small following and cannot do as much damage or bring the same ruin upon a country, he's called a thief or brigand. Not being book-learned, I won't quote a swarm of authorities but go on with the story I began.

Phoebus' wife sent for her lover, and they at once satisfied all their fleeting lusts. The white crow hanging in its cage saw them at work and said never a word. And when the master of the house came home the crow sang, 'Cuckoo! Cuckoo! Cuckoo!'

'What, bird!' cried Phoebus. 'What kind of a song is that? You used to sing so merrily it delighted my heart to hear your voice— but what kind of song is this, alas!'

'By the Lord, it's very suitable,' he answered. 'Phoebus, in spite of all your beauty and worth and breeding, all your music and singing and all your vigilance, you've had your eye wiped by one of no account—not worth a gnat compared with you, as I live and breathe! For I saw him screw your wife in your own bed.'

What more would you have? Without mincing matters the crow then told him the great shame and wrong his wife had done him by her lechery, giving him good proof of it and repeating that he'd seen it with his own eyes. Phoebus turned away; he felt his unhappy heart must burst in two. Then he bent his bow and strung an arrow to it and in his rage slew his wife. And that's how it ended; what more is there to say? But in his remorse he broke his instruments of music, harp, lute, guitar, and psaltery; then he broke his bow and arrows and said to the bird:

'Betrayer!' cried he, 'your scorpion tongue has brought me to my ruin. Why was I born? Why am I not dead? O dear wife, O jewel of delight, who was to me so constant and so true, now you lie dead with your face wan and pale—and wholly innocent, that indeed I dare swear! Rash hand that did so vile a wrong—O clouded mind, O heedless rage, recklessly smiting the innocent! O mistrust, brimful of mistaken suspicion, where was your wisdom, where your wit? O let all men beware rashness; believe nothing without absolute proof! Strike not too soon, before you know what you do; consider calmly and carefully before you wreak your rage on mere suspicion. Alas! Thousands have perished and been brought to the dust by reckless ire. Alas! I'll kill myself for grief.'

And to the crow he said, 'Treacherous villain! I'll soon pay you out for your lying tale. You sang like a nightingale once; now, false thief, you must lose your song and every one of those white feathers, and never speak as long as you live. This is the punishment of a traitor: you and your offspring shall be black for ever, and never again make a sweet sound, but ever croak before the coming of the tempest and the rain, as a sign that my wife was slain because of you.'

And with that he rushed upon the crow and tore out all its white feathers. Then he made it black, took away its song and faculty of speech, and slung it out of the door to the Devil—to whom I commend it. For this reason all crows are black.

I pray you, gentlemen, take note of the parable and mark what I say. Never in your life tell a man that another has pleasured his wife or he'll be bound to hate you with mortal hatred. Learned scholars say that the great Solomon teaches us to keep a good guard over our tongues. But, as I said, I'm not book-learned. Nevertheless this is what my mother taught me: 'My son, for heaven's sake remember the crow! Watch your tongue and keep your friend, my son. An evil tongue is worse than a devil; for, my son, against a devil we may cross ourselves. My son, God in his endless goodness walled the tongue with lips and teeth so that a man should think before he speaks. Scholars have taught us, my son, how often many' have perished through talking too much; but generally speaking nobody is ever harmed through talking seldom, and then with deliberation. My son, you should restrain your tongue at all times, except when endeavouring to speak of God in worship and prayer. The first virtue, if you will only learn it, son, is to restrain your tongue and keep a good watch over it; this is what all children learn. My son, great evil springs from ill-advised loquacity where a word or two would have sufficed. This I was told and taught. Do you know the operation of a reckless tongue? Just as a sword hacks and hews an arm in half, so will a tongue carve a friendship in twain. A babbler is abominable to God. Read the wise and honourable Solomon, the psalms of David, read Seneca! Never speak, my son, when you may nod your head. Pretend to be deaf if you hear a windbag talking on a dangerous subject. The Flemings say (and you may find it useful) "Least said, soonest mended." My son, if you have spoken no evil you need never fear betrayal; but I tell you this, he who has spoken evil can never recall his words. What is said is said, and forth it goes whether he likes it or not, even though he should repent. He is in that man's power who says to him anything he may regret. My son, take care: never be a source of gossip, whether false or true, but wherever you may be, among the mighty or the humble, watch your tongue and remember the crow.'

By the time the Manciple had made an end of his tale the sun had descended so low that so far as I could estimate, its altitude was not more than twenty-nine degrees. By my guess it was then four o'clock, since at the time my shadow—give or take a little—was eleven feet in length, as against my height which is six feet. Further, the moon's exaltation—I mean Libra—was still ascending while we were approaching the outskirts of a village. Here, as usual, our Host took charge of our happy company and addressed us thus:

'Gentlemen all, we only need one more story now. My rules and ordinances have been carried out, and I should think we've heard a tale from each rank and condition among us; my plan is almost fulfilled. God send good luck to the teller of the last and jolliest tale!

'Master Priest,' he continued, 'are you a vicar, or perhaps a parish priest? Out with it, now! But be what you may, don't spoil our game, for everyone has told his story except you. Unbuckle and let's see what you've got in your bag. Seriously though, judging from your appearance you look capable of spinning a yarn on some weighty theme. Cock's bones! Tell us a fable here and now!'

The Parson retorted, 'You'll get no fables out of me. For in his Epistle to Timothy, Paul reproves those who turn away from the truth and tell fables and trash like that. Why should my hand sow chaff when if I wish I can sow wheat? So I say that if you'd care to hear some moral and edifying matter, and are willing to give me a hearing, then I'll be delighted (with Christ's blessing) to give you such lawful pleasure as I'm able.

'But I'm a Southron, don't forget; I'm not one for this rum-ram-raf alliteration, not that I think rhyme's much better, God knows; so if you don't mind I won't use such devices but tell you a satisfying tale in prose to wind up the game and make an end. May Jesus in His grace send me the wit to show you, in this endeavour, the way of that perfect and glorious pilgrimage known as Jeru-

*salem the Celestial. If you agree, then I'll begin my tale forthwith;
so please tell me what you think—I can say no fairer than that.*

'*Nevertheless I place the following homily under the correction of scholars, for I'm not versed in texts; you may be sure I only extract their general meaning. Therefore I protest to you that I stand to be corrected.*'

To this we soon assented; to give him the chance of a hearing and so end with something virtuous and edifying seemed the thing to do; and we asked our Host to say we all entreated him to tell his tale.

*Our Host was our spokesman: '*Master Priest,*' said he, '*the best of luck to you! Give us your homily, but make haste, for the sun's going down—bring forth your harvest, but don't take too long. May God send you grace to make a good job of it! Say what you please and we will gladly listen.*'*

And with that the Priest began his sermon.

THE PARSON'S TALE

[This is the longest of the tales, and it is not a tale at all but a sermon. Like 'The Tale of Melibeus' it is written in prose, and I have also omitted it as being unlikely to interest the general reader. Briefly, 'The Parson's Tale' is a sermon on Penitence in which is embodied a long treatise on the Seven Deadly Sins. It begins by defining (as the Parson had promised in his Prologue) 'the right way to Jerusalem the Celestial'—i.e. penitence. It is probable that 'The Parson's Tale' was written in Chaucer's old age when he realized he would be unable to complete 'The Canterbury Tales' as he had planned, and was a way of winding them up in conformity with the 'Retraction' which follows. D.W.]

THE AUTHOR'S VALEDICTION

Now I pray all those who hear or read this little treatise, if there be anything in it which pleases them, to thank Our Lord Jesus Christ from whom proceeds all wisdom and all goodness; and if there be anything that displeases them, then I pray them to ascribe the fault to my incompetence and not my will, for I would gladly have spoken better had I the ability. As the Bible says, 'All that is written is written for our instruction' and that has been my aim.

And so I meekly beseech you, for God's mercy, that you pray for me, that Christ have mercy upon me and forgive me my trespasses, in particular my translations and my authorship of works of worldly vanity, the which I revoke in this retraction: *Troilus and Cressida, The House of Fame, The Legend of Good Women, The Book of the Duchess, The Parliament of Fowls,* those of the Canterbury Tales that tend towards sin, *The Book of the Lion,* and many other books could I remember them; and many a song and lascivious lay; that Christ in His great mercy forgive me the sin.

But for the translations of the *Consolation* of Boethius, and other books of legends of the saints, and works of morality and devotion, for these I thank Our Lord Jesus Christ and His Blessed Mother and all the saints of heaven, entreating them that they should send me grace to lament my sins and study my soul's salvation from henceforth till the day I die; and grant me the grace of true penitence, confession, and penance in this present life, through the merciful grace of Him Who is King of Kings and Priest over all Priests, Who redeemed us with the precious blood of His heart; that I may be one of those who shall be saved on the day of doom. *Qui cum patre et Spiritu Sancto vivit et regnat Deus per omnia secula. Amen.*

Here ends the Book of the Canterbury Tales
compiled by Geoffrey Chaucer,
on whose soul Jesus Christ have mercy.

ABOUT THE TRANSLATOR

DAVID WRIGHT, born in South Africa, is himself a distinguished poet. He won an Atlantic Award in 1950 and Guinness Poetry Prizes in 1958 and 1960. His books of poetry include *Poems, Moral Stories, Monologue of a Deaf Man* and *Adam at Evening.* In addition to *The Canterbury Tales,* Mr. Wright has also translated *Beowulf* into modern English prose. He has edited several anthologies, including *The Faber Book of Twentieth Century Verse, The Forsaken Garden, Seven Victorian Poets,* and *The Mid-Century: English Poetry 1940-1960.*

Knight
↓
Squier